War Is All Hell

War Is All Hell

The Nature of Evil and the Civil War

Edward J. Blum and John H. Matsui

PENN

UNIVERSITY OF PENNSYLVANIA PRESS

PHILADELPHIA

Published by
University of Pennsylvania Press
Philadelphia, Pennsylvania 19104-4112
www.upenn.edu/pennpress

Printed in the United States of America
on acid-free paper
10 9 8 7 6 5 4 3 2 1

A catalogue record for this book is available from the Library of Congress.
ISBN 978-0-8122-5304-7

CONTENTS

Abraham Lincoln begged his fellow Americans to be "friends," "not enemies." It was 1861 and he had just become president of a disuniting United
States. He concluded his first inaugural address hoping that "the better angels of our nature" would save the nation from separation and war. Lincoln's
wish failed to come true. The "better angels" failed to materialize. God and his
heavenly hosts seemed absent, quiet, and dumb, unable to answer Lincoln's
prayers. These sacred forces often seemed idle during the next four years as
one government became two, as hundreds of thousands of men and then millions marched to kill one another, and as Americans destroyed so much of
what they had strained to build. In the decades preceding Lincoln's election,
God appeared just as impotent. When it came to the nation's most divisive
issue—people owning other people, or what is simply called slavery—the
Lord seemed either unable or unwilling to destroy the so-called "peculiar
institution."

Another angel incarnated instead and brought his legions with him. This
angel's dominion grew as the war raged. Known originally as Lucifer, most
Americans more often called this force Satan, the mythical fallen angel from
heaven who lorded over hell with his fellow devils. A demonic contingent,
not an angelic host, invaded every aspect of American society during the
middle of the nineteenth century. They seemed intent on transforming the
earth into hell. And as much as Americans feared these powers, fact was more
sinister than fiction. It was Americans who created the devils, unleashed
them, redesigned them, and cheered them as they wrought havoc. American
politicians, reformers, writers, artists, mechanics, foot soldiers, nurses, home-
workers, and countless others made and remade devils. Then, in acts of profound and brilliant misdirection, they accused others of summoning hell to
earth. During the Civil War, the war Lincoln hoped to avoid but nonetheless

presided over, Americans brought Satan, demons, and hell to bear on nearly every aspect of their country.

Only a few years before Lincoln's inaugural, another Kentuckian dreamed of angels. After artist C. R. Milne skimmed *Uncle Tom's Cabin* (1851), the antislavery novel from Harriet Beecher Stowe that captivated much of the world, he rushed to respond. The novel's story of heroic and silly African Americans, of kind and horrible whites, and of an overall societal structure of slavery that supported the most heinous of behaviors led him to manifest "a dream" on paper. Devils, dragons, and countless other bizarre beasts dominated the landscape. They grabbed; they pulled; they burned copies of Stowe's book. Some of them were armed with muskets; some were hybrid cannon machines: part creature, part mortar, all wicked. Several assaulted Stowe's body directly in a tunnel labeled "Underground Railway." They yanked on her clothes and limbs. One stuck her in the back with a pitchfork. Another shackled irons onto her feet. She defied them, holding her novel above her head. An exposed page of her book read "I love the blacks" (a sentence nowhere to be found in the novel).[1]

Before the middle of the nineteenth century and the wrenching Civil War, devils like the ones in this print danced throughout American society far more than the "better angels" of Lincoln's speech. The history of European expansion in the Americas, in fact, cannot be told without reference to Satan, the demonic, or hell. Even from their beginning, Europeans narrated their invasion of the western hemisphere with attention to evil forces. In his *A Brief Account of the Destruction of the Indies* (1542), Bartolomé de Las Casas explicitly invoked the demonic. Some English translators subtitled his book, "a Faithful Narrative of the Horrid and Unexampled Massacres, Butcheries, and all Manner of Cruelties, that Hell and Malice Could Invent." In the text, Las Casas wrote that "some wicked Devil" possessed "the minds of the *Spaniards*" and led them to "such Inhumanities and Barbarisms" that "no Age can parallel."[2]

In the colonial lands that later revolutionized into the United States in the 1770s, devils seemed to flourish too. For every Puritan who hoped to build a "city upon a hill," there were other English men and women, like poet Michael Wigglesworth, who saw in the new lands "hellish fiends . . . That Devils worshiped."[3] During witchcraft trials in the colonies, men and women testified routinely and almost nonchalantly to the presence of demonic figures and

influences. It seemed that just about anyone could be seduced and manipulated, or at least entreated, by the devil.[4] When American revolutionaries then
battled for their independence from Great Britain, some attacked the government across the sea as part of a grand conspiracy of the devil.[5]

By the middle of the nineteenth century, malevolent spiritual forces
seemed to be on everyone's tongue. Novelists toyed with gothic themes of
dark, uncertain powers working in the midst of Americans. Nathaniel Hawthorne not only revisited colonial witchcraft in *The Scarlet Letter* (1850), but
also updated John Bunyan's *Pilgrim's Progress* with one now set in the modern United States. Hawthorne's short story entitled "The Celestial Railroad"
(1843) featured the devil as the engine conductor of a locomotive. References
to sacred wrongdoers punctuated American society. Temperance advocates
of the age attacked the distribution and consumption of "demon rum," while
Protestants assailed religious innovations, such as spiritualism and Mormonism, as led by people who were deluded by "Satan." The prince of evil even
became popular entertainment, useful in the growing commercial realm of
amusement. By the 1850s, the most popular exhibit at Peale's Museum in New
York was a tour of the "Infernal Regions," where Beelzebub and Lucifer guided
onlookers on an excursion through hell.[6]

Nowhere did the presence of evil become more apparent or visceral than
in sectional debates over slavery. There, invocations of devils, demons, and
hell worked to fracture the nation, to disunite that which had been fragilely
united only decades earlier. It began with African American antislavery
voices. Many of those who had achieved freedom from slavery and told their
stories linked slavery to hell and slaveholders to demons. From there, concepts of evil moved into the speeches of white abolitionists, proslavery advocates, and Congressmen. These elected officials of the 1850s tore the country
apart rhetorically before they did so legislatively. When the war came, the
devil and demonic history became important players in the political culture
of the day, the commercialization and profiteering from the struggle, the ways
artists attempted to visualize key aspects of the conflicts, and the ways countless Americans expressed their experiences.

While most invocations of the demonic and hell were used to denounce
enemies, the forces of evil also became useful tools of self-identification. Many
military men and political officials began encouraging combatant forces to
fight like devils. Rather than destroy their demonic opponents, these soldiers

cheered actions and attitudes expressly labeled demonic. They embraced bringing hell to earth as a positive good.

Near the end of the war and after it, some white men became so distraught by the possibilities of losing their place at the top of the political and economic hierarchy that they abandoned all considerations for law and civil society and embraced vigilante terrorism. First as guerillas and then as Klansmen, these white men embraced being what African Americans had long said they were: devils. By the late 1860s, these white men did not dress as farmers, planters, lawyer, or soldiers. Now they appeared as demons with draped cloth over their bodies and horns upon their hoods. They were bent on destroying God's work, on making life hellish for anyone who supported justice and equality for African Americans. When the federal government moved to destroy the Ku Klux Klan in the early 1870s, its demonic performative culture became an important aspect of justifying expansive new federal laws.

Satan's influence in the American Civil War, or at least how Americans brought concepts of the devil, demons, and hell into every fabric of their lives and times, continued to impact the nation and its people after the war. When General William Tecumseh Sherman looked back on the conflict, he observed that war "is all hell." When Confederate President Jefferson Davis wrote his history of the war, he called the United States federal government "the serpent." Then when discussing the ending of slavery, he penned, "The tempter came, like the serpent in Eden, and decoyed them with the magic word of "freedom." When Ambrose Bierce wrote imaginative stories of the age of conflict, he incorporated demonic figures into the complex twists of his descriptions. He even published a new dictionary of the real meanings of words after the Civil War and called it *The Devil's Dictionary*. When African Americans recalled the age, some referred to the past with reference to evil. "Dem days was hell," one told interviewers in the 1930s. Although many Americans later came to celebrate the war, to honor the men who fought as heroes, to venerate the political and military leaders, and even to glorify the Ku Klux Klan, they could never exorcise that which Americans had put to so much work: the demonic and hellish.

War Is All Hell uses Milne's lithograph from the 1850s as a window into the eras of the Civil War and Reconstruction. What seemed unique about this image was not the presence of devils, but their plentitude. The demonic characters overwhelmed the drawing. There were almost too many to count. In several figures, devils vomited smaller devils to bring terror to the land. There was no flow to the image, no direction, no progression. It was violent chaos. Milne's dream was a nightmare.

And it was Milne's nightmare, not Lincoln's hope, that defined the 1860s. Little did Milne or others know that they would experience not one nightmare, but many. It is into those nightmares that this book plunges. The "better angels" of men did not define the moment, at least not according to the countless Americans who comprehended the age as one defined by devils and hell. In the crafting and deploying of those fallen angels we may see another reason for why the United States remains so disunited more than one hundred fifty years after the war, especially when it comes to the unredeemed violent legacies of people owning other people. One reason may be that most white American men have been so busy seeking to exorcise demons from others and to make heaven on earth that they have rarely looked into the mirror and seen the hell of their own making.

During the presidential election of 1860, a notable Philadelphia publishing house distributed a book-length poem, *The Devil in America*. The work was so potentially scandalous and polarizing that the author kept his or her name secret and used the pseudonym Lacon. An obvious adaptation of John Milton's *Paradise Lost*—that epic poem from the 1600s in which Milton added layers of detail to short and obscure biblical passages to create a lengthy tale of Satan's fall from heaven and subsequent scheme to tempt Adam and Eve in the Garden of Eden—the American version picked up where Milton left off. After being defeated by Jesus more than eighteen hundred years earlier, the devil and his minions turned their "attention to America." They dominated the continents for centuries. Native Americans worshipped the "demon of revenge" and adored "the god of war." Before "the Anglo-Saxon came," demons "ruled the savage hordes." But with the British came the bright light of Christianity and "the Red Man disappear'd." After 1600, the kingdom of heaven invaded, prevailed, and seemed to overwhelm Satan's soldiers.[1]

Hell fought back. Collectively, the demonic horde determined that the best way to undermine God would be to stir "up strife between the North and the South, producing insurrections, civil war, and a dissolution of the Union." In the years before 1860, they went to work.[2]

The devils attacked on many fronts, much like those in Milne's lithograph. Some sowed seeds of unbelief, trying to convince Americans that there was no god and thereby create "atheistic legions." Others endeavored to convince Americans that "all is God, and God is all," thereby watering down true religion. Along with the speciousness of Unitarianism and Universalism, other "superstitions" (which included Mormonism and Spiritualism for the author) became demonic replacements for Christianity. At the same time, alcoholic beverages served to poison men's minds and keep them from the redemptive waters of genuine faith.[3]

While all of these created division within the country, Satan had an end game: disunion. He planned to achieve this by tempting Americans to put faith in a political and social concept called "freedom." This "higher law," a term used widely by antislavery activists and some members of the Republican Party of the 1850s, would seduce some Americans in the North to believe that slavery was evil and that acting beyond the legal restraints of civil society was justifiable. By the time the devil's will would be done, the entire nation would be in an uproar. Women would be convinced that they were enslaved. They would "hate the sphere for her design'd." Devils would lead "demagogues" to "infest the Congress halls." Men would "sacrifice their country's good" and then "ere long, the Union will dissolve."[4]

The devil's primary weapon would be "Black Republicans," those who were "white without / But black within, and known by kinky thoughts." These men and women were "a frightful horde" who would attempt to alter God's natural order of slavery. Naming names, the poet maintained that the same evil spirits that had once terrorized biblical characters now worked through white abolitionists who included Harriet Beecher Stowe, John Brown, Gerrit Smith, and Joshua Giddings. They and other abolitionists became "lying legions everywhere" who "through papers, pamphlets, sermons, and reviews / Through novels, poems, and books made for schools / Through teachers, preachers, and professors learn'd, / Through orators, editors, and statesmen, / Through societies, and in conventions, / In college walls and legislative halls" wrought "agitation everywhere."[5]

Satan ended his discourse by summoning all his fellow demons to the United States. "Wide ope, ye gates of chaos, night, and hell, / And let the foulest, blackest legions forth." He demanded that the "demon of Murder . . . send forth your hosts." Their goal was to bring "Hell's bloody hounds of carnage and of war!" The result: "And all the elements of strife break loose, / And desolation has her work commenced / North and South become a dreary waste."[6]

This pseudonymous poet presented his work as satire. He poked fun at the foibles and frustrations he and many other Americans found in their society. He and the publisher also capitalized on these conflicts through book sales and royalties. In doing so, the author and press revealed an important element of American society during the contentious presidential election that would ultimately result in disunion and civil war: the devil could simultaneously be considered to be working in their midst and to have been created by Americans for their own purposes. Whether through demonic intervention or from human harnessing, the devil and hell became present in the land. *War Is All Hell* investigates some of the obvious and hidden truths this poet invoked.

"The devil's in the details," and no epoch in American history has been more detailed than the Civil War. Before the war even began, Americans prophesied ad infinitum about the possibility of disunion. From the founding politicians of the 1770s to those in the days before the firing on Fort Sumter in April 1861, Americans anticipated a war between the states and often labored to avoid it. Nevertheless, as President Abraham Lincoln passively noted near the Civil War's end in March 1865, "the war came."[7]

During and after the titanic struggle, Americans produced an overflow of information. Just as devils invaded the United States in Lacon's poem and overwhelmed Milne's response to *Uncle Tom's Cabin,* so too did materials about the war supersaturate the land. Letters, speeches, judicial decisions, poems, stories, and diary entries stand as evidentiary peaks. Americans also created and exchanged a surplus of images for public and private consumption. They wrote and sang songs. They printed new currency, stamps, and envelopes. Over and over, Americans endeavored to make sense of the war, to explain it, to direct it, and to stamp themselves onto the story that seemed too big to comprehend.

As much as many Americans hoped that God was in control, as much as they pounded proclamations about providence—the notion that somehow, someway, the Christian God directed the course of human events—Satan and hellish minions stalked them at every turn.[8] The devil and his company invaded the United States because Americans conjured them. Like Milne and the poet of *The Devil in America*, they imagined and placed evil into their world in every conceivable way. They invoked him. They discussed him. They explained events and experiences by turning to the devil and to hell. They drew evil on paper. They sang evil into their songs. From the most moving of speeches to the most seemingly banal of visual renderings, Satan and his dark domain showed up just about everywhere.

Americans created the devil visually and sonically, mentally and materially. Men and women produced an incredible number of demonic items, and in some cases looked to make a profit from the prince of darkness. In the aural realm, hell pierced the sounds of nature. Instead of cows mooing or birds cawing, the soundscape now rang with bullets firing, cannons booming, and men screaming. The war unleashed hell on earth in the material and natural world.

War Is All Hell endeavors to accomplish three main goals: first, to place the devil on equal footing with the forces of God in American religious history; second, to emphasize the importance of extrabiblical resources for how Americans understood the Bible and the ways they linked Christianity to their lives; and third, to demonstrate to American historians in general that religion was crucial to every noteworthy aspect of the Civil War. *War Is All Hell* maintains that during the nineteenth century, a diverse array of Americans turned to notions of demons, hell, and Satan to understand the massive changes happening around them. Many of these Americans made use of ideas about dark supernatural evil to navigate issues as complex as slavery, secession, war, emancipation, politics, and extralegal violence. This study shows that the era of the American Civil War, how Americans made sense of it and themselves, and how they tried to transform their land can better be understood through attention to the many iterations of evil they created.

For too many years and in too many scholarly works, the forces of good have dominated renderings of American history and the Civil War in particular. God and Jesus most often play the leading roles. When the Public Broadcasting Service (PBS) aired a six-part series on American religious history in 2010, it was titled *God in America*. When Randall Balmer wrote a history of religion and the presidency during the second half of the twentieth century, he called it *God in the White House*. When Stephen Prothero attempted to find a unifying core to American religious history, he chose the title *American Jesus* and went so far as to claim that the United States was a "Jesus nation."[9]

This approach to American religious history has dominated the field of Civil War studies too. From Harry Stout's moral history of the Civil War to George Rable's expansive religious history of the war, historians have emphasized the ways Americans positioned themselves vis-à-vis God and Jesus. For Stout, this approach led him to maintain that an American civil religion was created during the war that conflated god with country. Although Stout despised this connection and hoped his work would challenge it, he paid little attention to considerations of evil during the age. If he had, he might have found that Americans were certainly interested and invested in darkness in their midst. He would have also found that at times they reveled in the immorality they knew they were making.

For Rable, his attention to God and Jesus led him to see providentialism as the key religious theme of the era, that most Americans held tightly to the notion that God was present and somehow in control. Even when Drew Gilpin Faust analyzed the overwhelming culture of death during the war, she focused upon re-creations of concepts of heaven. She made no effort to consider the place of the demonic in terms of death. In none of these works did Satan, or demonic legions, or hell play primary, secondary, or even tertiary roles. A perhaps connected phenomenon is that these works present religion as a secondary element—that the men, women, and children of the age had life experiences and then made religious sense of them.[10]

By diving into the demonic, *War Is All Hell* finds that some religious concepts were central, even pivotal, to how Americans understood, experienced, and created the war. This appears obvious as we address questions like these: why was Lincoln's most famous speech from before the war, "A House Divided," based upon a biblical story involving devils; why did Americans produce, purchase, and mail envelopes that featured demons by the thousands throughout the war; why did the most memorable musical anthem from the war, Julia Ward Howe's "Battle Hymn of the Republic," mention a serpent; why did a Civil War military leader come to the conclusion that war "is all hell"; why when Frederick Douglass waxed eloquent about the impact of black men's participation in the Union army did he borrow from the biblical book of Colossians to maintain that "there is no power on the earth *or under the earth*" that could deny their citizenship; and why did defeated white southern men fashion and then adorn themselves with elaborate horns and claim to be from hell as they terrorized African Americans after the war? These questions point to the clear importance of the devil, demons, and hell during the Civil War.

By drawing attention to spiritual evil, our book follows the brilliant works of W. Scott Poole and Kathryn Gin Lum. Poole's *Satan in America* offered a sweeping account of the place of the devil in American society, culture, and politics. He showed, and *War Is All Hell* elaborates upon, the ways in which Americans used Satan and hell for entertainment and commercial purposes. The demonic carried so much folkloric popularity that entrepreneurs found many ways to insert evil into American circumstances to assert political and social points along with making money. In many ways, the forces of evil could more easily be bent to those purposes because they avoided the stigma of overtly bringing God or Jesus into the realms of entertainment or commerce. In *Damned Nation*, Gin Lum emphasized that many Americans in the nineteenth century maintained a profound belief in hell and put the concept of damnation to work in their church lives, political cultures, and considerations of moral reform. When the question of "belief" arises, when we wonder if Americans really believed religiously in how they deployed devils around them, we rely on Gin Lum's work, which showcased how richly and powerfully Americans held the issue of damnation in their hearts and minds.[11]

In terms of extrabiblical sources, *War Is All Hell* examines how Americans made use of the Bible and Christianity. This study suggests that when Americans approached their Bibles to make sense of the Civil War, they did so not primarily with American philosophies or theologies but instead with historical resources from European popular culture. Many central story lines from the war, such as the equation of secession with Satan, the comparisons between prisons and hell, and the growing encouragement to "fight like devils" came not from the Bible, but from texts like John Milton's *Paradise Lost*, John Bunyan's *Pilgrim's Progress*, Dante Alighieri's *Inferno*, and plays by Shakespeare. In addition, when Americans visualized the devil and devils, they drew upon a long history of such conceptions in European art. The overall point is this: Americans were never simply "people of the Book," as much literature on the Bible in the United States suggests. Instead, they comprehended both themselves and sacred scriptures through nonbiblical expressions. "America's God" may have been a "shift away from European theological traditions," as Mark Noll argued famously, but America's devil was firmly tied to European roots.[12]

In drawing upon the European cultural roots of how Americans brought evil into the Civil War, this book uses concepts from several key studies on European religious history. First and foremost, we are indebted to the works of Jeffrey Burton Russell. His volumes on the long history of the devil and hell in Christianity showed how in the nineteenth century Satan became a "powerful and ambivalent symbol." On one hand, many people continued to believe in damnation and Satan, and this made them powerful. On the other, many did not or challenged conceptions of evil, and this made Satan's power seem suspect. There was no better example of this than in the decline of witchcraft accusations and trials. In the United States, there were no Salem witchcraft trials in the 1800s.[13]

Russell's point has a companion in the powerful work *A Secular Age* by Charles Taylor. He found the nineteenth century to be a critical hinge in the emergence of "the secular," in particular the emergence of societies that considered God as one possibility among others. Unlike previous centuries when God and the supernatural seemed unquestionable, in the nineteenth century it became commonplace for people to wonder about their realities and powers. Secularism did not replace belief, but instead heightened the ambivalence of religious figures. When Americans and Europeans invoked the devil, they had the ability in the nineteenth century to do so in many ways. They could mean it literally; they could mean it metaphorically; and Americans could consume references to devils, demons, and hell in those ways as well.[14]

Taken all together, the works of Russell, Taylor, and many others provide the backdrop for supposedly supernatural entities to be put to work on multiple levels of meaning. *War Is All Hell* embraces the ambivalence of evil during this age and maintains that this is one of the reasons Satan, demons, and hell could be invoked in nearly every situation.

Finally, this book hopes to convince historians of the Civil War that religious concepts influenced strongly every vital aspect of the age. Whether considering the political culture surrounding the secession crisis or the economics of print production, whether looking closely at the individual experiences of wounded soldiers or the broader views of military agendas, whether evaluating perspectives for emancipation or against it, and whether considering white terroristic violence after 1865 or the federal government's responses to it, religious concepts expressed in forms related to evil played definitive roles. The devil was in more than the details. Satan flowed in the mainstreams.

Because the devil, demons, and hell took so many forms and functioned in so many aspects of the war, *War Is All Hell* draws upon and combines a multitude of scholarly perspectives to untangle the many interconnected cords. When considering the origins and outcomes of disunion in the first chapter, we explore political culture, biblical interpretations, and print capitalism. The combination shows that an imaginative biblical origin story of Satan played an instrumental role in developing a Unionist explanation for Confederate activity and forming a militant response to it. When, in Chapter 2, we move to individual wartime experiences of combatants, we join disability studies and its emphasis on physicality to environmental studies and its emphasis on land and water, and to literary analysis and its emphasis on rhetoric.[15] Together, the three allow us to see how war became "hell" for many combatants because of the ways it ruptured their physical senses, replacing previous experiences of sight, smell, taste, and touch with new ones. In their struggle to articulate these embodied and experienced feelings many men turned to the language of other seemingly incomprehensible forces in their world: evil.

To examine emancipation, one of the most brilliantly and controversially analyzed issues of the war, we turn from the question of "who freed the slaves" to how Americans comprehended slavery's end.[16] For this, we look to visual culture of the era and use it to observe how artists endeavored to decipher invisible meanings with visible presentations. Many graphic portrayals of emancipation, of Lincoln, and of the war focused upon seeing the unseen. With etchings, paintings, lithographs, and even photographs, Civil War artists found in emancipation an exposure of things unseen, and often they created a dis-united states replete with devils and hell.[17]

The final chapters of *War Is All Hell* build upon recent works in guerilla studies, theater studies, and legal history to illuminate a new reality for Americans after emancipation: an embrace of behaving like Satan and transforming their landscape into hell. Americans continued to damn the actions and attitudes of their enemies as demonic, but also explicitly and overtly mimicked devils. As the war continued, "to fight like a devil" became a widespread compliment. Civil War soldiers ceased trying to act as Christian combatants and instead exerted themselves to shout, run, bayonet, and fire like demons in human form. Making hell on earth became a war aim for many in the North and the South. Then after the war, when southern white men felt the twin stings of defeat and African American citizenship, many resorted to dressing themselves, describing themselves, and behaving themselves as genuine devils. By the end of the Civil War and in its immediate aftermath, many Americans no longer hoped to defeat the devil. Now they wanted to be his minions. The most obvious expression of this came at night as members of the Ku Klux Klan.

These are just some of the ways Americans brought Satan, demons, and hell to bear on the eras of the Civil War and Reconstruction. It makes sense that the forces of evil would seem to define the age, because disorder seemed more prevalent than order, death more abundant than life, and fear more pronounced than courage. While historians have typically looked to how Americans conceived of God in order to understand their religious considerations of the war, we may find more, much more, by running with the devil.

Almost seventy years after the Civil War ended and in the midst of the Great Depression, the federal government commissioned interviews of aged former slaves. Carter J. Jackson, a man once owned legally by other men, answered the question of what slavery felt like directly: "If you's want to know 'bout slavery time, it was Hell." He then detailed a history of violence and malnourishment. Of the Civil War, he remembered it as "tough." There, he witnessed the death of his master's son, and even when emancipation came he nonetheless "worked on for Massa Rogers four years after that, jus' like in slavery time."[18] One woman told her interviewers "Dem days wuz hell."[19] Around the same time as these interviews, a black sociologist of the early twentieth century also spoke with elderly African Americans. One minister summed up his feelings about the past with these words: "Yes, in them days it was hell without fires. This is one reason why I believe in a hell. I don't believe a just God is going to take no such man as that into his kingdom."[20] For this minister and so many others, the age of slavery and Civil War proved not the existence of God, but of Satan. It is time, at least in terms of historical scholarship on the Civil War and Reconstruction, that the devil get his due.

CHAPTER 1

Slavery, Secession, and Satan

In 1861, just as the Civil War began, G. W. Henry, a blind Methodist preacher from the North, published a novel with a sentient cloth named "Tell Tale" as the main character. Tell Tale was made from southern cotton, lovingly cultivated and birthed by the laboring hands of African American slaves. Throughout his life, he became a rag, a piece of paper, and eventually one square of a missionary's garment. *Tell Tale Rag, and Popular Sins of the Day* was zany and comical, and it circulated widely in the North and in Britain. Although it was intended for children, Henry used the anthropomorphized Tell Tale to make religious, social, and political points. He also wanted to make money, as he sold the novel to fund his ministerial travels.

Tell Tale explored the most pressing matters of American society. In 1861, he began "a search for the initiative of SECESSION." Disunion had become the drama of the day, and Tell Tale hunted for answers. In response to Abraham Lincoln's victory in the presidential election, hundreds of white men throughout the southern states convened to debate whether to remain within the Union. Seven Deep South states determined to disunite formally. They based their decisions upon fears of emancipation, assertions of states' rights, and claims of social differences between the sections. They presented themselves as descendants of the American revolutionaries of the 1770s who chose independence over what they considered dependence. They understood their actions as preemptive strikes against servile insurrections and race wars, such as those that had occurred decades earlier in Haiti. Republicans and Democrats in the North rallied to stop secession. For them, disunion at this moment violated the contracts of civil society. Losing an election was no grounds for dissection.[1]

Tell Tale believed he had unearthed the seeds of secession below the time and space of the United States. He located its roots before the Constitutional Convention of 1787 or the Declaration of Independence of 1776. The origins reached back before human existence. "The first secessionist that history gives any account of was once a bright star in the galaxy of heaven," Tell Tale explained. The rag grafted stories from the Bible onto recent events in the United States, using the language of American politics to reconceptualize sacred Christian history. Tell Tale claimed that long ago the angel Michael was a "Free-Soiler" with "abolitionist friends." Their love for "liberty" enraged Lucifer, who became "the first secessionist." Lucifer and one third of the angelic host rebelled and endeavored to make "poor slaves" of humans. Michael intervened for freedom, constructing an "under-ground railroad from the brick yards of Pharaoh to the free soil of the spiritual Canaan." According to Tell Tale, secession "is the ancient landmark of the order of slaveholders." Satan is "their secession prince and leader." Tell Tale concluded that "a striking resemblance exists between the secessionist, Lucifer, and his Southern children."[2]

In the realm of nonfiction, Henry understood Satan to be both an active force and a useful analogy. In his autobiography, he discussed his travels throughout the United States, his work in the South among slaves, and his spiritual journey. Time and again, he experienced the devil in "whispers." Satan could speak through other people or within Henry himself. At the individual level, the devil focused on dissuading Henry from "trying to get religion." Beyond personal salvation, the powers of hell worked principally in the domain of slavery. After reading *Uncle Tom's Cabin* in the 1850s, the same novel that led C. R. Milne to imagine devils invading the United States, Henry became convinced that human bondage "comes from the devil, that's the short of it."[3]

As Tell Tale linked slavery, secession, and Satan, he tangled economic, social, political, and legal branches. He rooted all of them collectively in satanic soil. Radical evil served as the primary vehicle for Henry to explain through Tell Tale the pressing problems of this American moment. What followed during the next four years—the destruction and death, the liberation and exaltation, the puzzles solved and the conundrums concocted—originated with Satan. Just as Tell Tale began as a seed and came to life through cultivation so too did the conflict—irrepressible or not—that overtook the United States in

1861. If the Christian God had a manifest destiny for the United States, then disunited states could be explained by something, or someone, else: the devil.

Before 1861, Americans conjured the devil into a wide array of their circumstances, but in no place was Satan more omnipresent than in discussions over slavery and secession.[4] During the 1850s, the United States became the devil's playground because of what future generations would call the nation's original sin: slavery. Former slaves, white abolitionists, and Republican Congressmen sought to effect moral, social, economic, political, and legislative change through references to evil. Some southern whites and their northern conservative allies fired back that those who endeavored to overturn slaveholding were tools of the devil. The election of 1860 and its aftermath ignited even more mutual demonization. The Republican Party was branded "black"; while among Unionists, the notion that Satan inspired and sustained secession emerged as a central element of moral politics and Union loyalty.

In the run-up to the Civil War, Americans birthed and put into play an increasing number of devils. They attached them to social groups rather than individuals: slaveholders, abolitionists, and Republicans. The place of evil escalated from religion and culture to politics and governance and finally to violence and militarism. At every point of this trajectory, demons and devils helped Americans to make money, as a growing number of men and women capitalized literally on radical evil. At the start of the Civil War, Satan became a commodified political power as pro-Union forces used the devil to sell the war and their wares.

The Civil War saw a subtle but meaningful shift in the place of evil in American discussions. Pro-Unionists emphasized Satan's role in secession and minimized his links to slavery. This turn from a social economy to governmental politics moved the focus of debate from exorcising the evils of racial injustice to maintaining the glory of national union. That shift helped the Union win the war, but lose the revolution for equality.

The Atmosphere of Hell

In 1859, sculptor and abolitionist John Rogers endeavored to cash in on antislavery moralism and the growing divide between the North and the

South through a small piece he called *The Slave Auction*. It featured four slaves for sale. A man stood tall and proud with his arms folded in defiance. A woman cuddled a baby, while a child hid behind the woman's dress. In the center, the auctioneer held a gavel in his right hand and leaned forward to hear bids.

Viewed from the front, the scene seemed wholly of the natural and material world: humans being sold by a human; families enduring pain; men making money from the bodies of other men, women, and children. The back of the sculpture revealed a darker reality, one where otherworldly forces had invaded this world. The auctioneer's hair protruded in two areas to "give the impression of horns," as Rogers himself acknowledged. Below, a short tail bulged from under the auctioneer's coat. He masqueraded as a man. His animalistic features revealed his authentic identity: a devil in disguise.[5]

When Rogers used clay to deform a man into a demon, he followed recent trends in abolitionist culture and African Americans' depictions of slavery. Beginning in the 1830s, a number of black writers utilized references to devils, demons, and hell in order to explain what they endured in enslavement. Their work set the tone and stage for the 1850s when evil moved from the periphery of American political culture to its center. There, it helped fracture the nation.

Before the nineteenth century, antislavery whites and writers in the black Atlantic rarely invoked supernatural evil when discussing slavery. Neither Britton Hammon in his life story published in 1760, nor Olaudah Equiano in his "interesting narrative" published in the late 1780s, charged slaveholders with demonic activities. When African Americans in Massachusetts petitioned for freedom during the 1770s, they described themselves as living in the "bowels" of a "Christian country." They claimed that "nonexistence" would be preferable to what they experienced. At no point did they use the direct language of hell, devils, or demons.[6]

The individuals who most often labeled slavery an "evil" were those who put it into practice. In the years following the American Revolution, many whites who owned slaves or who justified the institution did so by calling it a "necessary evil." Throughout Thomas Jefferson's long life, he routinely criticized slavery as an "evil" social structure. In *Notes on the State of Virginia* from the 1780s, he referred to slavery as a "great political and moral evil."[7] One of his protégés, James Monroe, who owned hundreds of slaves himself, wrote in 1829 that slavery was "one of the evils still remaining" since the ratification of the Constitution.[8]

This shifted in the 1830s. A group of writers and activists began assaulting enslavement by using the language of religious evil. It became central to their rendering the social system of slavery. David Walker, a free black man in Boston, led the way. In 1829, he published an *Appeal to the Coloured Citizens of the World*, where he made direct and unequivocal proclamations against slavery and slaveholding. He attacked whites as "unjust, jealous" and "unmerciful." "We see them acting more like devils than accountable men," he charged. He referred to the actions of slavery as "infernal" and whites as behaving like "tyrants and devils." Their "hellish deeds" had created "hell upon earth." Overall, Walker used the word infernal on nine occasions, a form of hell six times, and variants of devil or demon eighteen times.[9]

Walker seemed to initiate a paradigm shift in the rhetorical struggle against slavery. After him, an increasing number of black writers routinely likened slavery to hell and slaveholders to demons. Henry "Box" Brown claimed in his autobiography, "It is true in more senses than one, that slavery rests upon hell." Their physical, emotional, and spiritual experiences in bondage led these writers to portray slavery as a comprehensive social organization best understood in terms of religious evil. "My sufferings I can compare to nothing else than the burning agonies of hell!" wrote Samuel Northrop. Sexual abuse and the selling of children from their parents led William Anderson to exclaim, "If there is anything like a hell on earth, New Orleans must be the place." Harriet Jacobs put the point succinctly, probably quoting white antislavery poet John Greenleaf Whittier: "Somebody has called it 'the atmosphere of hell'; and I believe it is so."[10]

African Americans demonized the bodies of slaveholders, just as John Rogers did later with his sculpture *The Slave Auction*. They called owners and traders "devils incarnate," "hellish fiends," and "demons in human form." Black writers also compared them to serpents. In so doing, they not only associated white men and women with evil but also with animals. William Walter discussed one particularly hated slaveholder, Dick Fallon, as "a demon" whose "glittering eyes . . . seemed to sit too far back in his head." This "made them glitter like the eyes of a deadly serpent."[11] Lewis Clarke viewed slave catchers "going about like Satan, seeking whom they might devour," and mistresses as "snake-eyed, brawling women, which slavery produces. . . . Of all the animals of the face of the earth, I am most afraid of a real mad, passionate, raving, slaveholding woman."[12]

Frederick Douglass leveraged this rhetorical analogy when describing Edward Covey, the "slave breaker" he made infamous. He "seldom approached the spot where we were at work openly, if he could do it secretly," Douglass remembered. "Such was his cunning, that we used to call him, among ourselves, 'the snake.'" Covey, at least in Douglass's rendering, contorted his body to mimic that of a serpent. "When we were at work in the cornfield, he would sometimes crawl on his hands and knees to avoid detection, and all at once he would rise nearly in our midst, and scream out, 'Ha, ha! Come, come! Dash on, dash on!'"[13]

For many African Americans, what slaveholders produced on earth followed them to times and spaces beyond. In the future, they would get what they gave: hell. These black writers concluded that slaveholding meant a one-way ticket to hell. Henry Box Brown came to believe that "*every* slaveholder will infallibly go to hell, unless he repents." Frederick Douglass maintained, "Slaves know enough of the rudiments of theology to believe that those go to hell who die slaveholders."[14]

When African Americans analogized enslavement as hell and insisted that slave ownership determined an afterlife of eternal damnation, they redefined Christianity and its connections between earth, heaven, and hell. Rather than focus upon how a person received salvation—whether through righteous works or through faith in Christ or through baptism—they emphasized the roads to hell. Slave ownership became the polar opposite of faith or works. It became a composite of evil—action and attitude—that destined one for the domain of demons.

Several social and cultural streams merged to facilitate African Americans' turn to the language of evil. A few of those streams flowed from one lake: liberty. When earlier writers of the black Atlantic like Equiano challenged slavery, there were few, if any, locations of liberty outside of Africa for people of African descent. All the British colonies had slaves, and so did the other European empires. When the American revolutionaries heralded "liberty" and some new states outlawed slavery, spots of freedom opened for African Americans. Then Britain ended slavery throughout its empire in the 1830s. With domains and denizens now on record against slavery, black writers could attack the institution directly. There were audiences that agreed: liberty was godly; slavery was wrong.

Another type of liberty made the turn to the Christian language of evil possible: religious liberty. Under the Constitution, the federal government refused to privilege any particular religious organization. Then the states detached church organizations from the operations of the government. In this milieu, Americans pursued their religious agendas. African Americans and many others formed their own religious congregations, published their own materials, and became active audiences for religious concepts. With religious liberty, African Americans became powerful and sometimes autonomous players in the realm of American religion and thus had increased legal and social space to make religious claims.[15]

Religious liberty was part of a broader tectonic shift in Western culture that scholars now call "secularism." During the late eighteenth and throughout the nineteenth century, conceptions of the sacred shifted. Religion became a choice rather than an assumed reality. Humans became buffered in their interiorities—meaning that supernatural forces could not invade humans as they seemed able to in earlier centuries. One indication of these shifts was the demise of witchcraft trials. Although some throughout Europe and the Americas continued to believe in witchcraft, states and governments stopped bringing those perceived to be in league with dark forces to courts of law.[16]

Secularism did not banish religion. Instead, it opened portals to multiple uses of religious language. The devil and hell became both literal and figurative. One could damn another as demonic without necessarily meaning the person was a literal devil. In the process, writers shifted the emphasis of evil from individuals to groups. The point was not to accuse slaveholders one by one of deals with the devil, but instead to indict an entire social system and those who participated in it as a group as evil.

For these black writers, hell and demonic concepts served several purposes. On the one hand, they constituted powerful metaphors to describe the social organization of slavery. On the other, they stood as literal places and experiences beyond this world where slaveholders would experience eternal torment. What slaves experienced temporally on earth—torture, sadness, horror—would become the everlasting reality for slaveholders in the afterlife.

An Agreement with Hell

An assortment of whites responded to these innovations by challenging, building upon, and redirecting associations of enslavement with hell and slaveholders with demons. South Carolinian John C. Calhoun attempted to shift perspectives on slavery from a necessary evil to a "positive good." He and his acolytes grew more vociferous in their claim that slavery benefited owners, the ones they owned, and society as a whole. A number of Christian leaders wrote works defending slavery as biblical and godly. The positive good position, along with antislavery denunciations of slavery, created polarized positions whereby debates over slavery became Manichean: good versus evil, depending on where one started.

Some whites took what African Americans offered and ran with it. William Lloyd Garrison benefited from African Americans and promoted them probably more than any other white American of his era. He did so primarily through his antislavery newspaper the *Liberator*, established in 1831 in Boston. Ten years later, in 1842, Garrison asked that the masthead of the abolitionist magazine be altered. Speaking before the Massachusetts Anti-Slavery Society, he hoped that these words would be placed alongside the imagery of an auction and emancipation: "The existing Constitution is a 'covenant with death, and an agreement with hell.' NO UNION WITH SLAVE-HOLDERS."[17] Garrison borrowed from the biblical book of Isaiah where the Hebrew prophet berated those who thought they could hide from the righteous judgment of God. Garrison and his colleagues also drew from the book of Revelation to damn southern white churches as "synagogues of Satan."[18]

Throughout the 1840s, Garrison and several other abolitionists continued to assert that the Constitution was a proslavery document and that northerners clasped governmental hands with monsters of hell. Garrison gave the line dramatic flair on the Fourth of July in 1854. Speaking in Boston, he burned copies of the United States Constitution and the Fugitive Slave Act of 1850. He used literal flames to expose the figurative hellish inferno from whence the Constitution and the Fugitive Slave Act came.[19]

Garrison and some other white abolitionists used a variety of references to hell to describe slavery and the constitutional union of northern states with southern ones. They aimed to persuade northerners to understand the Constitution as a "moral" contract with political, social, and economic outcomes. For Garrison, "union" with slaveholders was sin, not a sustainable civil society.

When Garrison deployed the language and literal imagery of hell, he followed, added to, and redirected attacks upon slavery previously made by African Americans. White writers added two important components to African American discussions of slavery as hell. First, white opponents of slavery, especially Garrison, focused their attacks on the Constitution and other aspects of federal law. Their attention to the nation-state turned the subject of discussion slightly from a social system (the institution of slavery) to laws and governance (the Constitution).

Second, whites like Garrison brought John Milton's *Paradise Lost* to bear on the situation. An epic poem published in the middle of the seventeenth century, *Paradise Lost* imaginatively told the story of Lucifer's fall from heaven and his decision as the now renamed Satan to turn humans against God. Many read and interpreted *Paradise Lost* as a saga about civil societies. Lucifer rebelled against the government of God and endeavored to bring anarchy to the theocracy that Adam and Eve experienced on Earth. Time and again, Garrison and his fellow white abolitionists included materials and language from *Paradise Lost* in the *Liberator*. After John C. Calhoun declared slavery "a good," an article in the *Liberator* retorted, "His statesmanship is nothing better, nothing less, than demonship. . . . He believes and acts in accordance with that belief that it is 'better to reign in hell than serve in heaven.'" Calhoun was "like Satan, as described in Milton's *Paradise Lost*."[20]

One striking difference between Garrison's deployment of the devil and those of African Americans was that Garrison and his comrades emphasized the political, legislative, and ultimately governmental. When Garrison struck against the Constitution, he called into question the entirety of American national government. As a white man receiving the rights and privileges of citizenship, Garrison could afford to do this even though his rhetoric led southern whites to place bounties on his head and some northern whites to threaten him with violence. He had far less to lose than runaway slaves like Frederick Douglass or Henry Box Brown. Whether Garrison meant it or not, whether he was speaking literally about destroying the government or just waxing with hyperbolic passion to draw attention to the unequal application of the Constitution, Garrison was an insider challenging a government established and working to benefit people like himself.[21]

Enemies of abolition also turned increasingly to the language of evil. In particular, they lambasted antislavery activists who seemed to challenge broader social norms. Becoming proslavery advocates, these southern whites found friends among northerners who desired harmony and to conserve the social order as it was. For instance, after antislavery orator Angelina Grimké addressed the Massachusetts legislature in 1838, some in the state turned her first name on its head, calling her "Devil-ina." The sight and sound of a woman speaking on political issues in public conjured chaos for them.[22]

Slave rebellions were labeled as moments of demonic behavior. Introducing the "confessions" of Nat Turner in 1831, Thomas Gray referred to Turner and his followers as a "band of savages" who had "hellish purposes" for the white people of Southampton, Virginia.[23] Even Harriet Beecher Stowe likened slave resistance to the devil. In *Uncle Tom's Cabin*, Tom refused to strike the vile Simon Legree and hoped that Cassy, Legree's concubine, would avoid violent reprisals, "O, Misse Cassy! for the dear Lord's sake that died for ye, don't sell your soul to the devil, that way! Nothing but evil will come of it! The Lord hasn't called us to wrath. We must suffer, and wait His time."[24]

In fact, Stowe endeavored to take African American literature and experiences and channel them into conservative reform. She did so in part with discussions of devils and hell. Stowe voiced African Americans' frustrations with slaveholders through the character of Aunt Chloe. After lamenting that whites rip nursing black babies from their mothers, she asked Uncle Tom, "If the devil don't get them, what's he good for?" Tom, in his supreme piety, responded, "Pray for them that 'spitefully use you, the good book says." Stowe raised the possibility that southern whites belonged to Satan, but then placed into Tom's mouth words to offset that connection. Then later, Cassy spit at Tom, "Everything is pushing us into hell. Why shouldn't we go?" Again, Stowe used Tom to deflect this extremity. He shuddered at such blasphemy and tried to overcome worldly pain with otherworldly faith.[25]

The antislavery versus proslavery battle had visual components in depictions linking ministers with devils. In the middle of the 1850s, Harriet Beecher Stowe's brother, Henry Ward Beecher, used his pulpit power to funnel rifles to antislavery activists in Kansas. Labeled "Beecher's Bibles," these weapons had the sanction and name of Christianity. Against him, a graphic artist created a print that depicted Henry Ward Beecher preaching with a devil upholding his text. Between the kneeling demon, two rifles served as a stand for Beecher's book, crossing at the perfect point to block visually the devil's genitalia.[26] By the 1850s, all sides seemed increasingly intent on their positions and the use of demonic rhetoric and imagery both expressed and furthered the growing chasm.

The Kingdom of Heaven or the Kingdom of Satan

The proslavery and antislavery perspectives entered American political debates and domains in pronounced fashions. This became most obvious in the 1850s. During that decade, political polarization sharpened. The Whig Party died and the newly formed American and Republican parties vied to become the primary challenger to the Democratic Party. In the South, a growing number of fervent disunionists became more vocal. Their detractors labeled them "fire-eaters" who wished to plunge the nation into chaos. Allusions to devils and hell, which had been the language of African Americans and radical reformers, became the rhetoric of campaigning and elected white government officials. It also became the basis for increasing physical violence among white men.

When Republican Abraham Lincoln challenged Democrat Stephen A. Douglas for his seat in the Senate from Illinois in 1858, Lincoln received a letter from an Illinois farmer urging him to remind the people that "the Bible teaches the same that is taught by the declaration of Independence—by the Constitution of the U.S. and by the fathers of the republic"—that slavery was evil and that liberty was divine. "As I view the contest," the farmer concluded, "tho we say it is between Douglas & Lincoln . . . it is no less than a contest for the advancement of the kingdom of Heaven or the kingdom of Satan."[27]

This Illinois farmer was far from alone. During the 1850s, exclamations that the kingdom of Satan seemed to have invaded the republic of the United States abounded. They could be heard repeatedly in the halls of Congress.

Before the middle of the 1820s, Congressmen rarely used the words "Satan" or "devil" or "hell." But in the 1850s, the numbers skyrocketed. Just about every month, a Senator or Representative invoked radical evil during discussions and debates. Almost every time, some aspect of slavery was the reason.[28]

Slavery, struggles over its extension, and the possibility of disunion led Representative Robert M. T. Hunter of Virginia to prophesy. In 1848, just as the United States took possession of Mexico's northern land with the Treaty of Guadalupe Hidalgo, he declared that if the federal government forbade slavery in new territories in the far West, a "civil war" would follow. When Hunter searched for a historical analogue for his concerns, where he could use the recorded past to explain the likely history he foresaw, he found none in the "realms of history." Instead, "we must turn to the gloomiest conception of Milton, who makes his Satan address 'old night and chaos,' and promise to extend their reign at the expense of light and life."[29]

Time and again, congressmen looked to the Bible or works like Milton's to explain what was happening in their midst. In 1858, after proslavery forces engineered a proslavery constitution in the territory of Kansas, Congressman Henry Bennett of New York insisted, "The offer contained in this act has no precedent or parallel. The only thing resembling it occurred more than eighteen hundred years ago." Then, "Satan tempted our Savior, and offered Him all the lands they beheld."[30]

Even the most explosive speech of the 1850s had Satan at its center. Over two days in May 1856, Charles Sumner offered the Senate a speech he called "The Crime Against Kansas." In it, he lamented that "the State" was in trouble. Not just Kansas, which experienced violent episode after violent episode as residents and those along its border turned to militancy over the issue of slavery; not just the United States either, which struggled to define itself as the conflicting systems of slave labor and free labor tore at every level of society. For Sumner, the entire notion of "the State" or what others might call "government" or "civil society" was in danger. The reason for the problems was clear: Satan. "One Idea has ever been present . . . as the Satanic tempter— the motive power—the causing cause."[31]

Sumner went to rhetorical lengths far beyond those of his colleagues. He used sexualized language to shame other white men, including another senator. He received almost immediate feedback from Preston Brooks, a congressman from South Carolina, whose uncle Sumner had impugned. Brooks entered the Senate chamber after a session and bludgeoned Sumner repeatedly. Badly injured, Sumner was unable to occupy his seat for four years.

Brooks's violent act after Sumner's vitriolic rhetoric matched American society of the 1850s: militarized and militarizing. Following the Mexican-American War and then the Fugitive Slave Act of 1850, everyday Americans increasingly turned to violence to protect themselves or obtain their objectives. The Fugitive Slave Act created an atmosphere of tension and potential violence. It established a volatile environment where African Americans felt unsettled and whites could be marshaled into protecting slavery even if they desired to be left alone. Then, when popular sovereignty became the organizing principle for the Kansas and Nebraska territories, all hell seemed to break loose. Supporters of the expansion of slavery flooded the territory and endeavored to sway elections and laws. In response, antislavery activists became more militant, sending men and arms to the region to fight fire with fire.[32]

The man most remembered from the struggle over "Bleeding Kansas" was John Brown, and he understood himself to be a member of God's army set to destroy Satan's sentinels. In 1859, he, a few of his sons, and several young African American men transformed the quiet town of Harpers Ferry into a war zone when they overpowered its federal arsenal and occupied it. The goal was militant liberation: grab the cache of arms, distribute them to slaves and anyone else who would fight against slavery, and baptize with blood those who had long used violence to hold African Americans in bondage. The inspiration was spiritual devotion. Brown believed that slavery was an evil that followers of Christ should destroy.[33]

"You know that Christ once armed Peter," Brown wrote to a friend several months after the raid failed. Two of his sons had died when marines led by Robert E. Lee overran the arsenal, and now Brown sat in prison awaiting his execution. Writing quietly from his jail cell, Brown did not despair. He repeatedly mentioned how "cheerful" he was and felt himself a neo-Peter for his abominable age. "So also in my case I think he put a sword into my hand, and there continued it so long as he saw best, and then kindly took it from me."[34]

By mapping Christ's redemptive work onto the days of antebellum slavery, Brown linked his militant crusade to the cosmic battle that set the forces of God against those of the devil. As early as 1854, Brown had identified the struggle as one against "*Satan* and his legions." Five years later, when Congressman Clement Vallandigham asked Brown, "Who sent you here?" Brown replied, "No man sent me here; it was my own prompting and that of my Maker, or that of the Devil,—whichever you please to ascribe it to, I acknowledge no master in human form." Baffled by Brown, one lieutenant asked, "But don't you believe in the Bible?"[35]

John Brown did believe the Bible, just not in the same way as his captors. Another Bible believer of the age, Thomas Jackson, kept watch the day the commonwealth of Virginia executed Brown for treason. In only a few years, Jackson earned the nickname "Stonewall." He became the Confederate general his northern antagonists most feared and most envied. On that cold day in December 1859, Jackson was a major in the United States Army and an instructor at the Virginia Military Academy. He observed Brown at the gallows. Although Brown had a "very solemn face," Jackson wrote home to his wife, he "ascended the scaffold with apparent cheerfulness." Jackson was, at first, "much impressed with the thought that before me stood a man, in the full vigor of health, who must in a few minutes be in eternity."[36]

Jackson did his Christian duty and prayed for Brown, "that he might be saved." The major meant from damnation, not execution. He did not have much hope, however. "Awful was the thought," he concluded to his wife, "that he might in a few minutes receive the sentence 'Depart ye wicked into everlasting fire.'" Jackson assumed God would banish Brown to hell because Brown wielded arms against slavery and against his nation. These acts, rather than faith in the redemptive power of Jesus Christ or a baptism into a particular church, determined his final destination in the mind of Jackson. Historian Kathryn Gin Lum was certainly right when she wrote, "The threat of hell influenced prescriptions for what it meant to be both a good Christian and a good American" during the nineteenth century.[37] In this moment and many others, civil religion overpowered Christian values. American events pushed views of damnation. When thinking of Brown's ultimate destination, his actions relative to society and the nation-state outweighed belief.

In less than two years, Jackson followed Brown in at least two ways. He brought violence against the federal government and also attacked Harpers Ferry. Like Brown, Jackson acted in the name of God. Like Brown, Jackson died for it and perhaps met his maker just as Brown had.[38]

Black Republicans and Selling Satan

Throughout 1860, antislavery activists continued to attack slaveholders as Satanic. Charles Sumner returned to the Senate in June 1860 after four years away following his beating by Preston Brooks. In his first speech after arrival, he told his colleagues he would never stop his verbal assault upon slavery. The devil remained a core rhetorical hammer. "I oppose the essential Barbarism of Slavery," he declared, "whether high or low, as Satan is still Satan."[39] During 1860 and 1861, the devil took a new role in American politics, and amid the political chaos several entrepreneurs and politicians found ways to sell Satan to increasingly bellicose consumers and voters.

These trends came to a head in the presidential election of 1860 and its aftermath. The victory of the candidate from the young Republican Party, Abraham Lincoln, and the subsequent secession of several states from the Union added new elements of radical evil to the now disuniting United States. New demons danced across the landscape, as Americans had to run with the devils they conjured.

Throughout the election campaign and during secession discussions, southern whites rarely used the direct language of radical evil. Only on rare occasions did they call Republicans demons and devils. One South Carolinian, for instance, denounced them as "selfish & envious sons of Satan."[40] A white Virginian borrowed from John Bunyan's *Pilgrim's Progress*, the famous and widely known English allegory from the late seventeenth century that emphasized the difficulties of believers making it to heaven, when he complained to his wife that William Seward, Lincoln's secretary of state, was "the Apollyon of the Republican Party—'the power behind the throne greater than the throne itself.'"[41] These references were far and few between. Most often, southerners did not accuse Lincoln of being in league with the devil. During official discussions at the Mississippi convention about secession in 1861, no member used the word Satan. Only once was the word "hell" used. The same was true for the word "demon." In Texas, none of these words were used. The same was the case in Alabama. Unlike the members of Congress during the 1850s whose references to "Satan," "hell," "devils," and "demons" routinely echoed through the chambers, southern secessionists did not call to their aid direct demonization.[42]

Southern whites had many reasons to disdain abolitionists and northern Republicans, but they did not desire to destroy them. Southern whites showed no interest in violently overthrowing the Union government or of invading the North to kill abolitionists. They wanted their liberty and the liberty to deprive others of those rights. They wanted their Christianity. These points limited their expressions of animosity toward northerners.

Leveraging the language of radical evil was difficult in their particular circumstances. They could attack antislavery activists for upsetting the social order, but they could not denounce general concepts of freedom since they themselves cherished independence. Secession itself was an act of independence. In addition, although southern whites came to understand the Constitution as a contractual compact that could be terminated, they did not see it as wicked or evil, as William Lloyd Garrison did. They interpreted the Constitution as a document that supported slavery and limited the powers of the federal government. For this reason, southern whites did not damn the United States in its entirety or its history, but they feared how northern Republicans would govern.

Rather than make explicit references to radical evil, southern whites created a catchall phrase and then repeated it over and over: "black Republicans." Beginning in the middle of the 1850s, anti-Republican writers took the criticism of French revolutionaries as "red republicans" and repurposed it, denouncing American Republican candidates, voters, and policies as "black." With increasing numbers and rhetorical ferocity, the conjoined terms "black" and "Republican" cast the party as depraved in several ways. It was "black," as in it was aligned with African Americans. It was also "black" when it came to morals and religion. Thus, "black Republican" became a means to vilify political partisans as pro-African American and anti-Christian. It was not, however, an explicit link to the rulers of hell.[43]

Some southern whites may have recognized that damning Republicans as "black" could trouble their home front. When southern blacks heard these words, some came to believe that northern Republicans were black physically like them. Since these politicians inspired such agitation among their white masters, perhaps these "black Republicans" were allies to the slaves. Some slaves guessed that Abraham Lincoln was "a black man, and the son of a queen."[44]

To handle this dilemma, southern whites in local conversations with African Americans described and depicted northerners as literal demons, not as men with black skin. "Ain't I always told you Yankees has horns on their heads?" one slave recalled her owner remarking. "They'll get you." Some masters claimed "the real, genuine Yankee had only one eye, set in the middle of his forehead, and a horn on the top of his head." Another African American man recalled, "Mas'r said de Yankees had horns and tails." Regarding Abraham Lincoln in particular, one slave recounted that local whites described him as having a "tail and horns."[45] Because southern whites knew that these claims were spurious, they spoke them in private and not in public. The public demonization of Lincoln emerged only after he began pursuing emancipation.

In the North, some radical abolitionists heralded secession as a godsend. Since they deemed the governmental inclusion of slaveholders as immoral, they now reveled that the alliance with them was no more. Abolitionist Wendell Phillips revived Garrison's words in January 1861, rejoicing that the "Covenant with Death is annulled—the Agreement with Hell is broken to pieces."[46]

Most northern whites, however, opposed secession. They refused the idea that southerners could dismember the nation because of a fair election. The vast majority longed to maintain the Union and expressed willingness to fight. Referring to the secessionist movement as "satantic," Jupiter Hesser spoke for many when he wrote to Abraham Lincoln, "If you want me, I will be Soldier to[o], I am only 61 years and 9 months of age."[47]

Events that followed November 1860 created the environment for Americans to fashion a new conception of Satan in the United States. This one caught on like wildfire. This one became prominent in Unionist politics. This one made money: it was the idea that Satan inspired secession. Secession prompted northern whites to seek rationales to put an end to it. Northerners looked for ways to render secession illegitimate, illegal, and ultimately evil. Although American revolutionaries had only eighty years earlier declared their independence and announced proudly the right to disunion, northern whites now had to justify opposing independence. For this, many Unionists turned to conceptions of radical evil. John Milton's *Paradise Lost* became central to their political claims. Rebellion was justified against tyranny, such as they understood the case of the American Revolution. But rebellion against a good government, as they understood the United States, was best compared to Lucifer's battle against heaven. These northerners brought Milton's conception of Christianity into their public and political realm, mixing the political, religious, European, and American.

One of the first to make and cement this equation was William "Parson" Brownlow of Knoxville, Tennessee. Editor of the *Knoxville Whig*, Brownlow long despised those who jumped at the chance for dismembering the United States. He considered the American government "the greatest and the best the world has ever seen." For Brownlow, the system of checks and balances through the Constitution meant that there were many avenues to obtain one's objectives according to the rule of law. If, for instance, Abraham Lincoln won a fair election, then that would be lawful. If he used his executive position to outlaw the internal slave trade, then Brownlow recommended seeing if Congress endorsed it with a law. If Congress passed such a law, then Brownlow counseled filing a suit that would end up in the Supreme Court. Only after exhausting all these lawful actions would secession be reasonable, because the totality of the government would have turned against what Brownlow believed was clear in the Constitution—the traffic of commodities, including slaves, across state lines.

Brownlow looked to both American and sacred history for the origins of disunionist claims. He located them most recently in 1832 during the nullification controversy. Brownlow remembered his time in South Carolina then and how southern churches sent forth ministers and missionaries to preach the gospel of nullification "like the deluded followers of Mahomet." Nullification had an insidious history, one even more vile than any connection to Islam that Brownlow made. Nullification "has been attended with the worst of consequences in all ages." It was there in the beginning of humanity. "In the garden of Eden, our first parents were induced by the devil, in the form of a serpent, to *nullify* the laws of God." Brownlow then marched through the worst events of the Bible—Cain murdering Abel, the Egyptians enslaving the Jews, the inhabitants of Sodom and Gomorrah opposing God's angels—and he attributed the cause of every one to nullification. In Brownlow's rendering, the true origin of nullification—and hence its true father as a political option in the United States—was the devil.[48]

Living in Tennessee when state leaders determined to secede, Brownlow was jailed and then expelled from his hometown. He then went on a speaking tour of northern cities. In Cincinnati he blamed and demonized radicals on both sides, claiming that if only a few years before he had been authorized to select "two or three hundred of your most abominable anti-Slavery agitators in the North, and an equal number of our God-forsaken and most hell-deserving Disunionists at the South, and had marched them to the District of Columbia, hanged them on a common gallows, dug for them a common grave," the nation would not now be embroiled in civil war.[49] Brownlow wanted to return to Knoxville and see his enemies sent to hell. As he put it, he wished to "point out to the triumphant Federal army such men as deserve to hang, and suitable limbs upon which to hang them! Nay, I desire to tie the rope around some of their infernal necks."[50]

James W. Hunnicutt, a minister and editor from Fredericksburg, Virginia, made similar points. After the war forced him to flee to Pennsylvania, he gave speeches in favor of union and attacked secession with a book he titled *The Conspiracy Unveiled: The South Sacrificed; or, The Horrors of Secession*. He labeled secession as "treason" and called it a "hellish liquid." When remembering debates within Virginia over secession, he cried, "Hell was spread out miscellaneously among the people, and all the discordant passions of the whole mass were stirred up, and the devil let loose generally." With the title of his fourth chapter, Hunnicutt minced no words: "Secession like the Devil." He announced, "Secession is as much like the devil as the devil is like himself: the more you try to compromise it, the more devil it is."[51]

Northern editors, speakers, and politicians echoed these sentiments. All types of Unionists employed this rhetoric: Republicans, Democrats, abolitionists, and conservatives. In the *Atlantic Monthly*, James Russell Lowell denounced southern whites as performing like Lucifer in *Paradise Lost*. The analogy was obvious to him, referring to Lucifer as "the first great secessionist." Elliot C. Cowdin, a businessman sent to France as a diplomat at the beginning of the war, addressed a group in Paris. There he declared that the rebels were "bold, daring, desperate." He cribbed from *Paradise Lost* and explained that they were "determined to rule or ruin, deeming with Satan, 'tis / Better to reign in Hell than serve in Heaven."[52]

Joseph Holt from Kentucky, who had served as secretary of war under President James Buchanan, was a southerner, a Democrat, and a slaveholder.

After both waves of secession, he gave a speech in Louisville damning secession. He declared that "Lucifer was . . . the first secessionist of whom history
has given us any account." The parallel seemed clear: "He rebelled because
the Almighty would not yield to him the throne of heaven. The principle of
southern rebellion is the same."[53]

These editorials and speeches reverberated throughout the North. They
did so, in part, because of reprinting and repetition. Brownlow republished
several of his main points, including ones relating disunion to the devil, in
the book *Sketches of the Rise, Progress, and Decline of Secession*. In the middle
of 1863, a Pennsylvanian wrote to his local newspaper: "What a fearful retribution will be visited upon these traitors, who, like satan, dissatisfied with
prosperity, with a government the most benignant ever known . . . and with
an enslaved race to produce the necessaries of life . . . attempted at one fell
blow to dash down their government."[54] Cowdin's speech was reprinted in
the *New York Times*. Holt's address became iconic. Frank Moore included it
in his *Rebellion Record* from 1862, but it also became a regular feature of
school readers to educate northern children. Unionists were dedicated to
convincing themselves and their children that secession was more than illegal: it was satanic.[55]

Along with reprinting and repetition, this concept worked because it
tapped into many Americans' genuine beliefs about the relationship between their nation-state and Christianity. They fused loyalty to the government with religious faith. In fact, it may have been that merging that allowed
Christians from diverse backgrounds to agree. Ministers from a variety of
traditions and political opinions eagerly gave these perspectives religious
backing. When members of the Tenth Massachusetts Volunteers left, the
pastor from the First Congregational Church of West Springfield told them
to resist "the tricks of that great secessionist, the devil." Conservative Presbyterian Charles Hodge, who condoned slavery, wrote an essay where he
opined that "the rebel is as truly a sinner as was Satan when he seceded." Another Presbyterian, one who opposed slavery, stoutly preached, "This fallen
angel is the first secessionist." Similar expressions could be heard from Uni-
tarians and New Thought religious spokesmen.[56]

By speaking Satan into the saga of secession, Unionists brought sacred
history to the present and the present to the sacred past. Using biblical stories
and Milton's creative extrapolations of them, they rendered southern secession

more than a political or governmental act: it was a sacred betrayal. More-over, by affixing the word secession to Satan, they transported con-temporary American events into holy history. In this way, they created a sacred-secular echo chamber where understandings of the past and present reinforced one another into one concrete truth. Secession was evil.

The widespread claim that Satan inspired secession led to the commodi-fication of the idea in print culture. When the war began, printers saw a fi-nancial opportunity. With thousands (and then millions) of men away from home, the demand for mailing paper and envelopes skyrocketed. Although small and inexpensive, envelopes generated huge amounts of capital: more than ten million dollars annually in postage stamps alone.[57]

To sell their wares, a number of publishing houses produced patriotic paper. Often with American flags or representations of the Constitution, these pages and envelopes marketed patriotism. With time, envelopes featured he-roic soldiers and military generals. Soldiers and their families could support the nation, the Union, and government through symbolic acts of paper pur-chasing.[58]

Product differentiation was difficult in this environment, however, when just about every printer tried to capitalize on patriotism. A few turned to pa-per products with anti-Confederate imagery. Often these images displayed demons. Two New York publishing houses created lines of envelopes connect-ing the devil to secessionist states. Both companies produced an individual card for each seceded state and featured a devil. By manufacturing envelopes that featured specific states, the publishing houses targeted individuals with family members serving in those areas.

Reagles and Company printed a winged, horned, and tailed devil who stands with a spear and seven-starred flag in his right hand. With his left arm, he holds a shield emblazoned with a state seal. To his left, large, capitalized words read THE REBEL STATES. The name of the individual state floats across those words. In this rendering, the devil defends himself with the secession-ist states. Militant and prepared for combat, his opponents can defeat him only by going through the rebel states.[59]

Charles Magnus, a German-born printer, joined the war effort and prof-ited from it in several ways. He produced patriotic song sheets with music and images for pieces like "Yankee Doodle" and "John Brown's Body" to in-spire war-making. More strategically, he produced several maps for military

movements and deployments detailing roads, rivers, and canals. He also ran
a series of devil and individual state envelopes. On the left side, a winged,
feminine angel floated beside a waving American flag. On the right stood a
circular state seal; a horned devil with sharp claws on his hands and feet
emerged from it. In this case, the devil seems to play a game of peek-a-boo
or perhaps to be pulling the seal down from behind. Although less martial
than the Reagles and Company demon, this devil also has a mischievous and
somewhat crazed look on his face.[60]

Another publisher highly attuned to the market used irony and parody
to hawk his wares. Samuel Upham created and sold several unique envelopes
with demon figures set in the South. One, *The Root of Treason: Found in the
"Sacred Soil" of Virginia*, made a devil appear as a series of roots. His arms,
legs, and tail looked like roots and had smaller roots running off them. Roots
formed a broad outline of wings. In this case, Upham turned the concept of
"sacred soil" into sarcasm.[61]

Upham followed the agricultural theme with another envelope, *Uncle
Sam Cutting Down the "Secession Tree,"* In it, Uncle Sam in a top hat and pin-
striped pants wields an axe and chops into a palmetto tree topped with the
Confederate flag. The "planter," a winged and horned figure, wags his finger
and asks Uncle Sam not to chop down his special tree.[62]

For Upham, the deployment of the devil was one facet of his wartime fi-
nancial enterprise. He began the war as a small-business owner in New York
City. In early 1862, after he received bills of Confederate currency, he began
to print his own versions and advertised them for sale in magazines and newspapers. While it would have been illegal for Upham as an American citizen
to produce American currency, there was nothing illegal about counterfeit-
ing the currency of a government whose legal existence his government denied. Upham sold the bills as novelties and souvenirs, but others understood
them as potentially powerful weapons against the Confederacy. If northerners could flood the South with Confederate currency, they could devalue the
bills and intensify the inflation already growing there by leaps and bounds.
Perhaps inadvertently, Upham had stumbled upon a way to use the power of
the press to depress the Confederate economy.[63]

A host of other printers peddled envelopes that linked the Confederacy
with Satan. One powerful figure holding a trident and having the words
"The Devil" emblazoned across his chest was titled *The First Secessionist.*

Another featured a devil presenting a Confederate flag to Jefferson Davis, who bows his head in submission before the demon. On one, a nude devil sits on a bale of cotton.[64]

The envelope devils varied in appearance. Some were clothed; some were nude. Some had elongated noses. The lengthy nose mimicked European artwork of previous centuries that grafted stereotypes about Jews onto demonic figures. Most often, the devil's skin tone was dark or darker than whites in the images. The blackest of the devils was *The First Secessionist*. This hulking devil was far blacker and more muscular than the others.[65]

By presenting the devil as a dark figure, these artists followed the tradition of blackening evil. In the American context that associated blackness with African Americans, this paralleled the "black Republican" charge of southern whites. One white minister of the era wrote, "It is common to represent Satan as *black*, and the place of his abode as the 'blackness of darkness for ever.'"[66]

Darkness and blackness, along with elongated noses, were clear folkloric imports from Europe. They also conveyed meanings through the physicality of these demons. The wings connoted the angelic. They reminded viewers that devils in the Christian tradition were fallen angels. They had lived in heaven. They had power. The horns, hooves, and tails indicated animality. Rendering demons with animal features was a way to denigrate them as below humans. Although created before humans and more powerful than them, devils debased themselves through rebellion, and the physical markers of animality became the symbols of that denigration.[67]

Presenting devils as above humans spiritually but below them in their animality, these artists offered another link to African Americans, far more subtle than the darkness of skin. By the middle of the nineteenth century, some whites had come to believe that darker-skinned people had greater spiritual and religious sense than whites. Midcentury racialist and racializing thought presented people of color as possessed of greater insight on religious sentiments. Harriet Beecher Stowe put this bluntly in *The Key to Uncle Tom's Cabin*, writing, "The negro race is confessedly more simple, docile, childlike, and affectionate, than other races; and hence the divine graces of love and faith, when in breathed by the Holy Spirit, find in their natural temperament a more congenial atmosphere."[68]

At the same time, there was a tradition of likening slaves to animals. According to scholars Anthony Pinn and Mia Bay, African Americans of the nineteenth century often found themselves confronting laws and attitudes from whites that rendered them as such. On many occasions, African Americans wondered if whites viewed them as humans or as "beasts of burden."[69]

Alongside the racial and racialized aspects of these images, the envelopes displayed hallmarks of southern and Confederate society and linked them to radical evil. In so doing, they undermined any claims to respect southerners. Their economy—cotton—was attached to the devil. Their symbols—flags and seals—were created by or used by demons. Their leaders served Satan. At a simple level of war-making and othering, publishers used the devil to present Confederates as others in every capacity.

There were deeper meanings in the details. Rather than demonize secessionists or Confederates themselves, these illustrated envelopes took another tack. They manifested the devil and devils into southern society as figures leading southern whites. Jefferson Davis and other Confederates were not devils. They were disciples of devils. They were not incarnations of evil. They were tools of evil.

This was an important distinction and one that applied to the Union cause and not to the secessionist one. Unionists invaded the Confederacy to keep it. Yankee soldiers killed not to separate themselves from southerners but to hold southerners close. For these reasons, Unionists could not regard southern whites as some abolitionists had: irredeemable demons. Rather, Unionists portrayed secessionists as manipulated tools. Defeating the devil and banishing the demons from the land, politics, and government would bring southern whites back to reason, back to salvation, back to the heavenly government of the United States.

At the same time, few of these envelopes directly linked the devil with slavery or slaveholding. In one exception, slavery was a secondary issue to secession. In *An eminent southern clergyman,* a fully robed minister stood behind his pulpit and Bible to preach. Behind him, a winged, horned, and tailed devil extended his right arm and hand to direct the minister where to read. The caption demonstrated that Confederates were not devils themselves, but led by demons. It read: "During an eloquent discourse," the pastor "is

wonderfully assisted in finding scriptural authority for Secession and Treason, and the divine ordination of Slavery."[70]

None of these images presented slaveholders as embodiments of the demonic as African American authors had done. One of Upham's envelopes
referred to Satan as a "planter" and italicized the word for effect, while another
associated the devil with cotton. In their overall effect, the envelopes emphasized secession as satanic and demons using or working through Confederates, the Confederate states, and Confederate symbols. This was a critical
shift. By seamlessly moving the focal point of evil from slavery to secession,
these artists and other Unionist proponents made the nation-state, and not
the quality of life for people or the makeup of civil society, the ultimate goal
for redemption. This helps explain the overwhelming emphasis on "union"
for so many northern whites, most important, Abraham Lincoln.[71]

Commodifying the devil through visualization was a brilliant tactic. As
historians R. Laurence Moore, Amanda Porterfield, and others have shown,
Americans of the nineteenth century routinely mixed their Christianity with
their capitalism. But they were ambivalent, particularly about using Jesus or
God to market wares. At the beginning of the Civil War, then, Satan served
as the best means to elevate current political problems into spiritual concerns.
Picturing evil allowed artists, printers and others the means to tap into Christian faith, American civil religion, and folkloric fears about the devil.[72]

As devils proliferated with the start of the Civil War, they invaded just about
every nook of American society. From the most august political speeches to
the ephemera of print life, the demonic found places in the road to disunion
and the conflict itself. Satan figured as an important part of the great slavery
debates. He animated the rhetoric of politicians and understandings of elec-
toral meanings. He was an aspect of American entertainment and business.

Satan even entered courting culture.

Charlie Tenney was one of hundreds of thousands of northern men making war in the South. He left in Ohio his family, and most important for
him, Adelaide Case. He adored her. He probably hoped to marry her when
he returned home, to raise a family, to grow old and lie side by side under
gravestones. In his letters to Addie, he discussed his surroundings, his political views, all the while trying to be playful, cute, and coy to win and keep
her affections. In one letter from late July 1862, for which he may have used

an envelope featuring the devil, he underlined a particular phrase, the one that seemed just about everywhere after Lincoln's election: "*The first secessionist was Satan.*" Charlie never had the chance to discuss this or his other overtures with Addie in person. One year later, near Harpers Ferry, Virginia, where Stonewall Jackson had prayed and John Brown had hung, a bullet put an end to Charlie's mortal life.[73]

CHAPTER 2

An Earthly Hell

Fifteen years after the Civil War ended, Gen. William Tecumseh Sherman addressed a crowd in Columbus, Ohio, that included former soldiers and sailors. It was an august affair. Preceding him, President Rutherford B. Hayes heralded the men for their courage and valor. He explained that "our country's prosperity" resulted from their willingness to fight, kill, and die for the government. Sherman expressed far less enthusiasm. He spoke in particular to the "boys" in attendance, those who pined for war but had not experienced it. He warned those who considered "soldiering as all glory" that in actuality war "is all hell."[1]

Sherman painted with a broad stroke. He did not say that the Civil War was hell. He did not say that long wars were hell or that they were hellish or mostly hell. He claimed that war itself, war as a category of time and experience, "is all hell." As a soldier and military leader, Sherman had fought in many wars. He battled Seminoles in Florida and Kiowa on the frontier, and he often expected armed conflict with Mormons in the West. When the American Civil War began in 1861, he wrote to his brother: "We are on the eve of a terrible war." He was right. Sherman witnessed devastation; in fact, he often ordered his men to be its instruments. He lamented in 1863, "Our armies are devastating the land and it is sad to see the destruction that attends our progress—we cannot help it. Farms disappear, houses are burned and plundered, and every living animal killed and eaten."[2]

In the war, Americans destroyed so much of what they held dear. What they had cultivated they now killed; what they had raised they now razed: the land, their buildings, their animals. The experience led Sherman, a career soldier who became a hero for the victorious side, to denounce unequivocally, universally, and utterly the horror of war.

This phrase became popular. It was the only part of his speech remembered. Usually shortened to "war is hell," newspapers throughout the country, even in the South, echoed it time and again.[3] Historians of the war routinely used it as a pithy catchall for the horrors that Americans experienced during the war. How and why did the totality of this war become reduced to one word: "hell"?

"Hell" became the lexical shorthand for the Civil War not simply because the combat involved suffering and pain or killing and dying. There had been and were after the war many conflicts that Americans did not label as hell. No Americans of note designated the War for Independence as hellish. American leaders, politicians, and soldiers did not regard the imperialistic wars of the late 1890s and early 1900s as demonic. For many Europeans, the first World War felt like hell, but the next one received the sobriquet "the good war," at least from Americans. Only the American war in Vietnam came close to paralleling the Civil War in descriptions and depictions of evil and darkness. Yet many who participated in the American Civil War experienced it as so encompassing, so totalizing, that even one of its most heralded leaders regarded all war as "all hell."

The location of damnation became a useful point of perspective for many reasons. In part, hell could be used because of secularization and secularism. With organized Christianity detached from the federal and state governments, and with the rise of unbelief or irreligion as options, concepts previously considered "religious" became fair game to explain other phenomena. Neither religion nor Christianity were banished from the public sphere. Instead, the words and models of Christianity became useful for many other expressions. This included emotion; it also included physical sensation. This meant that when Americans used religious language, it is impossible to vivisect their claims into those believed and those used purely for rhetorical effect. Religious language functioned as both. At the time of the Civil War, then, Americans had access to use hell and evil as concepts to speak of this world.[4]

The Civil War rent the prior associations of religion, war, nation, the land, and bodily experiences. Before the 1860s, most Americans valorized war as heroic, exciting, and godly. But very quickly, many men who volunteered for combat found their experience to be anything but. Just as slavery and secession allowed Satan and the demonic to be utilized in new and expansive ways, the war transformed how Americans experienced, talked about, and comprehended the presence of evil in their midst. The exigencies of combat, the devastation of the terrain, and the extent to which soldiers suffered led to an intense upswing in references to hell.

The notion that evil had invaded America found expression publicly and privately. Hell and the demonic became useful tools to express altered views of people and places, time and space, bodies and beliefs, experiences and values. Labeling enemies as devils and demonic became a wartime strategy for combatants and politicians on both sides of the conflict. For everyday soldiers, hell became their method to explain the unexplainable, conveying meaning when meaning seemed elusive. Increasingly, men and women represented themselves, their country, their fields, their ravines, their prisons, and their flesh with references to hell. Evil came to define the war for many as men beat plowshares into swords, as they turned from nurturing the ground to marching it down, and as their concept of manifest destiny succumbed to feelings of moribund solemnity.

Unlike fears of damnation to hell after death, the pain of this worldly life became explainable with references to evil. When all was said and done, when millions of men had been through this fire, it made sense for many to embrace the notion that war "is all hell."

From a Godly Country to the Devil's Domain

In the spring of 1861, Abraham Lincoln and Jefferson Davis called for almost 200,000 volunteers to join the Union and Confederate armies respectively. Tens of thousands of young men jumped at the opportunity. Volunteers on both sides swelled the rolls, and they were chock-full of romantic notions of war. They envisioned themselves as true to the nation, their god, and their heritage. Most Americans webbed together war, heroism, patriotism, and religious faith. From the Revolution to the antebellum age, the nation's heroes were men of war. George Washington became a secular saint, while Andrew Jackson rose to prominence after being the "hero of New Orleans." Americans lionized their land as much as their warriors.[5] John O'Sullivan's essay on the annexation of Texas in 1845, in which he voiced the concept of Manifest Destiny, resonated with many: it was the people's "manifest destiny to overspread the continent allotted by Providence for the free development of our yearly multiplying millions."[6] Many Americans understood themselves and their land to be chosen by God.

When soldiers and civilians voiced religious perspectives early in the war, they articulated abiding faith in providence: the belief that God had everything under control. When applied to the nation-state, providence easily fed into civil religion. Months after the war began, Grace Elmore wrote in her diary from Columbia, South Carolina, "We are in God's hands."[7] When Charles Johnson of Pennsylvania joined the Union forces after first Battle of Bull Run, he had a clear sense that God was in command of this world. "I hold most emphatically and seriously that no man dies until his allotted time has ran its course," he wrote to his wife several days before he encountered enemy fire. "If the Lord wills that my days are near an end, saltpetre will not save me, and on the other hand if *he* decrees that I should live for years to come, all the balls in secceshindom can not carry me off before *he* is ready." Neither the material artifacts of life, such as saltpeter, nor the political currents of the day, such as Confederate secession, would determine his destiny. For him, providentialism made being a soldier "easy."[8]

Men did more than volunteer for war. They yearned for combat. Anticipation and excitement radiated from their letters. "I hope we shall be reckoned in for I want to see what we are made of," wrote one Union soldier to his brother in October 1861. His camp was "a gay place." Then a few weeks later, he explained, "I never done anything yet that I like so well as I do Soldiering."[9] Charles Johnson wrote to his wife, "We have had a sight of the rebel videts and I hope soon will get much closer, so as to take the color of their eyes."[10]

Leaders from both sides hoped that Christianity would mark the war. In one of their few alterations to the United States Constitution from which they borrowed, the authors of the Constitution of the Confederate States of America asked in the preamble for "the favor and guidance of Almighty God." George McClellan, the Union's first military hero and the leader Lincoln hoped would topple the Confederate leadership in Richmond, Virginia, explained to the president his theory of war in July 1862. The war "should be conducted upon the highest principles known to Christian Civilization." By "Christian," McClellan meant that the war should be fought against armies, not people, and that the rights of private property should be respected, including rights to slaves.[11]

McClellan failed, and Lincoln replaced him with John Pope. Brought east in June after capturing 7,000 rebels at Island Number Ten on the Mississippi River and an aggressive advance on Corinth, Mississippi, Pope took command of the newly designated Army of Virginia. Pope soon declared war on McClellan's limited war policies and the Confederacy (soldiers and civilians) alike. McClellan's friends in Pope's army dissented—quietly— from his policies of confiscation, which allowed soldiers to forcibly take materials from their enemies that were considered necessary for the war effort. Pope's order, in fact, allowed soldiers to confiscate slaves. For some in the Union, this was too much and an affront to Christian warfare. Brigade commander Marsena Patrick of New York viewed Pope's confiscation policy as encouraging volunteer soldiers to indulge their worst impulses. He blamed the "Order of Pope's" as having "demoralized the Army and Satan has been let loose."[12]

Both sides attempted to emphasize the Christianity of their cause with expansive chaplaincy programs. These would help maintain the fidelity of Christian soldiers and perhaps convince unbelievers to convert. While the United States military had begun commissioning chaplains during the American Revolution, the reliance on volunteers during the Civil War and the massive numbers needed on both sides led to a huge increase of men employed by states to minister to the religious well-being of the men. The rough ratio was one chaplain for every thousand combatants.[13] During the war, the line between chaplain and combatant blurred and often disappeared. A number of chaplains chose to fight or—particularly on the Confederate side— were recruited from the armed ranks and continued to partake in combat. Chaplains blended combat with church. If individual chaplains were known as fighting parsons during the Revolution or during the war with Mexico, they became ubiquitous in the 1860s. A number of military clergymen gained fame as "fighting chaplains." Taking up rifles meant that these men could very well send the soldiers of the opposing army straight to hell (or heaven) by personal action. Before the war, this seemed beyond the bounds of civilized warfare as practiced by Christians and military tradition.

Before combat began and in the early months of war, Americans were reluctant to label one another as demons or demonic. During his first inaugural address, Abraham Lincoln hoped that the people would remain "friends." He hoped that the "better angels of our nature" would prevail. Less pleasant,

southern whites routinely described Union men as "Vandals," a reference to
the Europeans who invaded and plundered the Roman Empire centuries
earlier. Unlike Unionist claims that Satan inspired secession, which likened
Confederate actions to an era before the emergence of humans and into tran-
scendent realms, the metaphor of Vandals was fixed in this world and its
human history.[14]

Occasionally during the initial months of war, some Americans used demonic references when discussing their enemies. This was most pronounced
when it came to the Union "Zouave" regiments. These units designed and
wore French-style uniforms to imitate the light infantry chasseurs, including their kepi headgear. The original French Zouaves were recruited from the
Kabyle of northern Africa, denizens of the Ottoman Empire colonized by
France. This may have explain why American soldiers dressed as they did
could be demonized.[15] The Kabyle were not only African but also Muslim.

When the Zouave members of the Fourteenth Brooklyn made repeated
charges at Thomas Jackson's brigade on Henry House Hill, the Confederate
leader and devout Presbyterian called them "red-legged devils."[16] When Jackson called them devils, he invoked the potential for racial as well as religious
animus to southern portrayals of Yankee Zouaves as the worst possible kind
of "Black Republicans" under arms. In other words, the fact that many Union
recruiters emulated Muslim soldiers known for their aggressive (or "savage")
battle tactics could be exploited by Confederates as a sign of the diabolic nature of Union invaders whose embrace of non-Christian warriors was em-
blematic of their evil intentions.

Increasingly, northern and southern whites referred to one another as
devils. Demonization of the opposing military became common, as it often is
during war. This helped pave the way for many Americans to see and experience their land as saturated with evil. One song from the South positioned
Confederates as on the side of "the right." It boasted that southern whites were
powerful enough, perhaps because of their Christian faith, perhaps because of
their physical strength, perhaps because of both, to overcome Satan himself:

> They said we could not Sumter take,
> And of her strength they'd tell;
> But we can make old Satan quake,
> And breach the walls of hell.[17]

In Virginia, the wife of a Presbyterian minister lamented the "cruel, savage, unjust war," wondering "how can the Yankees persist in it? Strange they cannot see they are fighting against the Almighty and strange they should persist in it when they have been so signally whipped and defeated time after time." Jane White, whose husband was Stonewall Jackson's antebellum pastor, appealed to God to "continue to help us, thy oppressed people," conveniently forgetting the prayers of the enslaved. "Blindness seems to be resting upon all the Yankees, total blindness. They seem to be given up to the devil."

White had charity enough to ask God to "bring them to repentance for their enormous sins," while commenting that northern "ministers of the gospel . . . [were] urging on this iniquitous hellish war. Blood thirsty monsters!"[18] Six months later she persisted in her conviction that God "will bring good out of evil" despite the Union blockade of southern ports, "our country invaded, and desolated by the ruthless invaders, even our houses and wardrobes pilfered." Now she argued that the "cruel, wicked Yankees" forced the "hellish work" of civil war upon Virginians, and that northerners worshiped a different deity from southern Christians. "Who can believe in their religion, their religion of hate, and bloodshed."[19] The question remained how her faith would fare if her precious son Hugh was lost in the slaughter or if her town, Lexington, was occupied by Yankees.

A Methodist minister from Alabama confessed to his brother his "deep christian and inextinguishable hatred toward the demons of the north." He believed "it is doing God service to kill the diabolical wretches on the battlefield."[20] Another Methodist pastor noted "the most martial manner" of occupation commander Nathaniel P. Banks's triumphant arrival, for the general rode "in a carriage driven by four white mules." The pastor was amused at the remarks of a "youngster who stood near watching the Yanks go by. 'Why, they look like *people*, don't they?' he exclaimed. No doubt he had been told that the Federals were devils."[21]

"My heart grows sick at this unholy, this horrible war, without a prospect, nay without the faintest signs of peace," Virginian Robert Taylor Scott wrote his wife from George Pickett's (mostly) Virginia division on the last day of 1862. "When, Oh! when will it come? I am confident it will be achieved and that success will crown our efforts and repay all our sacrifices; no set of miscreants, barbarians, thieves and scoundrels, disgraces of humanity, as the *Yankees*, can ever succeed. Words cannot express my feelings towards them,"

Scott confessed, for to him "they [were devils] incarnate and I loathe and detest them [like he would a] toad or a viper." All Unionists were in his mind curses upon "the human race. I some times think the avenging anger of a righteous and just God will ultimately blot them out of existence or make them a prey to their own miserable and fiendish hearts. My heart is bitter against them," despite his best efforts to "soften my feelings."[22]

Hell could even be humorous. When John Preston Sheffey wrote home to his wife in September 1863, he mentioned rumors of "armies of ghosts" and "strange noises." He found it "very romantic" and compared it to "the spectral Moors with which Irving embellished the pages of the Alhambra." While some hoped it was a sign that Union soldiers would leave the South, others "more inclined to make fun of these serious matters say that the realms of Satan are filled so full of Yankees that he can accommodate no more, and many therefore are doomed to walk the Earth in the unrest of the wicked."[23]

Union leaders and soldiers also engaged in the language of demonization. Jeremiah T. Boyle sent a telegram begging for reinforcements to President Lincoln in late August 1862. Without them, he and other Kentucky loyalists would be captured by "the Devil & his Imps."[24] A medium also wrote to Lincoln, claiming to speak the voice of God. "It is time already that this Devilish power should be broken up forever," God told Lincoln. While "the Devil himself has had the control of affairs," God was now ready to act through Lincoln. If the President wished to know God's will and put an end to this "Devilish war," he should consult this medium. If he failed, he would "suffer the consequences."[25] After the Battle of Antietam, a popular song described Irish Union soldiers as driving "the devil out of hell."[26] In letters to his brother, John W. Chase of the First Massachusetts Light Artillery routinely referred to Confederates as "devils." Chase hoped he would have the opportunity to "kill several of the yellow skinned devils." Almost a year later, he wrote to his brother that all "we want is to catch the devils in an open field and death is their portion."[27] During the cataclysmic Battles of Shiloh, Ulysses S. Grant wrote, "By God, I want nothing better than to have at the Rebels come out and attack us. We can whip them to hell!"[28]

In the first two years of war, no one was depicted as more devilish than Benjamin F. Butler, an antebellum Democratic politician, who strode into the task of keeping order in New Orleans with a 10,000-man garrison. Butler's greatest trouble came not from paroled Confederate prisoners of war or even male civilians, but from women.[29] The elite women of the city flaunted their political views by cursing at Union soldiers, spitting on them, pouring the contents of chamber pots on soldiers' heads, and crowding northern occupiers off corduroyed planks into muddy streets. They assumed that their gender would protect them from northern reprisals. Sometimes these gendered acts of rebellion ended up in embarrassment for all involved, as when one woman flung herself off the sidewalk and into a gutter rather than suffer the indignity of walking next to two Union officers. When the men came to her aid, she expressed her preference to lie in the gutter rather than be helped by a Yankee. General Thomas Williams commented that "such venom one must see to believe. . . . I look at them and think of fallen angels."[30]

Less than a month after assuming responsibility for the occupation, Butler issued General Order No. 28, declaring that any further disrespectful acts by the city's women would leave a participant open to treatment as a "woman of the town plying her avocation," or a prostitute.[31] Butler claimed "the devil had entered the hearts of the women . . . to stir up strife."[32]

By depicting southern white women as "fallen," Williams and Butler echoed broader sentiments in the North that slavery and secession had demonizing effects. In a *New York Times* article from April 1862, the author compared Confederate leaders to the "King of Dahomey" for their "barbarism" and then drew particular attention to "the evil tendencies" wrought by "slavery and secession." These forces, "which have made devils of so many men, seem to have made furies of the women." According to this author, proof of the South's wickedness was that even "women urge men to evil."[33]

What Butler dished out, he got back in heaps. Confederates demonized him vociferously. From Jefferson Davis on down, Confederate leaders took Butler's order as condoning the rapes of pro-secession white women by northern mercenaries. Jefferson Davis outlawed Butler as "a felon deserving capital punishment," damning him as an instrument of Satan—if circumspectly so, commenting that northerners were "the only people on earth who do not blush to think [Butler] wears the human form."[34] According to the editor of the Richmond *Examiner*, Butler's actions were so infuriating that they would lead southern men to rise up and be "content to die if they can send a single Yankee devil back to hell." A year later, the editor referenced one of Butler's speeches "as pompous as Satan's speech to his legions in the bottomless pit."[35]

Other prominent rebel leaders offered financial rewards for his capture and subsequent execution.

Southern women—including South Carolinian diarist Mary Boykin Chesnut—labeled Butler a "wretch" and "beast." She even called him a "hideous cross-eyed beast." The label stuck. Combining notions of wicked animality and the Christian concept of Satan as the Beast of end times who would try to devour God's people, Butler became the embodiment of a demonic enemy.[36]

Butler became a lightning rod for political discord in the North as well. Lincoln removed him in December 1862, but this did not stop Butler from converting to the Republican Party. This freed Northern Democrats to demonize Butler as a traitor to their party. "Your rotten-hearted carcass must be deprived of vitality, your thieving soul of life, so prepare to meet your cohort, the Devil, who wants you more than this country does," a New York newspaper told Butler as he prepared to leave New Orleans.[37] The concept went far and wide. Mildred Bullitt wrote from Philadelphia to family members in Kentucky of walking by a store with "a portrait of Gen. Butler" on exhibit. Bullitt reported that when a little girl observed the image, she "screamed, clung to her mother + with the greatest alarm cried 'O mama, is that a wild beast, or the devil.'"[38]

In the first months of the war, while Americans in the North and South vilified some leaders like Butler, they for the most part understood themselves and their own actions as Christian. They often fused their faith in God with their loyalties to their nations, and the result was men marching to war believing themselves to be moral, just, and good. In 1862, this changed for many of the combatants. Their embodied experiences in war and the lack of imaginative tools to comprehend their surroundings drove many from considering devils out there to hell right here. Hell became a primary metaphor for the world and life they now endured.

It Is a Perfect Hell on Earth

In mid-November 1863, four months after the titanic battle at Gettysburg, Pennsylvania, Abraham Lincoln offered one of the shortest speeches in American history, and one of its most enduring. In the fewer than three hundred words of his Gettysburg Address, he eulogized the men who died in combat for the Union. He called it "a great battle-field" that had been "consecrated" by those soldiers. Lincoln believed that their nobility could inspire others in the nation to continue to support the fight. He concluded by hoping that "this nation, under God, shall have a new birth of freedom."[39]

Lincoln with his few words did not mention hell, demons, or Satan. The man who followed him, the main speaker for the event, did. Edward Everett was known far and wide as one of the finest orators in the country. Former senator, governor of Massachusetts, secretary of state, and president of Harvard University, Everett had achieved far more than Lincoln before the 1860s. While Lincoln's speech lasted two minutes, Everett's went on for two hours. In it, he emphasized the place of evil.

Everett wished to define this war. "I call the war which the Confederates are waging against the Union a 'rebellion.'" This word choice was vital for Everett because according to the Constitution and all the laws of "every civilized country, 'rebellion . . . is by every civilized government regarded as the highest [crime] which citizen or subject can commit." Rebellion violated laws of state and those of churches. And for Everett, the rebellion was "an imitation on earth of that first foul revolt of 'the Infernal Serpent,' against which the Supreme Majesty sent forth the armed myriads of his angels, and clothed the right arm of his Son with the three-bolted thunders of omnipotence."

According to Everett, the American government must mimic the heavenly government. This way, it could work with "that gracious Providence which over-rules all things for the best." For Everett, if the Confederates followed Satan, the American government and military must follow God. Only by bringing war against the rebels could they stop the country and world from becoming "an earthly hell."[40]

Neither Everett nor Lincoln were soldiers. Neither knew what it was like to drill for days, camp in the rain, tremble when cannons roared, and worry that the sound tolled for them. Although many noncombatants offered perspectives on the meanings of the war, it was the men and women who fought in it and endured it who knew what Sherman meant when he said war "is all hell."

Typically, when scholars consider the Civil War as "living hell," they draw attention to the obvious. With increasingly large battles, men witnessed bodies blown to pieces, they saw legs, arms, and hands severed from bodies. They beheld blood, guts, and then flies and maggots rushing into bodies. With loved ones dying far away from home and often impossible to recognize, many on the home front had to mourn without being able to see or touch the flesh of their loved ones. All of this certainly led many to liken their experiences to hell on earth.[41]

For many, evil overcame them far more subtly and its usefulness for expression brought religious concepts into their everyday lives. Many soldiers experienced the war as a total transformation of their reality, a shift of the massive and the granular. Changes to small and often overlooked elements of life altered their views of the connections between the natural and supernatural worlds. Wartime experiences altered the sights, sounds, smells, and physical sensations they experienced. It changed their daily routines, actions, and social company. Marching, shooting, and getting shot were merely the tip of the iceberg. Life in the army shifted overall senses of self from how they treated the land to the sounds they heard at bedtime. The experiences of combat shattered the eagerness of thousands of American men. For instance, one Union soldier in the summer of 1862 lamented, "I have seen sights the last week that would draw tears from a stone."[42] One outcome of this overwhelming change was that some American soldiers understood themselves to be experiencing hell.

War became hell for many of these men because of how their experience overturned their sense of God's order for the world. The sounds, smells, and sights of this war challenged all they had been taught about God's providential design and left them questioning their understandings of Christianity itself. Ultimately, some found that as godly rationalizations failed to explain what they experienced, the devil and hell would do.

While some soldiers continued to link their faith to the fight, others suggested that the struggle challenged their concepts of Christianity. "I feel that I would like to shoot a Yankee," inspector general of Mississippi William Nugent confessed to his wife in August 1861, "and yet I know that this would not be in harmony with the Spirit of Christianity, that teaches us to love our enemies & and do good to them that despitefully use us and entreat us."[43] By May of the next year, with Union forces invading the northern counties of his home state, Nugent changed his tune. "Kill, slay & murder them," he wrote after he had exchanged his desk job for a post in a cavalry regiment. "Give them no peace; for unless we do; we do not deserve God's mercy."[44] Reflecting on "the horrors of war," Hamlin Coe penned his thoughts in his diary.

"Will God forgive men for such work is a question I often ask myself, but I receive a silent reply and utter my own prayers for the safety of my poor soul and my country."[45]

Part of the problem was the transformation of Sundays. Bred to revere Sunday as "the Sabbath," a special day of the week to attend church, sing hymns, listen to a sermon, and rest from work, men and women during the war lost the uniqueness of the day. It wore on them. Annie Starling of Kentucky wrote in her diary, "We did not go to church this morning or tonight either on account of our church being used for a hospital for the sick soldiers."[46] "This has been a Sabbathless Sunday. In the morning we had no divine services because of the appointed Inspection, which, after all, was postponed."[47] Another soldier complained, "It don't feel like Sunday here . . . boys don't seem to be religiously inclined to day at all."[48]

For some soldiers and civilians, wartime experiences devastated their providential views. For Charles F. Johnson of Pennsylvania of the Eighty-first Pennsylvania Volunteer Infantry, his view of providence fell as he viewed this world and his flesh degrade. He wrote home that the particularities of Civil War combat countered God's designs for the land. "All nature appears in a calm enjoyment of the blessings of the Almighty," he wrote to his wife of twelve years, Mary, "and yet this day the 'Dogs of War' are ready and man stands prepared to commit a 'legalized murder.'" Human death was only one disconcerting factor. The sound of the struggle ripped through the cosmos as well. When the "mouths" of cannons opened, they produced "noise sufficient to reach the high heavens itself." The "clatter" of the rifles and muskets added to the cacophony. Charles lamented to Mary that in his letter he could only provide "some faint idea" of the sound that reached such an "extensive scale."

After spending the fall of 1861 in Virginia trying to kill Confederate soldiers and then the winter trying to keep warm, Johnson complained in a letter to Mary that it had been one month since his last "natural stool." The color and consistency of his excrement troubled Colonel Johnson. He explained with exclamation points, "it is utterly impossible to get a glass of water free from *mud*!; if the male population of the north are not troubled in *future* with the 'gravell' from drinking this infernal 'sacred soil,' it will be because their bladers were so antagnistical to the 'southern soil' as to be able to hold the 'infurnal stuff.'"[49]

Johnson was not alone in his attention to the ground. Various soldiers expressed the idea that the land and landscape held new demonic meaning for them. One remembered marching into the South and feeling "if there is such a place as hell, this piece of road is a sample of the road leading to Satan's residence."[50] For many northern soldiers, the southern land was cursed either by slavery or by war. The "sacred soil" of the South was being transformed into a hellish wasteland. Even before battles, some experienced the weather as devilish. "the weather here is a devilish sight more Changeable than it is in New England for some times it changes about four times a day."[51]

Some Confederates also regarded the land and environment as polluted. Clara Solomon in New Orleans maintained in her diary that one of her friends "did not wish to remain after a Yankee foot had polluted our soil." She also felt the air around her as different. "When I am in the street I do not seem to breathe a free atmosphere. It is not free. Laden with the breadth of those invaders." Although Solomon began the war referring to Yankees as "vandals," she ended it routinely by calling them "devils."[52]

After Johnson complained of the soil, he complained of diarrhea; and then a smattering of bullets whizzed through the air, tore through his uniform pants, crashed into his thigh muscle, and ripped open the scrotal skin that protected his testicles. Thus began Colonel Johnson's hospital days. Together, the water, the mud, the thrashed flesh, and immobility changed Colonel Johnson.

The landscape was matched by the soundscape as a domain of the devil. For Charles Johnson, during his physical pain and hospital immobilization, he could not stop himself from violating the moral edicts of the divine in terms of sound. Just as he could not stop the infernal from exiting his body as excrement, he could not stop his mouth from vomiting filthy words. It was not just what happened to him in combat, but what he could no longer stop from doing in the hospital. Charles wrote despondently to Mary that he could not refrain from fracturing the natural sonic morality God had put into place. "God forgive me if I should do any extra amount of 'cussing,'" he wrote to Mary, "but it is enough to make Job himself abjure his faith." Then one week later, with Job still on his mind, Charles told her, "Job had it and as he was not such great 'shakes' I do not see why I can not have it to—so patience—patience, say I."[53]

Charles Johnson's hospital scenes showcased the dynamic interactions among this world and ones beyond in space and time. The war had made his body into a conduit for infernal stuff, in this case "cussing," and when writing to Mary he linked that which was done to his body, that which his body did, and the biblical figure of Job. In these letters, Job was the referent not simply for how Johnson understood his suffering but also for how he maintained a sense of relationship to the divine amid so much pain. The biblical Job had experienced a whirlwind of suffering centered upon his material possessions, his livestock, his family, and eventually his own body. Satan was the star of this biblical saga, the one who inflicted the pains upon Job. Job was a test and a testimony for God. Johnson positioned himself beyond even the pains of Job, and the evidence was what came from his body: neither of which he felt he could control.

The soundscape, as historian Mark M. Smith has described, became an atmosphere of hell for many Americans during the war. Cannon fire, bullet explosions, humans and horses running, bodies and bayonets crashing into one another: the sounds of war were distinct from those of peace. As one Connecticut soldier recounted, the "echoing roar of the cannon contrasted strangely with the serenity and stillness about us." During and after battles, groans and wails punctuated the air. Then the silence of dead men's bodies came, and the whizzing and whirling of bugs and buzzards to pick at the flesh. After detailing the sounds of the struggle, one soldier wrote, "Such a seething hell will never be enacted on this continent."[54]

Perhaps no sound signaled the legions of Satan as much as the "Rebel Yell." Although never uniform, the idea of a Confederate battle scream emerged during the war. Reporters emphasized how the shouts differed from those of northern and European soldiers in significant ways. Soldiers from both sides compared it to the noise of devils. An Alabama soldier described it as a "wild yell, that sounded as if all the demons of hell had broken loose, went up from our lines." A Confederate nurse described one regiment "yelling like unchained devils."[55] One soldier wrote of it, "Then arose that do-or-die expression, that maniacal maelstrom of sound; that penetrating, rasping, shrieking, blood-curdling noise, that could be heard for miles on earth, and whose volumes reached the heavens." According to this soldier, "such an expression as never yet came from the throats of sane men, but from men whom the seething blast of an imaginary hell would not check while the sound lasted."[56] A Union surgeon wrote that when rebels advanced, they moved "through the woods yelling like devils."[57]

White Americans had experienced and categorized extreme combat vocalisms before this war. According to one reporter, southern whites "learnt it from the Indians, I believe."[58] Throughout the nineteenth century, one way white Americans differentiated themselves from Native American soldiers was through representations of sound. Time and again, white writers referred to the yells of Indians as "war whoops." When J. K. Callaway wrote home in September 1863 with a description of the Battle of Chickamauga, he observed that when the men offered their "War whoop" they sounded "like a gang of mad tigers or demons."[59] "War whoops" had long been a feature of white American representations of Indians. Americans contrasted the "shrieking" of Indians with the discipline of white soldiers, and this was further evidence of the evil of Indians. When rendering a battle during the War of 1812, one American writer noted how the "Indians raised the war-whoop" and then "the savages, like an army of demons, poured over the walls upon the weak and helpless."[60]

One soldier who experienced many of these changes and looked to hell as a primary vehicle to express the changes in his life was Lewis Bissell of Connecticut. He was twenty years old when he enlisted with his friends in September 1862, and his initial letters home told of the food, the crowds in Washington, DC, and how "the men are all well and in good spirits." He heard the war, the "sound of the enemies' cannon," long before he saw it or fought in it. He enjoyed his local surroundings. The Capitol "is magnificent. No pen can describe it."[61]

Even before he experienced bullets whizzing by him, cutting down his fellows, and littering the fields with bodies, Bissell noticed the changes to the landscape. Where trees had grown now only stumps remained. He reported to his brother, "Thousands of acres of woodland have been cut over by McClellan's Army." Graves were only "a stone's throw from our camp." He saw stragglers and prisoners of war, many "of them barefoot with nothing but shirt and pants to their backs and legs." As the war raged, he viewed deserted homes, windows "minus sash and glass" and walls with "holes . . . where a cannon ball had passed."[62]

Committed to his Christianity, Bissell often wrote to his parents about the chaplains, prayer times, reading his Bible, and his belief that those who trusted in Christ went to heaven after death. The war, however, altered the routine of his Connecticut home. "Sunday we pitched Sibley tents," he explained to his father in November 1862, "Was very busy all day. It did not

seem much like Sunday—the camp was all bustle and confusion." In fact, after
joining the military, Bissell went three months before attending a church
service or hearing a "good sermon." Through these early months, he maintained his providential belief that God was in charge of everything—from
who was elected to when men died.[63]

While the lack of church services and the disfigured landscape began the
shift in Bissell's moral imagination, the realities of battle upended it. After
the Battle of Fredericksburg in late 1862, Bissell and his comrades helped carry
the wounded from the battlefield. The familiar and unfamiliar collided to
confuse his senses. "The first thing that attracted my attention was the slaughter house smell caused by the wounds of the men. . . . It was a sight never to
be forgotten by me." "It was a sickening sight," he continued, "Some were shot
in the legs. One had a ball through both legs below the knees. . . . One other
had been hit in the head, was speechless and one arm and one leg was para-
lyzed." The smells and sights, he finished to his mother, were "enough to melt
a heart of stone."[64]

As one day of horror turned into weeks of horror and as those weeks
turned into months, young Lewis Bissell started to wonder about the nation.
"To me things look very dark," he set down in late January 1863. Disease
struck him and countless others as diarrhea left a stench and stain of its own.
Casualties were no longer listed as "killed" or "wounded," but just the lone
letters "k" or "w." By the middle of 1864, he found no joy in the war. "If there
is ever again any rejoicing in this world, it will be when this war is over." Bissell claimed that only those who experienced combat knew what it really
meant. "One who has never been under fire has no idea of war."[65]

Then for his June 4, 1864, letter home, Lewis Bissell did something he had
never done before. He altered his geographical location to include a moral
one. Typically, Bissell let his family know where he was at the beginning or
ending of a letter. "Near Fort Lyon," he would write. Or "Headquarters . . .
Alexandria, Va." After all he had seen, smelled, witnessed, and done, Bissell
now identified his location as "Cold Harbor and Hell."[66]

"Hell" became a geographical and spatial marker during the war for many
Americans. As Union soldiers closed in on the Confederate capital in Richmond, Virginia, in 1865, they laid siege to Petersburg. There they constructed
several forts, one of which they named officially Fort Sedgwick. Unofficially,
it became known as "Fort Hell" because of its proximity to Confederate forces.

When William P. Hopkins created a map years later, he titled it *Plan of Fort Sedgwick generally known as Fort Hell.*[67]

Only a few hundred yards away, Confederate forces constructed Fort Mahone, named after Gen. William Mahone, who earlier in the war had been largely responsible for atrocities against African American Union soldiers. Fort Mahone was better known as "Fort Damnation." By 1865, both Union and Confederate forces used the language of hell to refer to their physical spaces.[68]

While for many men the war rendered chaotic their physical senses, it also provided moments when their gendered conceptions were overturned. This became true particularly when they encountered violent women. One Union soldier, for instance, recalled a moment when "another She-Devil shot her way to our breastworks." With both hands wielding "large revolvers" she killed several men and when she ran out of ammunition she stabbed three men with a knife.[69]

Many men joined Bissell in a chorus of writing to declare that war was evil—that war was hell. Those who had longed for combat and who had boasted of it as part of their patriotism, manhood, and religion, now considered the land to be drenched in darkness. John Chase wrote his brother in late 1863, "without any joking I don't see when or where this War is going to end for it looks darker and darker to me every day." Later he wrote to his brother in December 1864, "it is a perfect Hell on earth to be there."[70] Confederate cavalryman James Bates from Texas wrote to a friend, "such is manifest destiny—God has brought this war to humble a wicked & corrupt people, & until the country & all its inhabitants are ruined I fear we will have no peace."[71] They had had enough of war and wished it to end. South Carolinian John F. Lanneau concluded in his personal journal, "War is an evil."[72] J. K. Callaway wrote home to his wife, "may the Lord hasten the happy time when the demon of war shall be driven from our bleeding land."[73]

Hell Is a Palace to It

As Charles Johnson battled diarrhea and his distress over hospitalization, he turned to reading the book of Job and to penning a personal diary. While his letters home detailed some aspects of his agony, his diary allowed him to express inner thoughts and feelings he could not share with his family.

Darkness and despair marked the pages. "I cannot sleep, cannot read," he bemoaned. His environment depressed him: "rough walls . . . ragged floor . . . empty!" The inside of the cabin matched his soul. He felt "loneliness that resembles dread." Life, he declared, had become "as a desert—a wide waste of bareness, a desolation."[74]

Johnson could not live as he had before. Immobilized in a hospital bed, he could not provide for his family or participate in the war. When he healed somewhat, he joined a new federal organization of wounded soldiers called the Invalid Corps. Labeled an invalid, Johnson not only lost his sense of God's control of the world and found darkness everywhere, but also felt a profound loss of his manhood and whiteness. "I am getting tired of this life and begin to feel as if I would like to *live* and *be* a *white man* once again," he wrote to Mary.[75]

Other soldiers who lost the ability to fight shared Johnson's sense of loss of manhood and whiteness. This seemed to equate to hell, particularly for men who were captured and imprisoned. For Union soldiers in the South, the experience of bondage recalled that of African American slaves. This descent in the experience of status led many to turn to the language of evil in pronounced and visceral ways.

During the four years of war, about 700,000 of the three million men who served as soldiers spent time in captivity. "I don't like to think of our men suffering in southern prisons," Lincoln noted after the debacle at Manassas in July 1861. "Neither do I like to think that the southern men are suffering in our prisons."[76] All in all, Union and Confederate forces operated about 150 distinct prisons.

Early in the war, both sides often exchanged captured soldiers. This kept prison numbers low. However, after the Emancipation Proclamation went into effect in January 1863, Confederates and Union leaders refused to exchange their prisoners. Prisons swelled with combatants even though neither side was prepared for the logistics of mass incarceration. The results were unsanitary, overcrowded places filled with starving and sick men.[77]

In various writings during and after the war, soldiers tried to evoke their horrible experiences by turning to the language of radical evil. "They wish to reduce us to rags, wretchedness and disease as rapidly as possible; and this they are fast effecting," wrote Capt. William Wilkins during his captivity. He believed this was a Confederate policy for "the fiends desire, in order that we may be disabled from rendering further service to our Gov't. And yet these are white-men like ourselves, and pretend to be civilized and *call themselves* Christians."[78]

Prisoners routinely describe what they encountered as "infernal" and "hellish." Often soldiers referred to the prisons simply as "those hell-holes," "the confines of hell," and "this living hell."[79] One prisoner stated baldly that life in prison was "the closest existence to a hell on earth."[80] Another went so far as to say that prison was worse than hell. In his diary William Dolphin called one prison a "lousy dirty hole. Hell is a palace to it."[81]

Many of the reasons for these references were obvious. Packed into small areas, fed with inadequate rations, and medically neglected, prisoners developed disease, discontent, and depression. Rats became so ubiquitous in and around prisons that soldiers sometimes labeled particular rooms "Rat Hell."[82]

Arriving at prisons and living within them, prisoners viewed their environment as hell on earth. Seeing Andersonville Prison in Georgia for the first time, John McElroy saw "the fires blazed up and showed us a section of these, and two massively wooden gates, with heavy iron hinges and bolts. . . . We were in Andersonville." These "infernal dens," he wrote, could never be fully described.[83]

Forced to live outdoors or in poorly constructed buildings, prisoners experienced wide fluctuations in the weather and temperature. The soldiers noted the impacts on their bodies and cast about for metaphors and analogies. Time and again, they turned to conceptions of hell. One southerner explained that Johnson's Prison in Ohio "was just the place to convert visitors to the theological belief of the Norwegians that Hell has torments of cold instead of heat."[84]

While Americans drew quotations from and referenced Milton's *Paradise Lost* during political discussions, several prisoners turned to another European classic: the first book of Dante Alighieri's *The Divine Comedy*, popularly known as *The Inferno*. George Erwin Comstock, a soldier from Iowa, noted how prison life transformed his body and those of the men around him. "Our men begin to look like anything but United States soldiers," he wrote in his diary, "more like beggars than anything I can think of, poor, pale, lean, lank, slender shanked, some no shoes, some no shirts, no pants. . . . It is a stiff battle now against insanity, we are so hungry." This prisoner felt close to hell but not quite there. In August 1863 he wrote in his private diary of "hot steaming sands under food, a place not unlike Dante's Inferno, where you freeze and fry alternatively." He held onto hope, though. "We are not yet quite to the Inferno's doom, 'all hopes abandon, ye who enter here,' for still we dare to hope."[85]

The taking and transferring of prisoners offered northern and southern whites opportunities to demonize one another directly. When southern whites viewed the Union men, they often wondered if they were demons in disguise. According to John McElroy, when young white women viewed Union soldiers wearing hats, they "immediately jumped at the conclusion that the projections covered some peculiar conformation of the Yankee anatomy—some incipient, dromedary-like humps, or perchance the horns of which they had heard so much."[86] Other camps could rival Andersonville in suffering, if not in the death toll. At the Cahaba camp in Alabama, a guard allegedly went unpunished after shooting four Union prisoners at random, "the unprovoked deed of a demon," in the words of one survivor.[87]

Edward M. Van Duzee of an Iowa regiment recalled a southern boy shouting "Where are the Yankees?" as he and other captives marched into a prison. When told that the men were Yankees, the boy replied, "Oh, you don't fool me—where are their horns?" Van Duzee compared and contrasted this perspective with the concept of "black Republicanism": "The lad had evidently heard and believed that the 'Yanks' were a kind of beast allied to the devil himself. I have since seen southern men and women, who really believed our late Vice President Hamlin was a negro, and President Lincoln a mulatto; but such mistakes were slight indeed compared with that which traces the Yankee's pedigree to a hotter country than Africa."[88]

For Union soldiers, the leaders of Andersonville, Henry Wirz and John Winder, became the embodiments of prison evil. De Will Spaulding described Wirz as "the most curious specimen of humanity I ever saw hump backed round shouldered his legs are three fourths the length of him and one might take him for old satan himself."[89] Their actions and words were demonic. Of one of Winder's quartermasters, Ezra Ripple wrote, "The diabolical acts of this inhuman monster were too numerous and too horrid to recount. He was a fit instrument of the master devil, General Winder, who no doubt prized him as one who was ready and willing to carry out his hellish schemes."[90]

As they traveled, some prisoners viewed the landscape as devoid of God. There travels seemed to take them into hell. As John McElroy moved through southern Georgia he described it as "teeming with venomous snakes, and all manners of hideous crawling things." Spanish moss, which many called "death moss," was everywhere, and the now weaponless soldiers felt "Alone on a wide, wide sea, / So lonely 'twas that God himself / Scarce seemed there to be."[91] A woman from Massachusetts wrote to Lincoln in 1864 asking that that the president appoint a special day for funeral services to recognize the many men who had died in the South. In particular, she expressed concern for the "unnamed dead heroes, lying forever unrecognizable in the ditches around those hells, Andersonville and the other prisons of the South."[92]

When Union soldiers depicted their prison experience as hellish, they echoed many of the metaphors used previously by African Americans who had been enslaved. Before the war and mass emancipation, many black writers had described slaveholders as demons, horrible living conditions as hellish, and violence committed against them as Satanic. For white men of the war, life as a prisoner was the closest thing they ever experienced to that of enslaved African Americans.

Like slaves, the men were divested of their property upon capture. Their bodies were inspected for disease. They were often separated from those they knew. They were moved physically without their consent. On the way to prisons and behind the walls, civilians gawked at them. Before imprisonment, captured soldiers experienced social shame. Guards and locals demanded that for their entertainment the incarcerated men sing. "The people flocked to see us," wrote one former prisoner from Iowa, "manifesting the keenest curiosity and most malignant hatred."[93] Southern jails were often repurposed slave holding cells. All of this looked eerily similar to the internal slave trade. U.S. Sanitary Commission workers who interviewed former inmates of Libby Prison in 1864 noted that the overcrowding at the officers' prison compelled the men to huddle together "like slaves in the middle passage."[94]

Life in prison left many white men looking dark-skinned. In part, this was due to exposure. Often the men had little reprieve from the sun's rays. The dirt and dust, coupled with the lack of water and soap, left the men even darker. McElroy recalled that "Any one of us could have gone on the negro minstrel stage, without changing a hair, and put to blush the most elaborate make-up of the grotesque burnt-cork artist."[95] Another prisoner recalled that "we could not be distinguished in color from the negroes."[96]

Some prisoners took advantage of this resemblance. One soldier recalled that when two prisoners hatched an escape plan, one prisoner "blackened his face thoroughly with lamp black" and another "rubbed his face with a piece of bacon rind." The effect was that the men looked like African Americans, at least enough to fool the confederate officers who "mistook him for a 'niggah.'"[97]

The hellish experience of immobility, disease, and exposure to the weather led some imprisoned Union soldiers to liken themselves to slaves and devils. One Iowa soldier wrote to a general, "The deaths of prisoners were announced as follows: 'Died, a Yankee prisoner,' among the deaths of slaves—no name or rank being given."[98] Another mentioned that they had been placed "in a brick jail, previously used for jailing negro slaves."[99] "Privation and abuse have made me Selfish and more like a Devil than a man," a prisoner from the 103rd Pennsylvania in Andersonville noted in August 1864.[100]

For all these similarities, white prisoners' experience of hellishness was quite distinct from that of African Americans. Whites endured prisons for a season, months, or sometimes years. None spent their entire lives in captivity. None experienced the wrenching childhood revelation that the law rendered them property. Few watched family members being beaten, sold, or raped. The vast majority of imprisoned white men choose to fight in the war and they knew that captivity could be one of the consequences.

Even after the war and in the years when northern and southern whites made overtures of forgiveness toward one another, those who had lived in the prisons persisted in their hellish descriptions. Writing a preface in the late 1870s for John McElroy's prison autobiography, Robert McCune claimed that the evil of Confederate prisons sprung from the evil of slavery. "The system of slavery," he asserted, "had performed a most perverting, morally desolating, and we may say, demonizing work on the dominant race." Those who could have "used whip and thumb-screw, shot-gun and blood-hound, to keep human beings subservient" were clearly not prepared to treat prisons of war with "chivalric tenderness and compassion." McElroy's narrative, McCune concluded, was "an exposé of the inner hell of the Southern prisons."[101]

Ezra Ripple felt similarly. When, decades after the war, he remembered what he and other prisoners had endured, he wrote, "Thirty thousand prisoners, helpless, many sick, many dying, unable to take any offensive part themselves, to be opened upon with grapeshot at close range because there was danger that they might be liberated. Does history record anything more devilish? This was not war, it was hellish hatred seeking the chance to commit murder." Although he was a believing Christian, Ripple found these crimes unforgiveable. "It is over 40 years ago that all this happened," he concluded, but he still felt that history did not "record anything more devilish."[102]

In later years, Americans held onto their wartime letters and diaries. Some became family heirlooms that eventually made their ways to archives. Scores of men and women used their documents to publish reminiscences of the war. By the 1880s and 1890s, these works became increasingly popular. In one of them, published in 1888, Orvey S. Barrett sounded a lot like William Tecumseh Sherman. He recognized the place of hell and the demonic in the war. Of the Battle of Mechanicsville in June 1862, he explained that "Men, of human form divine, became demons." Then, when recalling another day of the struggle, he wrote, "the battle raged all day with great slaughter, on both sides. . . . The thunder of cannon was awful: clash of arms, shouts of combatants, was deafening. Such a seething hell will never be again enacted on this continent. It would be impossible to repeat it, in all its details."[103] When Robert Loudon Drummond gave a reunion speech to his regiment in the early twentieth century, he explained, "Even from the Federal standpoint, war has been defined to be 'Hell.'" As he remembered back to his wartime and prison experiences, he explained, "By the time the last ambulance has gone by, I am ready to say with the master of the Art, General William T. Sherman, 'War is Hell.'"[104]

After the war when former soldiers talked about their time in prison, they routinely described it as indescribable. For McElroy, the hellishness of prison life could never be depicted. "No living human being, in my judgement, will ever be able to properly paint the horrors of those infernal dens."[105] Another former prisoner wrote, "It is not my purpose, if I could, to make this more horrible than it was. There was much to be seen there every day so horrible that it goes beyond my power to describe it."[106]

In some ways, these authors echoed Walt Whitman's perspective on the war. Although Whitman neither fought nor spent time in prison, his hospital labors gave him an up-close-and-personal view of the war. He often used hell as a referent to explain the events. One piece he titled "Deserters—A Glimpse of War's Hell-Scenes." In another essay, "The Real War Will Never Get in the Books," Whitman reflected that "future years will never know the seething hell and the black infernal background of countless minor scenes and interiors." For him, it was "best they should not." While Americans could read about and perhaps understand grand armies and titanic battles, they could never know the fleshly intimacies of the affair. For Whitman, the truth of the war—the "interior history" would be "untold and unwritten." It would be "buried in the grave, in eternal darkness."[107]

While Whitman, Ripple, and many others used ineffability as a means to draw attention to the horror of the war, many other Americans looked beyond the medium of words to present what the conflicts meant for them. They turned to visual culture to depict elements of the war, including political divisions, sectional disagreements, and most emphatically emancipation. In addition to the outpouring of writing and speaking, many Americans made and viewed political cartoons, paintings, and photography to comprehend the war. When it came to notions of evil, they produced visible images of the invisible. While others found that words failed to express the evil invading and swirling, American artists used graphic illustrations to present the evil all around them. In the process, they fashioned another space where devils had dominion.

CHAPTER 3

Masks and Faces

Years before William Tecumseh Sherman declared that war "is all hell," his friend created a photograph of it. George N. Barnard spent a great deal of time with Sherman during the conflict. Appointed as the official photographer for the Military Division of the Mississippi in 1863, Barnard followed Sherman's forces as they "marched to the sea" in 1864 and 1865. When the war ended, Barnard published a collection of his photographs with a simple main title: *Photographic Views of Sherman's Campaign.* The sixty images showcased generals and battlefields, cityscapes and ruin-scapes. Usually the titles were simple descriptors of the people, places, or properties photographed: *Sherman and his Generals, Trestle Bridge at Whiteside, Interior View of Fort Sumter.*

There was one exception. He titled the twenty-seventh photograph *The "Hell Hole," Battlefield of New Hope Church, GA.* The image was stark. In the center stood a leafless tree, split halfway up so that its peak leaned to the side to form what appeared as gallows. A tree line ran along the background while brush dominated the foreground. Hidden behind the bushes and branches, the remnants of a wooden split-rail fence showed that the place once bore the marks of human civilization.[1]

Without the title, the photograph could have been any number of locales during the war. It could even have been a landscape after a tornado or other natural disaster. Together, the text and image offered meaning to viewers. It was not any grouping of trees and brush; it was located geographically at New Hope Church, Georgia. It was not any kind of hole; in fact, there are no discernible dips in the ground. It was instead a particular hole: a "hell-hole."

Barnard's publication, photograph, and title highlight several elements of the place of evil during and after the war. First, the textual was never purely textual. Americans viewed words in contexts and material forms. Words had weight, literally printed on paper or imprinted on plaster or stone or other physical objects. Personal letters looked and felt different than newspapers or pamphlets. Words often had visual designs surrounding them, such as drawings and photographs. Second, images were rarely, if ever, just images. They were routinely framed by textual markers and directives. This was most obvious in political cartoons where written words served as key identifiers to comprehend the political points. Text boxes or bubbles animated political cartoons, while titles and textual descriptions offered viewer-readers layers of meaning to bring to their own consideration of the paintings and photographs.

Third, words and images usually cost money. The publishers priced Barnard's album at $100. According to the reviewer for *Harper's Weekly*, the book was worth every penny, but that price point would leave the book "not very popular."[2] Many other expressions of devils, Satan, and hell were much cheaper, and these artists created a commercial enterprise by combining folkloric imagery of evil with contemporary politics and military affairs of the day.

Fourth and finally, neither Barnard's photograph nor his title involved people. The *"Hell Hole"* offered an environment and a geography. It featured trees and forest. Detaching from the logocentrism of those writers like Walt Whitman (who wrote famously that the "real war would never get in the books" or "be written") allows for a subsequent detachment from anthropocentrism: neither words, nor humans constituted the center. They were not the ultimate objects or subjects of this world or ones beyond. When it came to visualizing hell, Barnard presented nonhuman entities.

Americans endeavored to convey, create, and capitalize upon meanings of the war through graphic imagery. In the process, they further brought devils and hell into the mainstream of American entertainment culture and politics, a process that saw Satan and evil move from everyday folklore to widespread commercial consumption. Along with envelopes, the beginning of the war also featured the rapid rise of snakes as signifiers of evil. Americans and Confederates cast treason as demonic. Unionists characterized southern secession and then opposition to the federal government's pursuit of war as demonic, and then anti-abolitionists presented Abraham Lincoln and emancipation as inspired by the devil. When Abraham Lincoln followed African Americans who had pursued freedom and Congress which had legislated against slavery, several artists transformed him from a person into a demon.

Artists turned and twisted beyond human forms to represent the world and worlds elsewhere. Displays of evil came to include the environments altered by war. During the first years of war, artists transformed humans into nonhumans; in the final years artists represented the material and animate nonhuman as expressions of hell on earth. These various visualizations provided another expression of how Americans understood and created the war as beyond humans and fused the material and the spiritual. The struggle encompassed the totality of their known universe, including animals, trees, buildings, humans, and demons. The visual imagery of the era, and the texts tied to those images, displayed the war as one where earth and hell existed on a shared terrain.

Scholars of the Civil War and the nineteenth century in general have ingeniously analyzed many of the features of the age. Some examined cartoons to comprehend political culture. Others scrutinized photographs to consider the moods and feelings of society. Still others found race constructed and racism furthered through visual renderings.[3] Looking at presentations of evil shows that visualizations became avenues to new meaning. Artists did more than create the visible to reveal the invisible; they attempted to conjure the invisible through their pencils, pens, paints, and cameras. Although their work can easily be called political cartoons or drawings or paintings or photographs or statues, it was much more. These were attempts to reveal hidden truths. In a way, they became acts of revelation.

Snakes in a War

In the years and decades before the American Civil War, a variety of graphic artists had portrayed the devil and demons at work in the atmosphere of the United States. The war, however, ushered in a new era for visual displays and the place of evil within them. As Americans hankered for news on the war, they grabbed illustrated newspapers, read and viewed them, and often retained them as keepsakes. Recognizing this market potential, publishers and artists rushed to document the war visually. Along the way, several created new views of evil in the country. Perhaps nothing illuminated this transformation more than the explosion of scenes featuring serpents.

Snakes had not been representatives of the demonic in American politi-cal culture before the war. In fact, they had been quite the opposite. They had been desirable symbols. More than one hundred years earlier and before the United States came into existence as a nation-state, Benjamin Franklin pub-lished an image of a snake to appeal to his fellow colonists. In 1754, he printed a simple woodcut that featured a serpent severed into eight discrete pieces. The title read *Join, or Die* and it provided a visual analogue for his hopes that the colonists could unite in a coordinated fashion to oppose their French and Indian rivals. Several printers throughout the colonies copied it, and two de-cades later when the War for Independence began, printers refashioned Franklin's image into propaganda for American unity. The goal was not to kill a snake, but to become one.[4]

During the American Revolution, another snake entered American pol-itics: a coiled rattlesnake with the phrase "Don't Tread on Me" printed under-neath. Designed by South Carolinian Christopher Gadsden, it gained notoriety with its vernacular punch. Just as the clear and pointed rhetoric of Thomas Paine's *Common Sense* appealed to everyday colonists, Gadsden's flag and words expressed the desire of many colonists for liberty from govern-ment intervention.[5] During the war, Congress approved a flag for the mili-tary that featured a rattlesnake with a banner that read "This We'll Defend."[6] These three visual representations continued to be well-known in the decades after the War for Independence.

Only rarely before the Civil War did Americans turn to snakes visually as references for evil when it came to their military, political, or legislative affairs. Far more often, snakes were positive symbols akin to the bald eagle or the liberty cap. Snakes served as emblems to mobilize political and mili-tary action. They were not denigrations.

Then when the Civil War began, another desirable snake slithered onto the American scene. Gen. Winfield Scott offered Abraham Lincoln a plan to compel southern whites to remain within the Union: he recommended that the navy blockade the Atlantic Ocean and that the army gain control of the Mississippi River. Effectively, Scott hoped to strangle the South geographi-cally. This would make imports and exports difficult and thus compel south-ern whites to rejoin the Union or die. Friends and foes of the Scott's strategy called it the "Anaconda Plan." One political cartoon from 1861 titled *Scott's*

Great Snake featured a map of the United States with a serpent coiled around the southern states.[7]

Evil took another visual turn with snakes during the war. Northern artists rushed to create various types of serpents and put them on display to expose the wickedness of disunion. It constituted another element of how Unionists linked Satan's "secession" from heaven to the actions of white southerners. As Christians had long done, they conflated the serpent tempter of Eve and Adam in the biblical book of Genesis with the Lucifer and Satan of later biblical passages. When artists created visual referents for the actions of secessionists, the rebellious and conniving snake of the Bible became their key symbol. By turning to snakes to depict the evil behind political acts, these artists abandoned one American artistic tradition and created another. They shifted the focus of evil visually from the shackles holding African Americans in bondage to the snakes of secessionist political actions.

Snakes animated an array of anti-secession and anti-Confederate depictions. Only a few months after the war began an artist for *Harper's Weekly* created a haunting image of Jefferson Davis titled *Jeff Davis reaping the harvest*. It featured a ghastly looking Davis holding a sickle in his right hand and a bundle of stalks with small skulls on the top of them. Behind him a vulture perched atop a barren tree with a noose hanging from it. Below him, almost hidden at his feet, a snake flashed his fangs, ready to strike.[8]

Snakes became ubiquitous in letter envelope productions of the Civil War. Often, the eagle of liberty battled a host of snakes. Sometimes there was only one snake; sometimes many; sometimes the Constitution was featured as a book in the background and sometimes a bust of George Washington was present as well. On one, a serpent attempts to slither up a pole with an American flag at the top. Another featured a nude woman who knelt, cowered, and covered her face. She had a snake coiled around her. On it were the words "Free Speech at the South."[9]

A number of these productions featured a devil working in concert with snakes. One presented the Goddess Liberty attempting to spear an unclothed devil. Running away, the devil, who has a serpent wrapped around his body, holds a Confederate flag in one hand. The envelope instructed its viewer to "Resist the devil, and he will flee from you."[10]

Serpents also spent time with Confederate leaders. In one, Jefferson Davis hung from a palmetto tree with a snake hissing into his face, as if speaking to him. The intimacy of the image, along with the directness of the serpent, emphasized an affinity between the Confederate leader and evil along with an authoritative direction. In this case, Davis listened while the serpent spoke. Davis did not give orders; he took them.[11]

Several envelopes used snakes and other symbols to juxtapose the godliness of the Union with the villainy of the Confederacy. One elaborate envelope read across the top "Liberty or Death." It featured a shield with a liberty pole and cap emerging from behind it. Two books sat beside: one was the "Holy Bible" and resting atop it was the Constitution. Beneath was a snake with an arrow through its neck.

On some occasions, artists labeled the snakes with words. Most often they used either "Secession" or "South." A few times they wrote "Dixie." By rendering the political act or the geographical region as evil, these graphic artists participated in the shift of the presence of the demonic from the social structure of slavery to the political and military particulars of the present moment. Put this way, devils had invaded the United States recently in the form of treason. Satan was not so deeply rooted in the totality of the national experience through the long-standing realities of human bondage.

The association of secession and the Confederacy with snakes even took the form of a board game. In 1862, a Philadelphia print company distributed "The Game of Secession." A dice game where players moved forward based upon the numerical value of their role, but could then move forward or backward based upon the space they landed, it featured a few dozen small images. There was Lincoln, McClellan, the shelling of Fort Sumter, a lion to represent Great Britain, and even a devilish-looking Confederate riding an African American slave who appeared as a bucking bull. The more than one hundred spaces consisted of pieces of a long snake that wound throughout. At the top, the eagle of liberty bit near the head of the serpent. For players, the war took place and shape within the context and upon the terrain of a lengthy snake.[12]

The link between secessionists and serpents continued to be pictured throughout the war. As Confederate hopes for victory appeared to be dying in 1864, an artist's cover for a new song, Jeff Wants to Get Away, featured snakes hissing and coiling around Confederate people and symbols. The image centered upon Robert Breckenridge blackening the face of Jefferson Davis so that he can hide from Union soldiers. The two men stood on bales of cotton, and a large serpent coiled around Breckenridge's feet. Behind them, another snake slithered up the pole of a Confederate flag turned upside down. The song lyrics made no reference to the snakes and focused instead on the blackness of Davis—his body and soul—and the triumph of the federal government over the Confederacy.[13]

This song sheet, the board game, and the other examples showcased the movement of snakes, devils, and Satan into the mass-produced commercial culture of the nineteenth century. Whether to sell envelopes or music, magazines or board games, Americans manufactured visual depictions of evil. Artists and publishers leveraged religious concepts not only to make political points but also to make money in the expanding sphere of American consumerism.

Along with these visual items, many Americans used graphic rhetoric and word selections to associate Confederates with serpents. Before the war, Abraham Lincoln did so with an anecdote: "If I saw a venomous snake crawling in the road, any man would say I might seize the nearest stick and kill it; but, if I found that snake in bed with my children, it would be another question. [Laughter.]" The future president proceeded: "I might hurt the children worse than the snake, and the snake might bite them. [Applause.]" He continued the story with obvious allusions to contemporary political debates: "Much more, if I found it in bed with my neighbor's children, and I had bound myself by a solemn contract not to meddle with his children under any circumstances, it would become me to let that particular mode of killing the gentleman alone. [Great laughter.] But if there is a bed newly made up, to which the children are to be taken, and it was proposed to take a batch of young snakes and put them in with them, I take it no man would say there was a question how I ought to decide. [Prolonged applause and cheers.]"[14]

Unionists unmasked the metaphor. Alfred West, a Kentuckian who was living in New Orleans in 1860, enlisted in the Union military. When he wrote home in August 1861, he sounded similar to African Americans when they described slave masters. There was one small change: West claimed to observe physical likeness between snakes and secessionists, not snakes and slaveholders: "If you can imagine anything sneaking or treacherous + cowardly then you may have some idea of a Secesh. . . . Those in this part of the country are the most miserable shiftless looking set of people you ever saw."[15] This idea also found expression in contemporary fiction. In *The Unionist's Daughter: A Tale of Rebellion in Tennessee*, published early in the war, the author had an African American describe Jefferson Davis and other Confederates as "a mean, sneakin', toad-hoppin', snake-crawlin', house-settin'-on-fire lot."[16] Both of these instances emphasized secessionist bodies, not slaveholding ones.

The ties between secession and serpents also had small, seemingly innocuous, influences on word choices during the war. Perhaps the most famous example of a snake in Civil War musical culture could be found in Julia Ward Howe's "Battle Hymn of the Republic." In her amalgamation of the American war and biblical concepts, perhaps the quintessential expression of American civil religion, she wrote, and thousands have sung ever since:

I have read a fiery gospel writ in burnished rows of steel:
"As ye deal with my contemners, so with you my grace shall deal;
Let the hero, born of woman,
Crush the serpent with his heel."[17]

Howe connected one prominent Christian interpretation that related Jesus to the book of Genesis. After God cast Adam and Eve from the Garden of Eden, God told the man, woman, and serpent what their lives would be like in the days and years to come. To the serpent, God declared that it would slither on the ground, that it would bite the heel of the man, but that the man would crush its head with his foot. Many Christians read this as prophecy for what Jesus would do through his death and resurrection.

The word "crush" was very different than the legal and technical phrase "suppress" sometimes used to describe the Union's aim with regard to secession. When Abraham Lincoln called for volunteer troops in the middle of April 1861, he did so with the explicit intent to "suppress" any "combinations" forming to undermine the federal government. He used suppress because it was the language of the Militia Acts from the 1790s. Two years later, when Lincoln endeavored to defend his suspensions of habeas corpus, he did so with a public letter where he maintained that he had every legitimate right to enact any "lawful measure to suppress the rebellion."[18] This was also the word choice of Congress when it amended the Militia Act in 1862 to allow African

Americans to enlist in the military and to emancipate slaves in rebellious areas.[19] In the realm of constitutional law, suppress was the appropriate verb.

But the vast majority of northerners preferred the word "crush." The difference underscored an important point about northern views of secession. Defeating the Confederacy went deeper than protecting the Constitution. It tapped into the how they understood God's creation of the world and their nation. Even Lincoln turned to "crush" instead of suppress at times. In his first annual message to Congress in early December 1861, he challenged the notion that foreign nations would naturally come to the aid of the Confederacy. He maintained instead that arguments could be made to persuade Britain, France, and other nations to help "to crush this rebellion." One envelope titled *Old Uncle Abe will crush secession forever* featured an arm reaching down from the cloud. Labeled "O.U.A.," the arm had a snake wrapped around it, but the hand was squeezing its life out.[20]

Crushing the rebellion could be heard and read far and wide. One captain wrote to his brother: "My first object is to crush this infernal Rebellion."[21] In Edward McPherson's collection of statements regarding the war published in 1864, he recounted numerous leading Americans calling for "efforts to crush the rebellion."[22] In 1862, the *New York Times* drew particular attention to this word: "There is no word that so completely expresses the duty of the Government toward the rebellion as the word 'crush.'"[23]

The concept of crushing the rebellion also took graphic form. David Gilmour Blythe's painting *Lincoln Crushing the Dragon of Rebellion* featured a strong and sinewy Lincoln in the midst of striking a four-legged, long-tailed dragon. With its mouth open, its tongue was angled to look like a red lightning bolt. The dragon's tail cracked and pulled down a pillar representing the nation. An Irish Democrat tried to stop Lincoln by attaching a shackle to Lincoln's right foot.[24]

In the background, scribblings on a wall read: "The rebellion *must* be crush'd!"[25] For this painting, Blythe mingled Genesis and the Book of Revelation. While evil slithered as a serpent at the beginning of the Bible, Satan returned as a dragon at the end. Blythe's painting featured several other demonic characters as well. Behind the devil, the world has been rent open and evil flowed through it in the form of lightning and dark clouds. For Tammany Hall, the New York City organization of Democrats, Blythe drew several letters that began the word—TAM—and then a face with horns.

Blythe incorporated urgency, invasion, presence, and absence. Below the dragon, where Blythe inscribed his last name, he included a palette of paint and brushes knocked over either by the dragon's violent movements or the artist's flight from the scene. The events were so terrifying that they invaded the world of the artist, and perhaps that of the viewer too.

At the end of the war and in the years after it, crush continued to be used far more frequently than any other word. According to Thomas Prentice Kettell's *History of the Great Rebellion*, published in 1865, after the initial battles of war, the North's "courage and zeal which rose above defeat, and a determination to put forth all her energies to crush out the rebellion."[26] In a tribute to the patriotism of men from Schuylkill County, Pennsylvania, the editor introduced the volume by claiming that the men volunteered "to assist the Federal government to crush rebellion." At the end of the work, the editor made the connection between crush and evil explicit: he declared that the men endeavored to "crush" a rebellion that was "unprovoked, unwarranted, cruel, [and] hellish."[27]

To crush the snake, ultimately, offered another perspective on how many Unionists expressed their involvement with and understanding of the war. Visually, snakes were distinct from shackles, the common way of graphically depicting slavery and freedom in paintings. Snakes had life. They could move; they were affiliated with the darkness of the devil. Moreover, killing a snake was extraordinarily difficult. Severing one piece does not necessarily kill the whole. They are also prophetic of the Second Coming, that time when Jesus would return to judge the quick and the dead, to bring a second Jerusalem to the world. Yet by investing so much symbolic meaning connecting snakes with secession, Unionists set themselves up for the problem of evil when the war ended. How could evil remain if and when secession no longer slithered?

Copperheads and Democrats

Pro-war Unionists took the snake imagery and applied it not only to their Confederate enemies but also to northerners who opposed the administration's prosecution of the war. Artists devalued their military and political enemies by transforming them into animals, associating them with the demonic, and sometimes both at the same time. One group especially received this particular treatment: pro-peace Democrats. Labeled copperheads, they found themselves attacked in visual and rhetorical culture as snakes in human form. Even when not called copperheads, Democratic politicians and candidates received attack after attack that linked them to evil.

The phrase copperhead held numerous meanings in the 1860s. It was a term for a penny, which at the time had Lady Liberty emblazoned upon it. It was also the name of a particular snake, the Scytalus Cupreus. According to one scientific writer, "After the rattlesnake, the copper-head snake is the most dreaded in the northern states." These snakes went by different names in different locations, but a typical copperhead ran about three feet long, and had a large mouth and yellowish-white fangs.[28]

For the Civil War, the application of the label to anti-war Democrats began with a direct connection to biblical evil. In several pieces published in the *Cincinnati Commercial* in the summer of 1861, the authors likened northern supporters of secession to serpents and copperheads. One suggested sarcastically that Ohio's Peace Democrats should take the biblical curse of the serpent in Genesis as a motto for themselves: "Upon thy belly shalt thou go, and dust shalt thou eat all the days of thy life." Readers at the time knew that the following curse and prophecy was that the serpent would have his head "crushed" by Adam's children.[29]

No work more obviously linked copperheads to biblical demons than *Ye Book of Copperheads*, published in 1863. Unlike Barnard's album of photographs that cost $100, this "Book of All Comic Books!" as it was advertised, cost only 25 cents. The publisher clearly priced and marketed it as a frivolity.[30] The front cover bore the pamphlet's title with a snake wrapped around a tree and an apple labeled "disunion" in its mouth. The biblical symbolism was obvious. This was the serpent of the book of Genesis who tempted Eve and Adam into disobeying God's directives against eating the fruit. The rest of the book linked Confederates and pro-peace Democrats in the North with Christian understandings of the devil in the Bible. *Ye Book of Copperheads* served as another example of Americans leaping back and forth between their present day and those described in the scriptures. On one page a snake coiled around a boot, and the text read, "There once was a Copperhead snake / tried to bit Uncle Sam by mistake." Unfazed Uncle Sam "crushed this pestiferous snake."

The other pages featured snakes seeking to undermine the war effort and emancipation. The snakes either attacked soldiers and Republicans or tried to dissuade them from war. After twenty pages of snakes working in tandem with devils, Confederate leaders, and any northerners who stood in the way, the work culminated with the forces of the Union crushing the snakes. On one, the eagle of liberty "with his bill did the Copperhead kill." On another, Union soldiers used swords, clubs, their hands, and their heels to "settle the Copperheads all." The final word of the visual tale was an elegant and simple linking of piety to politics: "AMEN!"[31]

By transforming political enemies into snakes, pro-war Republican artists trafficked in zoomorphic demonization. By ascribing animalistic characteristics to humans, they resembled to some extent the whites who often linked African Americans to animals. When slaveholders and others characterized black men, women, and children as subhuman, they mostly did so with the concept of "beasts of burden." These were animals that humans had harnessed for labor and resources. Blacks became like mules, horses, and cows—beings and bodies that carried materials, cultivated the ground, and provided food. When Republicans portrayed Democrats as animals in the shape of serpents, however, they did so with animals that offered no profitability or productivity. These snakes added nothing to the broader community or economy. They were abject and dangerous, mostly understood in the Christian tradition as demonic. The point was to crush snakes, not to capitalize upon them.

Along with copperheads, graphic artists transformed a number of people and political positions into hybrid animals and demons. One envelope, titled *G. T. Blow-Regard*, cast the Confederate general Pierre Gustave Toutant Beauregard as a strange devil. With horns or ears that looked almost like rabbit ears and a lengthy tail, this devil-animal blew into a bugle that was draped with a Confederate flag.[32] Another print featured Beauregard as an animal. This time, the artist portrayed him, Jefferson Davis, and Alexander Stephens as donkeys under the direction of a horned Satan. With bodies of donkeys, faces of men, and their last names emblazoned on their sides, the political leaders became amalgamations of humans and animals. Davis asked the question that opens Shakespeare's *Macbeth*: "When shall we three meet again?" The devil answered, "Very soon."[33]

Far more often, visual artists in the North depicted Confederate leaders as inspired or duped by the devil and not demonic themselves. For the graphic cover of the sheet music for the song "Emblem of the Free," an artist presented Jefferson Davis sleeping upon his arm on a desk. Behind him, a winged, horned, and cloven-footed devil placed a crown upon his head. In the background, the ghost of George Washington looked down disapprovingly and endeavored to direct Davis to the angels of liberty and justice behind him.[34] These graphic accusations mirrored statements made by American military men. One wrote from Hilton Head, South Carolina, to Jefferson Davis in April 1863 that he was fighting for "the liberty" to steal, sell, exploit, and kill humans. "This is the kind of liberty—the liberty to do wrong—which Satan, chief of the fallen angels, was contending for when he was cast into hell."[35]

Typically, Democrats rejected the copperhead label. In one print from 1863, however, an artist embraced serpents as a referent. This artist contrasted heroic copperhead snakes with a villainous Lincoln. Titled *The Great American WHAT IS IT? chased by Copperheads*, it featured several powerful serpents attacking Lincoln and African Americans. Shoeless, Lincoln raced away from the black men and tore apart a sheet that read "Constitution & the Union As it Was." He shouted back to the men, "Go back to your masters, dont think you are free because you are emancipated." The black men begged him for help: "FADDER.r.r.r Abrum," one called. Another intoned, "Take us to your bussum."

These snakes appeared powerful. One devoured a small man. They hissed. They spoke. One alluded to the caning of Charles Sumner a decade earlier with "hit him again." Another scolded Lincoln, "If you cant read that document drop it." In fact, the snakes were so ferocious and frightening that in the background the devil raised the bones of John Brown, and the two planned to flee to Canada. In this case, the serpents were not Satan. Their efforts would drive away the devil and his abolitionist minions.[36]

Sometimes, Republicans and Unionists did not bother with using snakes as surrogates for Satan. On occasion, they went straight to direct demonization for failures to support Lincoln's administration. In early 1864, for instance, Senator John Conness of California wrote to Lincoln regarding an old friend of his, James A. McDougall. In the 1850s, McDougall had been a Republican but shifted to the Democratic Party in 1860. Although elected to the Senate in opposition to secession and then known as a "war Democrat," McDougall opposed many of Lincoln's efforts. Conness felt "disgusted with McDougall" and enclosed "choice Extracts from Satan"—otherwise known as speeches from McDougall in 1862.[37] On another occasion, a spiritualist wrote to Lincoln about a séance where a spirit spoke through a medium to

say, "The traitors about you [are] under the influence of demons—once in the
form, and that their power for evil [is] past our comprehension."[38]

Republicans used the presidential election of 1864 as another opportunity to render the political points of their opponents as demonic. After Democrats at their convention in Chicago nominated George McClellan, the
former general who had hoped to convene the war on "Christian" principles,
Currier and Ives released an image titled *The Chicago Platform and its Candidate.* A two-faced McClellan stood atop a wooden platform upheld by
Jefferson Davis, anti-war Democrats Fernando Wood and Clement Vallandigham, and a devil. The devil looked directly at Davis and said with
resignation, "Well Jeff it's no use trying to hold up this rickety old platform."
The demon concluded, "I guess I'll leave you to your fate!" Davis responded,
lamenting the state of affairs. The Confederacy had lost Atlanta and Mobile,
and now "you who led me into the scrape threaten to leave me!!!!!" To the
left, a Union soldier holding a musket raised his right arm and hand toward
McClellan and stated, "Its no use General! You can't stand on that platform
and come that blarney over me, I smed brimstone!"

The imagery and text within it contain several layers of evil. While the
devil attempted to hide his horns under a scarf, the twin protruding features,
along with his dark skin and long nose, gave him away. His direct interac-
tion with Davis included his gaze, his words, and the physical proximity of
his body and his text bubble. Finally, the Union soldier used smell as prophesy for McClellan. The scent of brimstone indicated that McClellan and the
others would soon reside in hell.[39]

One week before the election, Thomas Nast webbed together copperheads,
devils, and Democrats. With *How the Copperheads Obtain their Votes*, Nast
presented Democrats examining tombstones to locate the names of deceased
soldiers. Their plan was to record their names as voting for Democratic candidates. Above the grave, the ethereal ghost of the fallen soldier emerged to
deliver "a curse upon you for making me appear disloyal." Then in *Election
Day,* the central image featured two demons named "Southern Rebellion" and
"Traitors North" hiding behind the angel of peace. They seemed to have
bound her hands and they wielded swords, ready to launch a surprise attack
on Columbia.[40]

Throughout the Civil War, visual artists twisted the political meaning of
snakes. Artists deluged the Union with images of snakes as symbols of treason.

In so doing, they pushed the origins of secession beyond the time and space of the material world to the scriptural stories and prophecies of the Bible. They also portrayed dissent as anti-godly. They did not cast anti-war Democrats as misguided political minorities who were expressing their opposition, but rather as sneaking serpents who wished to bring about the fall of the godly government. The conflation and merging of Christianity and nationalism was extraordinarily widespread, a way for printers to make political points more than religious ones. In the process, villainous snakes became central features of the commercial mass culture of the North during the war.

Emancipation

Democrats and opponents of abolition dished out demonization as much as they took it. During the presidential election of 1860 and then early in the war, southern whites and northern Democrats often used the pejorative "black Republicans" when referring to Lincoln and his comrades. While occasionally associating Republicans explicitly with demons, Democrats and southerners used direct demon language less often. Emancipation changed this. When Abraham Lincoln eventually followed the lead of African Americans and Congress in making the end of slavery an object of the war with his Preliminary Emancipation Proclamation in late September 1862, he became a lightning rod for anti-Republican sentiment. The preliminary and then actual Emancipation Proclamation became turning points for visual expressions of evil. In response to Lincoln's executive edicts, several northern and southern white artists represented the occasion as an ultimate moment of revelation. Lincoln unveiled himself not as a president, but as a despot. He also unmasked himself as a traitor—not against the nation, but against the white race. All of it added up to Lincoln exposed as the devil.

When most Americans look back to emancipation, they often share the view of artist Thomas Nast. He heralded Lincoln's proclamation with a glorifying print in *Harper's Weekly*. Emancipation featured in its center a multigenerational African American family. To the right, the fruits of emancipation were many: pay for labor, homes for families, and schools for children. The left side featured the world before emancipation. Nast used traditional abolitionist iconography, including depictions of slaves being beaten and sold. In the upper left corner, slave catchers chased African Americans through a swamp. One of the pursuers with horns atop his head emerged from a dark cloud, holding ferocious-looking dogs by a chain. Rather than focusing his gaze toward the runaways, however, this figure looked behind him menacingly at the goddess Justice who stood above the scene. Below this demon a snake slithered out of the darkness as well. For Nast, as for many abolitionists, emancipation was a godly act that could help the Union triumph over the forces of evil.[41]

Other artists characterized the move toward emancipation as an expression of and contributor to the demonic overwhelming the United States. Adalbert Volck, a Baltimore dentist, drug smuggler, courier to Jefferson Davis, and graphic artist, sketched a scene of Lincoln writing the Emancipation Proclamation where demonic materials worked upon him or through him. A winged and horned devil held Lincoln's inkwell, while occult rams' horns sat at the corners of the table upon which he wrote. Demonic forces provided the physical support for his paper, while the very ink of the edict came from a sculpted devil. The anti-emancipation graphic also featured Lady Liberty with a hood, a portrait of John Brown as a saint, and a painting celebrating the Haitian Revolution. Lincoln himself looked disheveled but not necessarily demonic. His material surroundings indicate that the president was a pawn, acted upon internally and externally to sign such a reprehensible decree.[42]

Another northerner blamed spiritualism for allowing Satan to inspire the war and emancipation. In a *Pictorial History of the Cause of the Great Rebellion*, the writer and artist maintained that "abolitionism" was responsible for dividing the people and the nation. "It commenced by dividing the Church," the writer began, with reference to earlier denominational schisms of American churches; "it ended by dividing the Union." The visual images showed the devil placing a strong arm on the back of a white American in 1844 and encouraging him to speak words that would cause dissension and strife, "Slavery is a national sin." Then in 1860, Satan revealed himself as a lion with words from the Republican platform: "Slavery may remain in the States where it now exists, but shall not be extended into the territories of the Union." Then, with emancipation, Satan pursued "Liberty, Equality, and Fraternity!!" With these horrid notions, Satan plunged a trident into the torso of a nude African American man. The points were clear: the devil leveraged abolitionism for his demonic work of disunion and then emancipation.[43]

While most of the anti-emancipation graphic images emphasized de-monic influences upon the president, one displayed the person of Lincoln as the disguise. The president of the United States was not human. He was not a wicked man seduced by Satan. He was Satan himself. In *Masks and Faces*, an artist for the *Southern Illustrated News* presented a horned devil dressed in a suit. In his right hand at his hip, he held a broken chain. In his other hand just to the side of his face, he held the face of Abraham Lincoln. The image title, along with a scroll dated "Jan 1. 1863" explained the unveiling: *King Abraham before and after issuing the Emancipation Proclamation.* Lin-coln's true face was that of a devil; his mask was that of a white man.

This presentation differed from other ways Americans demonized one an-other during the war. While Unionists likened secessionists to Satan, and while partisans from both sides condemned the other for behaving like dev-ils, this one cast Lincoln as the devil. The president was not human; he was a façade. Lincoln was not Lincoln. King Abraham was actually the prince of darkness. In some ways, this depiction mirrored antislavery portrayals of southern whites who benefited from slavery as demonic figures. Sculptor John Rogers placed horns and a tail on the back of his *Slave Auction* piece before the war, and the artist for the *Southern Illustrated News* centered upon the idea that Lincoln was actually Satan.

In many ways, this graphic work functioned as both revelation and proph-ecy. Published early in November 1862, it came out almost two months be-fore the January deadline for areas in rebellion to return to the nation peacefully and masters to receive potential compensation for emancipation. In addition, in the distant background, the Washington Monument has a noose on its roof. The artist appeared to suggest that this would be the ulti-mate result for Lincoln—or rather, the devil.[44]

Just as was the case with other visualizations of evil during the war, words matched images to create webs of associations. Many northerners opposed emancipation as well and associated any attacks upon slavery as part of Satan's work in the United States. G. W. Woodward, whom James Polk had nomi-nated unsuccessfully for the Supreme Court in the 1840s, stated after the Emancipation Proclamation: "Agitation on the subject of Slavery is Infidel-ity, and comes from the instigation of Satan."[45]

Similarly, after Lincoln publicized the preliminary Emancipation Proc-lamation in September 1862, a writer for the *Staunton Spectator* penned an article titled "Lincoln's Fiendish Proclamation." The piece began with a reference to "the time our first parents were expelled from Paradise" and then connected the "Arch-Fiend" of hell to Lincoln. The devil's programs "have succeeded in prevailing upon 'Old Abe' to issue a proclamation of emancipation which will send a thrill of horror through all civilized nations." The author echoed Woodward with the phrase "the instigation of Satan." "The devil triumphed," according to the article, and Lincoln's actions showcased his government as "the most tyrannical military despotism which has ever existed upon the earth."[46]

In this anti-abolition environment, a songwriter made many of these same points through lyrics, rather than graphics. It linked Abraham Lincoln to John Brown. The song's title answered Stonewall Jackson's question about Brown's final destination after his execution: "John Brown's Entrance into Hell" (1863). The lyrics featured "Old Satan" presenting Brown with a seat at his left hand. Perhaps riffing on George Root's melancholic tune "The Vacant Chair," a song that lamented the deceased of the war, Satan now pointed to "that vacant chair" that "I did prepare" for Brown. Satan reserved the seat to his right for one still in the land of the living: Abraham Lincoln. Together, the three would form an unholy trinity:

John at my left, Abe at my right
We'll give the heavenly hosts a fight;
A triune group we then shall be,
Yes, three in one and one in three.[47]

Many white Americans who opposed Lincoln's Emancipation Proclamation bristled especially at the text's end. There, Lincoln followed Congress's earlier revised Militia Act to state that the federal government would employ African Americans in the military. This threat of black men with guns, wearing military uniforms, receiving pay from the government, and aiming at and shooting southern white men, infuriated Confederates and some other whites. Frederick Douglass thought the arming and employing of black men was an incredible moment. "Never since the world began was there a better chance offered to a long enslaved and oppressed people." He marveled at the totality of the possible transformation. "Once let the black man get upon his person the brass letters U.S., let him get an eagle on his button, and a musket on his shoulder, and bullets in his pocket." He prophesied the result with a biblical reference to hell: "No power on the earth, or under the earth" would be able to "deny that he has earned the right of citizenship in the United States."[48]

Douglass hit the nail on the head. This is what terrified anti-black northerners and southerners. In late September 1862, the editor of the Richmond *Examiner* exclaimed, "Now comes the proclamation of Lincoln! . . . the call for the insurrection of four millions of slaves, and the inauguration of a reign of hell upon earth."[49]

Black soldiers caused Josie Underwood, a well-educated Kentucky woman in her early 20s, distress about the evil in the nation. On two occasions, she recorded in her diary that the presence of African Americans in the military revealed that "evil and only evil" came from Lincoln's government. Underwood considered herself a patriot, one who loved the United States and those who defended it. But when she witnessed her town "now garrisoned by negro troops" she wrote that for these "evil times . . . language fails."[50]

Two years later, after Lincoln won reelection, a British newspaper mimicked *Masks and Faces* with its own print. In it, the artist for *Comic News* portrayed Death as a cricket player. Wearing striped pants like Uncle Sam and surrounded by soldiers sprawled under broken-down cannons, Death holds a mask with Lincoln's face on it. In both cases, the artists used visualizations to reveal demonic presence hidden by a human face.[51]

For the 1864 presidential election, one northern publisher endeavored to defame Lincoln and encourage votes for George McClellan by printing and distributing *Abraham Africanus I: His Secret Life, as Revealed Under the Mesmeric Influence*. The title characterized Lincoln as African and the cover image darkened his facial skin to give him the appearance of blackness and also placed a crown upon him to depict him as a monarch. Neither the title nor the frontispiece image suggested any connection between Lincoln and the devil. The lengthy textual piece—part poetry, part prose—however, centered upon the devil. It featured Satan visiting Lincoln and promising to help make him king. Satan encouraged Lincoln to refer to himself as "Honest Old Abe" because it served as "a cloak for everything." He also instructed Lincoln on how to win the presidency and establish a monarchy for himself. Upon taking office, the president could achieve his dictatorship through unending war and by issuing "a Proclamation of Emancipation." In this story,

Lincoln had no interest in elevating African Americans but planned to use emancipation as a ruse. Black people would become "free" to labor on the plantations upon which they already lived.[52]

While the racial component of emancipation was obviously one reason these artists turned to devil imagery to characterize Lincoln, another element was the particularity of American politics. By referring to Lincoln as a "king," the artists and writers articulated a key point to their anti-administration agenda and an abiding theme of American politics: the hatred of despotism. Many Democrats and southern whites claimed that Lincoln overstepped his constitutional bounds throughout the war. They viewed him as violating the Constitution by taking actions reserved for Congress or without precedent. This combination of perceived despotism and clear abolitionism made him the chief symbol of evil, rather than Congressmen whose emancipatory laws during the war and the Thirteenth Amendment to the Constitution at its end did far more to bring about the end of slavery than Lincoln's proclamation.

War and Peace and Photographs

Along with these various characterizations of treason—whether with serpents to convey rebellion against the United States or in the form of a demonic Lincoln to render his undermining of white supremacy and the Constitution—artists portrayed the devil and hell in a variety of other circumstances in the final years of the war as well. Several white artists, in fact, integrated African Americans as part of the Union's destruction of demons, while others applied concepts of evil to nonhuman elements of the war. Photography became another visual venue where artists and writers unveiled the powers of hell invading this world. Photographers did more than chronicle the conflict through the scientific use of sunlight, paper, and chemicals. Some sought to reveal the presence of the unseen.

While anti-emancipation artists claimed with pen, paper, and paint that Lincoln's Emancipation Proclamation unmasked him as a devil in disguise, some northern artists reveled in the end of slavery and the arming of black men. In fact, some images featured African American figures as actors in the banishing of the demonic. Black soldiers became vital to the defeat of Confederate devilry. For instance, on the graphic cover of the song sheet for "Babylon is Fallen!; Sequel to Kingdom Coming," several uniformed black soldiers who aim rifles overtake the word "Babylon." Their physical appearance demonstrates their new identities as members of the military, and their heroic actions show them bringing the downfall of the evil land of Babylon.[53]

While soldiers often connected the hellishness of their experiences through discussions of the environment and other material factors, artists also linked these elements to evil. This was particularly the case when it came to war machinery that was new to Americans and had the power of surprise. Unlike the war on land, the conflict at sea rarely elicited the same turn to demonic rhetoric from combatants—in part because naval life was typically more humdrum than hellish. One exception was underwater explosives. Although torpedo-like weapons existed before the Civil War, their potential use led some northerners to damn them as "infernal," at least when Confederates attempted to create them.

When Confederates planted "torpedoes" in the water or when they attempted to use submarines to attack Union naval vessels, northerners called them "infernal machines." When depicting them, artists used no obvious symbols or visual references to the devil. One drawing by Alfred Waud showed the physical representation of the contraption with boats and people in the distance. When printed in the newspaper, however, the text read *Infernal machines discovered*. Another graphic image featured a submarine containing two soldiers, a tube reaching air above the water, and several levers. Once again, nothing in the visualization referred to hell. Its title was *Submarine Infernal machine*.

The textual titles alerted viewers to something deeper than the bombs below the waterline. The names marked the weapons as somehow beyond the confines of Christian or just warfare. Opponents of these weapons viewed this type of combat as secretive and hence unmanly. By calling them "infernal," northerners referenced both their fiery combustibility and their similarities to how the devil in Christian interpretations worked behind the scenes to tempt and destroy God's people.[54]

According to Waud, he based his drawing of the "infernal machine" on a photograph by James F. Gibson. During the war, illustrators and photographers often worked together; they routinely based their works upon one another's artistic creations and the lines separating one medium from the other were more about the technology than imagination. Although photography was and is often regarded as a "real" representation of visual subjects, it was and is as much a creation as other forms of visual art.

Photographers in the Union became indispensable for the war effort. Employed by the government, they created reproductions of maps and chronicled tactics such as entrenchments and fortifications. In 1863, for instance, Andrew J. Russell published a book with dozens of photographs depicting the best means to destroy bridges and railroad tracks, to construct small boats by piecing together and painting blankets, and to straighten tracks that had been bent. The photographs were an instructional manual for warfare.[55]

Other photographers presented their work as both war chronicles and artistic perspectives on American society, politics, culture, and religion. They recognized that Americans were familiar with photographs and that they comprehended them as having the power to reveal forces beyond the visible. Paradoxically, the belief that photography presented an accurate or real image became an argument that it had the power, more than other visual mediums, to make visible the invisible.

Although photography had been a young technology before the Civil War, most Americans, especially in the North, had become familiar with its many varieties. From daguerreotypes to stereoscopes to cartes de visite to photographs, Americans gazed at these visual images, sat for them, purchased them, collected them, and arranged them in their own albums. As Frederick Douglass marveled, the middle of the nineteenth century could easily be "termed an age of pictures." "Nothing," he told one audience of his era, "is it more remarkable than for the multitude, variety, perfection and cheapness of its pictures."

Douglass drew direct connections between religion and photography. He maintained that the creation and recognition of pictures differentiated humans from animals. As makers of pictures, humans had risen from creatures to "creators." He declared, "This picture-making power accompanies religion, supplying man with his God, peopling the silent continents of eternity with saints, angels, and fallen spirits, the blest and the blasted, making manifest the invisible, and giving form and body to all that the soul can hope and fear in life and in death."[56]

While some proponents of photography heralded it for representing "reality," others ruminated on the complex web of science, art, and even spirituality of the medium. When scrutinized, the process of creating photographs and the material visualizations themselves were marvels of inversion, akin to what religion often had the power to accomplish. Oliver Wendell Holmes articulated this most clearly. Writing in the *Atlantic Monthly*, Holmes took readers into "the sanctuary of the art" to walk them through the process of photograph production. After sunlight allowed the photograph to capture an image, the glass negative needed to be shielded from the light. It must lie "safe in utter darkness." The visual contents of the image were now "a ghost" held "imprisoned." At this point, there was only a "potential image in it,—a latent soul." As the image began to appear, light replaced shadow and shadow replaced light. Now able to see the image, the viewer observed "a reversed picture, which puts darkness for light and light for darkness." Although photographs appeared to simply capture a visual moment and convey it without distortion to viewers, Holmes knew there was more than met the eye.[57]

The war offered new spaces of meaning for photography. Before the 1860s, graphic artists emphasized heroic charges and gallant leaders when portraying war. Civil War photography trafficked in that register, but a growing number of photographers either emphasized material realities for practical purposes or centered upon the horrible and horrifying.

If before the war photographs promised to reveal God's grandeur through nature and bodies, wartime photography showcased destruction and the dead. It was difficult for Holmes to wrap his mind around this point, that the medium he adored could reveal the "ghastly" and the "sordid." Sunshine, he acknowledged, had the power to show everything, even "what a repulsive, brutal, sickening, hideous thing . . . this dashing together of two frantic mobs to which we give the name of armies."[58]

In particular, Holmes referred to the exhibition at Mathew Brady's New York studio, *The Dead at Antietam*. The images displayed contained multiple layers of death. First, many of the people shown had lost their lives on the battlefield. Second, as Douglass observed, in all photographs "a man always looks *dead*." Unmoving and mute, representations of individuals within photographs mimicked the deceased in everything but three dimensionality. A reviewer for the *New York Times* did not describe the exhibit with any direct references to evil, but he noted responses to the photographs with words like "terrible" and "horror."[59]

Photographers only rarely used titles and textual claims to point viewers toward the demonic. When they did, however, they made sure their points stood out from other photographs. Barnard's *The "Hell-Hole"* was one expression. Its title was distinct from the others in his album. When Alexander Gardner published a book of his photographs shortly after the war—many of which he had offered for sale from his shop in Washington, DC—he included a paragraph or two to accompany each image. Often, Gardner's images and texts drew attention to the effects of the war upon nature. Where once "grassy hill-sides . . . smiling to each other over the forests" had been the site of one battlefield, they had been "devastated by the army, and is now a wilderness." He repeatedly used the words "devastation," "ruin," and "crush" to refer to man's actions on the landscape.

His most famous photograph was also the one that pointed directly to evil. *A Harvest of Death* centered upon a dead soldier sprawled on his back. His right arm was raised above his head, while his left was at his side. His mouth gaped open. Behind him were strewn a set of men, and as a viewer looked from the central figure to the characters in the back, a vapor seemed to place the men and horses in an ethereal otherness.

When writing about this photograph, Gardner maintained that it held meaning beyond the men involved, the specific battle, or even this particular war. He sounded like Sherman: "A battle has been often the subject of elaborate description; but it can be described in one simple word, *devilish!*" So that his meaning would not be missed, he italicized the word—a graphic change of the text he did not use elsewhere. Noting that the photograph featured Confederate dead, he pointed out how they were "distorted" and "paid with life the price of their treason." After referring to the strife as "wicked," he concluded, "Such a picture conveys a useful moral: It shows the blank horror and reality of war, in opposition to its pageantry. Here are the dreadful details! Let them aid in preventing such another calamity falling upon the nation."[60] Gardner hoped that by unveiling the devilishness of war and displaying it to American eyes he could persuade his countrymen to avoid war at all costs.

Perhaps other than *The "Hell-Hole"* no other photograph conveyed war's resemblance to hell as much as *A Harvest of Death*. Others made nods at the presence of evil but did not linger. In one photograph of a bridge at Antietam, Gardner mentioned that a ridge in the area bore the name "the 'Devil's Backbone.'"[61] For his photograph of Fort Sedgwick, he included in the title the phrase *generally known as "Fort Hell."* Once again he drew attention to the inability of words to convey the meaning of war. "The scene presents a singular and grotesque appearance—to be appreciated it must be seen; no description will prove adequate." He then observed that even though its nickname may be objectionable to "ears polite" the spot "deserved the very euphonious name . . . as given by the soldiers, of 'Fort Hell.'"[62]

One photographer from the war did not need a title or textual description for his photograph to signal associations with evil. It was a photograph of the devil. Titled *Political Still Life*, this carte de visite featured a horned and winged devil with the legs and ears of a mule. With one hand, he held a gallows with a Confederate flag above it. A rope choked a small Jefferson Davis wearing a nightshirt and a cap, and clutching a doll. This not only connected Davis to the devil but also infantilized the Confederate president. In his left hand, the devil carried a pitchfork with six carte de visite portraits of Confederate political and military leaders.[63]

This complex photograph was the creation of one of the nation's most noteworthy photographers: Frederick Gutekunst. He operated a shop in Philadelphia where he photographed some of the most famous Americans of the era. Although Gutekunst created photographs after the Battle of Gettysburg, he spent most of his time and made most of his money marketing cartes de visite. His portraits of Ulysses S. Grant, for instance, sold remarkably as Grant pushed the Union military toward Richmond. With *Political Still Life* he created a carte de visite with other cartes de visite within it. The devil's personal album of photographs signaled that he had met with these men and probably exchanged images. Gutekunst suggested intimacy between the devil and Confederates through the photographs. He also blended sculpture with his brilliance for individual portraits. Like many other visual representations to reference evil, Gutekunst's photographic creation was simultaneously a political statement and a religious one. The war, these artists expressed, exposed the presence of evil, and their task was to reveal these realities, to make seen that which had been previously unseen.[64]

In the first half of 1865, Union victories piled up. It became clear that the Confederacy would not be able to continue, and during these months Union visual artists began to gloat and predict the future. Several created images consigning vanquished Confederate leaders to hell. In one, *Jeff and Beauregard on their Last Ride*, two devils carried Davis and Beauregard as they raced across the page. The poem for the envelope did not match the image entirely. It mentioned Davis and Confederate vice president Alexander Stephens as the ones "now *driven* . . . by the imps of *Old Nick*." The use of the word "driven" recalls on how masters typically drove slaves. In this case, the white men had lost their liberty and were driven by demonic beings.[65]

Another envelope featured a winged devil carrying Davis into hell. From his left hand, Davis dropped a Confederate flag and within the flames another devil held a pitchfork toward Davis. According to the caption, the demon in hell was "Traitor Arnold," who was about to give "Traitor Davis" a "warm reception." The visualization of Arnold as more demonic than human suggested that perhaps humans devolved into literal devils while in the abyss.[66]

In at least one graphic work, the artist depicted Union soldiers as responsible for sending Davis to hell. A song cover sheet displayed a large devil holding Jefferson Davis by the seat of his pants and about to drop him into the abyss of hell. From a distance, an African American soldier with a bayoneted rifle thumbed his nose at Davis with his left hand. "How do you like it Jefferson D?" the black soldier mocked Davis. The song instructed Davis that his best chance for survival would be to flee to Europe. The black soldier was now a member of the nation-state, while Davis needed to reside either abroad or in hellfire.[67]

One envelope produced in New York City near the end of the war featured a devil running as fast he could. Holding a trident with a Confederate flag attached to it in one hand and a bottle of liquor in the other, this demon said in the caption, "Secession is nearly played out, so I will go back to my H[ell] [H]ole." Dressed in a jester's outfit, the devil's head was exposed because his hood has been pulled back by the force of his flight. In this case, like that of the devil masquerading as Lincoln in the anti-emancipation print from the *Southern Illustrated News*, the events of the war led to an unmasking. With Union victory imminent, the devil's dash revealed his presence within the Confederacy.[68]

In only a few short years, southern whites would turn to masks to transform themselves from people to demons. After emancipation had become constitutional law and rights of citizenship and male suffrage followed in amendments to the Constitution, some southern whites decided to become what African Americans had long said they were: demons on earth. Before that, as the war took a major turn in 1863, soldiers, civilians, and politicians added another layer of evil to the war. To destroy their demonic enemies, citizens on both sides began to encourage their comrades to fight "like devils." By embracing evil to destroy evil, both sides transformed the war's focus from saving godly governments to bringing the heft of hell to the people and the land.

CHAPTER 4

To Fight Like Devils

Before the war, James Wadsworth wanted peace. The son of a wealthy New York family, he dabbled in politics, shifted from the Democratic Party to the Liberty Party, and then found a home in the Republican Party. After Lincoln's election and the secession crisis, he participated in the February 1861 "peace meeting" of prominent Americans who hoped to avoid war. When peace failed, Wadsworth volunteered for military service. Although he had no previous military experience, he received the rank of major general in May 1861.

Wadsworth worked alongside George McClellan during the first year of the conflict. Wadsworth watched as McClellan disappointed most northerners, especially Lincoln, for failing to destroy their Confederate enemies. When members of Congress sought to investigate McClellan's abilities, they called upon Wadsworth to testify before the Senate. He expressed nothing but disdain for McClellan, painting him as a coward. Near the end of his testimony, Wadsworth complained of McClellan's lack of aggression, "Who ever heard of a retreating army that was not pursued by the victors like demons, except in the case of rebel retreats?" Wadsworth continued, "No other nation but ours was ever guilty of stopping immediately after a victory. Other armies fight like demons after a victory, and annihilate the enemy, but we do not."[1]

By the early 1860s, Congressmen had become accustomed to references to Satan, demons, and hell. Representatives and Senators routinely demonized their opponents by associating their positions and actions with evil.[2] They quoted lines from *Paradise Lost* as often as they did any nonlegal or constitutional document. But Wadsworth brought evil to the government in a new way. He wanted American soldiers to become like devils. Rather than call upon "better angels," as Lincoln had, Wadsworth wanted men to act as fallen ones. In war, Christian men who aspired for heaven needed to act like demons who had forfeited their existence there. He encouraged Congress and the president to appoint generals who would encourage hell on earth. For Wadsworth, to fight like a demon was a desirable military tactic that leaders needed to cultivate.[3]

The various phrases that lined up "fight" or "fought," "like" or "as," and then "devils" or "demons" grew in prominence during the war. These developments signaled a change in governmental, military, and personal approaches to war. Although the war began for many as a romantic adventure where the men fought for God and government, and in time everyday soldiers started to experience it as hell overwhelming their lives, the encouragement to become like devils and the deliberate choice to make hell on earth could be heard more and more as the war continued. Between 1862 and 1865, Americans joined becoming like the devil to their desires to defeat the devil.

Showing the emergence of the concepts of fighting like devils and bringing hell to earth adds another side to considerations of the war. In *This Republic of Suffering*, historian Drew Gilpin Faust brilliantly showed how the Christian culture of the nineteenth century left soldiers more emotionally prepared to die than to kill. Americans, in her estimation, were more interested in having a "good death" than being good at killing.[4] But the simile of fighting like demons suggests an embrace of killing. No one during the war encouraged the men to "fight like angels," even though biblical angels did fight for God's army in the book of Revelation. Instead, they valorized destruction and killing through references to devils and hell. Evil became the positive means to pursue and win war.

As more and more Americans demonized their enemies during the struggle, they validated becoming "like devils" in order to win. It became an issue of fighting fire with fire. If one's enemy took heinous actions that could only be likened to the demonic, then some level of evil behavior became necessary in order for the good guys—one's own side—to win.

Of course, Americans did not wish to become devils or demons or to bring the literal hell to the earth. They used the similes and metaphors on purpose. The deployment of Christian language figuratively, rather than literally, fit with the secular transformation in the nineteenth century, wherein words and phrases previously bound to religious belief expanded to accommodate other circumstances.

This chapter looks first at the rise of fighting like demons as a compliment and a positive affirmation for one's military side. Then, it explores four particular occasions when Americans brought hell to earth. In each—the massacre at Fort Pillow, the battle of Cold Harbor, the struggle at the Crater, and Sherman's March to the Sea—soldiers, leaders, government officials, and civilians who experienced the violence not only characterized events around them with the language of evil, but also encouraged actions previously considered irreligious. Demonizing enemies and their actions paved the way for some Americans to endorse seemingly evil behaviors and attitudes. In short, to defeat demons many Americans determined to become like them.

Give 'Em Hell

When the Civil War began, many Americans agreed with Union Gen. George McClellan that the war should be fought on "Christian" principles. Men viewed themselves as going to war as a godly act. This changed as the war dragged on. Throughout the North and South, soldiers increasingly called upon one another to behave as Wadsworth asked: like devils.

On rare occasions in 1861, some Americans called for the bringing of evil to the effort. In late September 1861, for instance, William "Bull" Nelson wrote to the assistant secretary of the navy, Gustavus Vasa Fox, of his shift from the navy to the army. Although a naval officer, Nelson found it imperative to oppose secession in his home state of Kentucky. He raised an army in the middle of the state, an extremely important border state that Lincoln desperately hoped to hold. He explained to Fox, "As Kentucky is the real Key of the War, her wants should be attentively supplied." When it came to naval affairs, Nelson hoped that Fox would "send out a big expedition and give Charleston hell!"[5]

Comments like this were few and far between, and in this case Nelson wrote it in a letter he labeled *Private*. More often when the war began, Americans expressed their desire to fight in ways they termed "civilized" or "Christian." When they did liken soldiers to demons, they did so to assail their enemies. In late June 1861, for instance, Mary Chesnut recorded a conversation with Jefferson Davis where "he is despondent, does not see the end of this thing! Gives the north credit for *courage*—says they will fight like devils."[6]

About one year later, Sarah Morgan reported in her diary of events after Confederates pushed Union soldiers to the edge of a river, "The majority ran like fine fellows, but a Maine regiment fought like devils."[7]

Nowhere in the Bible did the writers encourage the people of God to behave like devils or demons. The closest biblical passage would be in the Gospel of Matthew when Jesus instructed his followers to be "as wise as serpents." The particular phrase "fight like devils" came not from scripture, but from Shakespeare. In *Henry V*, as the French prepared for war with the English, an official explained to another "give them great meals of beef, and iron and steel, they will eat like wolves, and fight like devils."[8] Before the American Civil War, with the exception of references to the military behavior of Native Americans, Americans did not apply this to themselves.[9]

As combat became real and it appeared that the war would not end quickly, the number of affirmative references to devils and demons rose. With the increase, moreover, came a growing number of compliments for nontraditional soldiers as fighting like devils. This was especially the case when it came to female combatants and then African American men, perhaps indicative of how upsetting the war was to the social and religious order. The Civil War so disrupted norms of American society that women and African Americans fighting in combat became both heroic and demonic at the same time.

Soldiers and leaders began describing their men as performing like devils. One of the earliest was Franc B. Wilkie, a reporter who embedded himself with the First Iowa Infantry. During their fighting in Missouri in August 1861, he reported one battle where a captain shouted to the men, "Now boys, keep cool, aim low, and give 'em hell!" When the battle ended, the regiment's major thanked the captain for the courage his company displayed. "Your fellows fought like devils, and if any man after this ever says to me that Volunteers won't fight, I'll make it a personal matter with him! Yes, sir, your men fought just like devils!"[10]

Throughout the North and South, combatants and civilian observers praised their men for behaving like fiends from hell. Charles F. Johnson wrote to his wife, "in an instant every man rushed forward, when they put spurs to their horses and over fences they went, and we (like so many devils) after them."[11] Another soldier boasted to his parents, "Our boys fought like devils, till nearly half of them were killed or wounded, and then retreated to Winchester."[12]

White soldiers from the Union even used this language to discuss female soldiers and African American soldiers, often expressing to friends and family at home their admiration for these combatants. The phrase "fought like demons" was so routinely used to reference women who took to arms that historians on the subject titled the volume with that line.[13] As an increasing number of white northerners embraced, or at least accepted, the employment of black soldiers, one way whites praised them was by comparing their heroism to devilry. After the battle of Port Hudson, a Wisconsin soldier wrote his father that the "negroes fought like devils, they made five charges on a battery that there was not the slightest chance of their taking, just (as their officers said) to show our boys that they could and would fight."[14] Another soldier from Wisconsin admitted, "I never believed in niggers before . . . but by Jasus, they are all hell in fighting."[15]

Especially after the war, when northern whites memorialized the war with attention to the lives of everyday soldiers, authors routinely mentioned the heroism of African Americans. A chronicler of the First Massachusetts Cavalry drew attention to "an infantry regiment of negroes" who "fought like devils all the way." Of another battle he maintained, "The colored troops went in grandly, and they fought like devils."[16]

This phrase, used equally to praise white and black soldiers, showed how the war could bring these two groups together. Although Frederick Douglass invoked evil in a different way when he described the importance of black soldiers, his point heralded important truths asserted during the war that equated the sacrifice and valor of black and white Union soldiers to vanquish an evil foe. Union "devils" were saints when compared to demonic Confederates.

As performing like a devil became a compliment, it had the power to cross racial and sectional lines. It became a rhetorical way for whites and blacks, northerners and southerners, to express respect for one another. One Confederate brigadier general in Arkansas wrote to a lieutenant colonel in October 1863, "My troops behaved well. The Federals fought like devils. No news."[17]

Remember Fort Pillow

Fighting like a devil became far more than rhetoric. It became a military strategy encouraged by political and military leaders on both sides. Union and

Confederate soldiers began to act in ways they understood to be demonic. In at least four pivotal moments, James Wadsworth got his wish: both sides perceived their enemies as evil, choose to become like demons, and then congratulated themselves while denouncing their opponents.

One description that linked African American soldiers to devils contained within it an important shift in the rules of combat that followed emancipation. A white lieutenant colonel at a skirmish near Vicksburg in March 1864 observed that "the colored soldiers fought like devils. There seemed to be a mutual understanding between them and the enemy that they should take no prisoners."[18] That final sentence touched on a major reason for the increased virulence from both sides. After Lincoln offered the Preliminary Emancipation Proclamation and then signed the final document, Confederate leadership exploded. Jefferson Davis declared that black soldiers would be executed, rather than imprisoned, and this led Lincoln to respond that captured Confederates would be treated similarly. This transformed combat for some soldiers. No longer could they be assured that capture would lead to prison captivity. Now the threat of death loomed even if men waved the white flag.

Nowhere did this become more apparent and disastrous than at the Battle of Fort Pillow. Black soldiers marched with the Union army that was decimated at the Wilderness, Spotsylvania, and Cold Harbor, but they did not fight—not yet. The new United States Colored Troops (USCT) regiments generally performed occupation and rear area duties—including the building of fortifications that would characterize the war in Virginia from mid-June. In large part this was because their white generals doubted their combat effectiveness. As late as September 1862, President Lincoln expressed concerns that black soldiers might panic upon confronting their former masters, thereby supplying ragged rebels with their weapons and uniforms.[19] As one engineer battalion commander commented, a "negro is worth two, if not three, white men to dig." He pushed men of the Thirty-fifth USCT to work all day and night on a battery emplacement near Petersburg without food. Sounding more like a slave driver than a slave emancipator, he explained that he wanted to "get all he could out of the d— niggers."[20]

On the banks of the Mississippi River, the rear guard and garrison duties of many of these soldiers brought them face-to-face with vengeful rebel troopers under Nathan Bedford Forrest. He had been a thorn in Sherman's side since the Battle of Shiloh in April 1862. "It is exceedingly difficult to deal with these Mounted Devils," Sherman confessed to his wife, "and I am sure all we can do is to make the Country feel that the People must pay for these wandering Arabs."[21] By June 1864, Forrest had been promoted to "the very devil" by Sherman in a letter to Secretary of War Edwin Stanton.[22]

Black soldiers serving beyond Virginia's borders proved their ability and willingness to face white rebel soldiers generally—and sometimes their former masters specifically—in the spring and summer of 1863. Both operations were part of the Anaconda Plan aimed at strangling the Confederacy by river and sea. On May 27 two regiments of black soldiers from Louisiana (one of them formerly a part of the state's rebel militia) took part in a costly assault in the ultimately successful siege of Port Hudson on the Mississippi River.[23] Nine days after the fall of Port Hudson—which, coupled with the surrender of Vicksburg, meant that the Mississippi River was now a Union-controlled thoroughfare—a regiment of black soldiers raised in Massachusetts won glory attacking Battery Wagner. One of the fortifications protecting Charleston, South Carolina, Wagner did not fall. Yet the death of the Fifty-fourth Massachusetts's white colonel and many of its men in the assault was ample evidence of the courage of black men under fire.[24]

These brave actions west and south of Virginia by no means convinced all white Union soldiers of the worth of African Americans in combat. Yet as one antislavery soldier from Wisconsin acknowledged, black troops had an extra layer of practical reasons to fight than the abstract ideals of white men. Chauncey Cooke noted in late July: "The poor black devils are fighting for their wives and children, yes and for their lives, while we white cusses are fighting for . . . an idea."[25]

Fort Pillow became a focal point in the early spring of 1864. A mixture of white loyalist Tennesseans and black soldiers garrisoned Fort Pillow— originally a Confederate battery constructed to guard the riverine approach to Memphis—in February 1864. The garrison was tasked with living off the surrounding land, recruiting southern Unionists into the army, and deterring rebel guerrillas.[26] The 600-odd garrisoned men had limited training and less combat experience before Forrest arrived on April 12.[27] After four hours of skirmishing, Forrest demanded the garrison surrender, for its defense of the fort "has been such as to entitle them to being treated as prisoners of war." Yet if he was refused, he could not be held "responsible for the fate of your command."[28] On two prior occasions (in 1862) Forrest successfully threatened Union garrisons with annihilation if they did not surrender and convinced them to capitulate.[29] During the truce, the black and white defenders of the fort allegedly taunted their opponents, claiming that "the last man [of the garrison] would die before surrendering."[30]

The garrison's officers opted not to surrender, and when Forrest's cavalry renewed the offensive, the men broke and ran "or rather tumbled down . . . [the steep bluff] & tried to get behind logs, trees, stumps, etc. to shield them from the rebel bullets."[31] Many of the garrison's soldiers, white and black, now attempted to surrender. Many of Forrest's men were from the same areas of Tennessee and Mississippi as the Union soldiers. A soldier-correspondent claimed that "the sight of negro soldiers stirred the bosoms of our soldiers with courageous madness."[32] "God damn you, you are fighting against your master," one trooper shouted at a USCT soldier.[33]

Many of Forrest's officers and troopers refused to take prisoners. "The slaughter was awful," Sergeant Achilles Clark recorded. "The poor deluded negroes would run up to our men[,] fall upon their knees and with uplifted hands scream for mercy but they were ordered to their feet and then shot down. The white men fared but little better. Their fort turned out to be a great slaughter pen," where blood "stood about in pools and brains could have been gathered up in any quantity."[34]

Forrest and his men valued close-range firepower, which sometimes enabled them to overcome foes armed with repeating rifles or carbines, and the two revolvers that each trooper carried helped them with close-range executions.[35] Some of Forrest's officers and noncommissioned officers attempted to stop the massacre, but failed because—as Sergeant Clark claimed—"Gen. Forrest ordered [the Unionists] shot down like dogs," although the more vengeful among Forrest's men may have facetiously used their commander's name to keep killing.[36] A number of black soldiers drowned in the Mississippi in their efforts to escape the slaughter, or at least to die on their own terms in a desperate bid for safety.[37]

While not addressing his complicity in the massacre, Forrest noted in his official report of the combat that the Mississippi "was dyed with blood of the slaughtered for 200 yards." The former slave trader "hoped that these facts will demonstrate to the Northern people that negro soldiers cannot cope with Southerners."[38] In his memoirs, Ulysses S. Grant noted Forrest's report, adding the wry comment that he "left out the part which shocks humanity to read."[39] Capt. John T. Young, one of the garrison's fallen officers, claimed that he saw the general shoot one of his own troopers who refused to cease firing at the surrendering Unionists, so there was at least one eyewitness to the argument that Forrest was aware of the massacre while it was in progress.[40] He did fence with Union generals over what he allowed to happen at Fort Pillow and whether he took black soldiers prisoner, corresponding with Cadwallader C. Washburn to the effect that "I regard captured negroes as I do other captured property, and not as captured soldiers."[41]

The Radical Republican-dominated Joint Committee on the Conduct of the War investigated the massacre. Unsurprisingly, the committee condemned "the brutality and cruelty of the rebels," claiming that Forrest's troopers "seemed to vie with each other in the devilish work."[42] Yet congressional committees had little power to bring Forrest to bay in wartime; only Union soldiers—not least vengeful black ones—could do so.

If Forrest never faced retribution from black soldiers, African Americans in arms in other theaters of the war heard of the massacre and vowed vengeance. A St. Louis newspaper warned "every colored soldier when going into battle remember that with him it is victory or death, and when called upon to surrender, let him 'Remember Fort Pillow.'"[43] Confederate soldiers defending Petersburg in late July claimed that the first time they encountered African American Union troops, their war cry was "no quarter" and "remember Fort Pillow," with deadly results for the black soldiers when the tide of battle turned against them. The idea seemed clear: to fight devilry with devilry.

Cold Harbor

Only a few weeks after the Fort Pillow atrocity, the battle of Cold Harbor in June 1864 prefigured the hellish combination of the trench warfare that would later define the World War I and those of the bloody maneuver battles of the World War II. This battle also became the occasion for many soldiers to search for language beyond the usual vocabulary of war, or perhaps beneath it. Soldiers at the time and after struggled to explain just what they had experienced, but many acknowledged that both sides had moved beyond the established category of war.

The year when trench warfare became de rigueur in Virginia was also the year that Confederates perpetrated racial atrocities in both western and eastern theaters in response to the increasing deployment of black soldiers by Union armies. The massacre at Fort Pillow in April demonstrated that African American soldiers could expect to lose their lives if they lost a battle. Their opponents saw the use of black troops as indicative of a Yankee effort to institute hell on earth via racial equality, and were accordingly motivated to butcher even African American combatants who attempted to surrender in order to decisively defeat this demonic campaign.

Cold Harbor was a bloodbath. In one hour on June 3, 1864, Confederates killed, wounded, or captured three thousand Union soldiers. Four thousand more fell before the end of the day. Not until July 1916, when 19,000 British soldiers were killed in a single day at the start of the Somme offensive. was the pointless slaughter of men charging against prepared defenses equaled. A British survivor of that catastrophe, John Ronald Reuel Tolkien, incorporated his experiences of the evil waste of war into the *Lord of the Rings* trilogy. After Cold Harbor, one of the few high-ranking Confederate casualties noted this battle for posterity: "It was not war; it was murder."[44] At the end of his life, Grant, who led the Union war effort in Virginia, admitted that the order to make the last assault at Cold Harbor was the worst of his military career. Maine Gen. Joshua Lawrence Chamberlain looked back fifty years from this battle and placed it in a list of with the Wilderness, Spotsylvania, and North Anna as "unspoken, unspeakable history." In May and June 1864 the "flower of Northern homes" was "plunged straightway into hell-like horrors."[45] Fittingly, this futile attack marked the transition from the forty-day Overland Campaign to the nine-month siege of Petersburg, which presaged the trench warfare of Europe's western front.

During the six weeks leading up to Cold Harbor, the Army of the Potomac and the Army of Northern Virginia clashed continuously. A combination of veterans and new draftees, the Union army was—crucially—under the supervision of the new general in chief of all Union armies. If he did not take personal command, Grant's presence with the army ensured that it would follow his unconditional surrender strategy of hounding Lee's army to the death. If its geographical target was Richmond, the capture of the Confederate capital was merely incidental to the defeat of the rebel army, which would presumably fight to the death rather than lose the city.[46] The combat at Cold Harbor marked the near end of this offensive and Grant's grudging acceptance of the siege of Petersburg, which inaugurated a new kind of hell for combatants on both sides.

In the campaign's first four weeks, Grant's army attacked Lee's multiple times, resulting in three major battles. Each battle was fought several miles closer to Richmond, and the first two each resulted in more than 20,000 casualties, or more casualties than the men killed, wounded, and captured at Antietam. At the Wilderness in early May, soldiers on both sides stumbled over the unburied skeletons of the fallen from the Chancellorsville battle exactly twelve months before.[47] The woods caught fire, burning dozens of wounded men as they lay helpless and assailing survivors with the smell of roasting human flesh. At least some immobile soldiers chose to enter eternity on their own terms as the flames crept closer, using their rifles to commit suicide to avoid an earthly lake of fire.[48]

Less than a week after the carnage in the Wilderness, a second major battle took place at Spotsylvania Court House, fifteen miles closer to Richmond. When initial Union attacks against Confederate defensive positions failed, a young colonel who graduated from West Point with George Custer in 1861 drew from the pre-gunpowder tradition of swords and spears to overcome the deadly stalemate of musket warfare. He drew up twelve regiments into a battering ram of a column that punched its way through a Confederate position at the point of the bayonet before being pushed back by reinforcements.[49]

Grant promoted this innovator, Emory Upton, to general and then ordered an entire corps (seventy-five regiments) to try a similar tactic two days later. They also plowed through a Confederate salient, but then stalled when boxed in by rebel reserves in a confined space. Bodies were shot to pieces, riddled with bullets or impaled on bayonets in hours of close combat at the "Mule Shoe."[50] The two bloodbaths in the first half of May demonstrated all too fatally that the moment that these armies stopped marching for the day, they dug in wherever they halted, determined that if a fight caught them they would be able to protect themselves from incoming fire. If in 1862 soldiers deemed the digging of trenches unmanly or—from the Confederate perspective—labor fit only for slaves—now spadework was a natural activity to preserve life and limb.[51]

The Union army exhibited the ill effects of constant marching and fighting as it moved on Cold Harbor. Most crucially, a number of the army's most aggressive generals, notably Winfield S. Hancock, were fatigued and no longer demonstrating their previous acumen. The new battlefield-to-be was a mere mile from the Gaines's Mill battlefield. Gaines's Mill marked the closest George McClellan's army had reached in its offensive against Richmond in June 1862 before being forced back by Robert E. Lee.

Some veterans referred to this earlier battle as "Cold Harbor."[52] As a soldier from Louisiana noted in July 1862, "I walked over the field early on the morning after the dreadful battle of Coal [Cold] Harbor and the dead lay almost thick enough in some places to have walked on." He noted that where "the battle raged the fiercest every twig was riddled and many trees not more than a foot in diameter had as many as forty balls in its trunk." Many of the enemy wounded were still alive, begging for food and water, while the Union dead "seem to have expired laughing while others clinched their teeth and hands and seemed to have perished in awful agony. Some were still clinging to their guns as if they died fighting."[53]

The soldier's words could have been applied to the hellish landscape on the same ground two years later. Now, in June 1864, the Union army could once again hear the church bells of the rebel capital, a melancholy reminder to the veterans of 1861—many of whose three-year enlistments were about to expire—of the massive losses and minimal gains of the intervening years. They might also have recalled that it was here that Lee—newly appointed to command the rebel army—demonstrated his willingness to attack in the face of long odds.

If Cold Harbor is now remembered as a suicidal Union frontal assault, on the day before the infamous attack Lee's army reminded the Army of the Potomac that it could still sting whenever they found a weakness in their opponent. While half of the Union army marched to Cold Harbor and the right flank of the rebel army, Lee hit the other half, which was holding its position. "Give 'em hell, boys!" a captain in the Forty-fourth North Carolina exhorted his charging company. "That field was a mass of yelling shrieking demons wild with pain, thirst, anger and excitement as we rushed, raged, swore, cried, laughed & laughed, raged, yelled, cried, & swore."[54] The "mass of yelling shrieking demons" bent the Union line back, but failed to prevent the army from carrying on to Cold Harbor. The day before, Union cavalry

under the youthful general George Custer advancing on Cold Harbor rode
into an ambush of Confederate artillery and infantry. "A perfect hell of fire
and smoke broke from the rebel works," a sergeant in the Fifth Michigan
noted. "Even the air we breathed seemed thick with lead and sulphur. It did
not seem possible for balls to fly thicker," and fifty men in this regiment fell
in a few minutes, a very steep loss for a cavalry unit.[55] Indeed, this ambush
elicited curses from Custer, the only time that one of his veteran troopers recalled the general calling on his men to "give them hell."[56]

Grant ordered an all-out offensive at Cold Harbor for first light on June 3,
keen to attack before most of Lee's army was in position and had constructed
more than the most rudimentary defenses. Union veterans heard the rebel
shovels all night and knew that the dawn offensive would fail. According to
the postwar account of one of Grant's staff officers, many of them pinned their
names to the back of their uniforms so that their bodies could be identified
after the slaughter was over.[57]

The moment that Union artillery opened up on at 4:30 a.m. it ignited "a
veritable tempest," which was immediately responded to by Confederate cannon, worryingly as if they "have been anticipating it. It had the fury of the
Wilderness musketry, with the thunders of the Gettysburg artillery super-
added."[58] In other words, at least one veteran noted that the cacophony of this
battle combined the worst kinds of combat he had heretofore experienced.

Frightening as the sound of massed artillery was, things only got worse
for the Union soldiers when they went "over the top" to charge their rebel
counterparts. A Confederate officer noted his artillery "firing double-shotted
canister . . . at a distance of a hundred yards was cutting side swaths through
their lines at every discharge, literally mowing them down by the dozens,
while legs, arms, heads, and muskets were seen flying high in the air at every
discharge." Yet the "wide lanes made in their columns were quickly closed"
and "on they came, swaying . . . like great waves of the sea, until one upheaval
from the rear would follow another, hurrying them nearer and nearer . . . to
the murderous fire from our works."[59]

"Fought like hell and got licked like damnation," was the succinct account
of one lieutenant thirty years later.[60] "Truly we had marched into the jaws of
death and the mouth of hell," a New Yorker recalled.[61] The most poignant epi-
taph for this battle at the beginning of June was the supposed final diary
entry of a Union soldier found dead on the field: "June 3. Cold Harbor. I was

killed."[62] Sergeant Major Joseph Hume of the Thirty-sixth Massachusetts was wounded at Cold Harbor on June 3, and a comrade wrote the final entries in Hume's diary: "Joseph received his death wound" and "Died in consequence of the above."[63] It was in this moment that Lewis Bissell, a heavy artillery-man from Connecticut, wrote to his father with the geographical referent: "Cold Harbor and Hell." Bissell doubted after this bloodbath that there would "ever again [be] any rejoicing in this world" until the war was over.[64]

Soldiers at the time and after strained for words to explain the events. A lieutenant of the Eighth New York Heavy Artillery marveled "that a single man escaped the hail storm of bullets and shell."[65] "We felt it was murder, not war," another survivor from New York recorded, "or that at best a very serious mistake had been made."[66] "It could not be called a battle," a third New Yorker commented. "It was simply a butchery, lasting only ten minutes."[67] A soldier from New Jersey resorted to a biblical story from the second volume of Chronicles, likening the winnowing of his comrades to the plague that struck down the armies of Sennacherib, an Assyrian king who had invaded Israel: "An arena of horrors and the appearance of these bodies, strewed over the ground for a quarter of a mile, and in our view for days."[68] Other biblically literate Union soldiers might reflect on this account and wonder whether they were somehow on the wrong side, for Sennacherib's Assyrian host was fighting against the people of God and struck down for the evil act of attacking the Chosen People.

Even as enslaved people spaded soil over the Union dead at Cold Harbor after the battle, both armies marched toward the James River. In crossing, Grant's army turned its back on the repeated efforts over the past month to catch the Army of Northern Virginia in the open and fight a battle of annihilation. Having defied fire in the Wilderness and surmounted the waters of the James, Grant's army would now tunnel under the earth in another effort to enter Richmond and destroy the Confederacy.

The Crater

When Frederick Douglass encouraged black men to join the Union military in April 1863, he maintained "Once let the black man get upon his person the brass letters U.S., let him get an eagle on his button, and a musket on his shoulder, and bullets in his pocket," then citizenship would become his. Douglass exclaimed that nothing could stop this change, not even "power on the earth or under the earth."[69] For Douglass, the idea of power "under the earth" referred to the legions of hell. More than one year later, and shortly after the battles of Fort Pillow and Cold Harbor, Americans made a literal hell from "under the earth": they called it the Crater.

Less than two weeks after the carnage at Cold Harbor, Grant's army was besieging the city of Petersburg. No stranger to this type of warfare, Grant had successfully taken the key Mississippi River town of Vicksburg after two months' investment in 1863. Petersburg would be a tougher nut to crack, and Grant was keen to break through the Confederate defenses. Sixty thousand Union soldiers had already been killed, wounded, or captured, or half the Army of the Potomac when it set out in May.

The colonel of a regiment from Pennsylvania's anthracite coal mining region went to Gen. Ambrose Burnside with a novel proposal: excavate a mine under the rebel line and blow a hole from which men could attack. A successful exploitation of the breach by a division or more could capture Petersburg, then Richmond, and end the war. For just over a month the men of the Forty-eighth Pennsylvania dug their tunnel.[70] By the end of July, the mine was ready.

The question of who was to lead the assault remained. As Burnside's corps received the task, he picked the all-black division led by Edward Ferrero to be specially trained. This included fanning out on both sides of the crater to widen the breach instead of running into—and getting trapped by—the hole. Burnside's superiors worried that if the green USCT units were defeated, the northern newspapers would have a field day, claiming that the black soldiers were deemed expendable and therefore led to slaughter, that "we were shoving those people ahead to get killed because we did not care about them." They were also largely untested in battle, which worried General George Meade.[71] As a result, the white division of James Ledlie was substituted at the last moment. Although General Ledlie was to lead them as if demons emerging from the depths of hell, he himself struggled with another devil: liquor. His alcoholism had a profound impact on the success of this desperate plan.[72]

When the mine exploded—blowing sky-high and burying several hundred rebel soldiers—the division went forward, Ledlie was nowhere to be found. Leaderless and improperly trained, the division poured into the crater rather than widening the breach in the rebel line. The eight USCT regiments of Ferrero's division followed, and in the face of growing rebel resistance, poured into the crater as well. As they reached the Confederate works, they supposedly yelled *"No quarter for the d-d rebels. Remember Fort Pillow."* If true, the soldiers intended to pay back evil for evil. Rebels from Virginia determined the black soldiers "would give no quarter to us and rest assured received none."[73] "Kill 'em! Shoot 'em! Kill the damned niggers!" yelled South Carolinians.[74]

Two brigades of William Mahone's Confederate division, including five regiments of Virginians—many of them from Petersburg—rushed to seal the breach. The commander of the Sixty-first Virginia "never felt more like fighting in my life," after he saw the race of his foe.[75] "Our men were maddened and wild with rage," the colonel remembered, "deep and loud curses were hissed between clinched teeth as bayonets were thrust into men and drawn from the bleeding bodies of the dying or as the butt thud brought strong men to their knees."[76] The fighting was face-to-face and hand-to-hand. "Our men would drive the bayonet into one man, pull it out, turn the butt and knock the brains out of another, and so on until the ditch ran with blood of the dead and dying," another Virginian officer recalled.[77] William H. Stewart of the Sixty-first Virginia noted that the bloody mud was "shoe-sole deep" in places.[78] "Save the white men but kill the damn niggers," a captain in one of Burnside's white brigades heard the rebels yell.[79] Morgan Smith Cleveland, an officer in the Eighth Alabama asked some of the trapped (white) Union soldiers, "Why in hell don't you fellows surrender?" A Union colonel replied: "Why in the hell don't you let us?" The adjutant of the Fourth Rhode Island tied a white handkerchief to his sword, raised it up, and the soldiers around him began laying down their arms.[80] Race would matter in who would be allowed to surrender, however.

White Union soldiers trapped in the crater, seeing no escape but surrender, realized that their lives were still in jeopardy so long as they were mixed in with black soldiers. The maddened rebel soldiers were not keen to take prisoners while living black men stood in front of them. Several USCTs fell victim to unfriendly fire by their fellow Union soldiers "in order to preserve the whites from Confederate vengeance," which may have been the sad lesson learned by white Unionists from Fort Pillow.[81] Overcome by the chaos and carnage, and now facing deadly violence from their fellow Unionists, it was no surprise that USCTs sought escape, "crowding, swearing, yelling, making frantic endeavors to get through; some were down and others treading over them; and those in front were pushed on by the dense mass behind."[82] If "brave in their charge," a white officer of the USCTs noted more sympathetically, they were "wholly unmanageable, and totally demoralized in their defeat."[83] After the failure of the assault, many of Burnside's white soldiers blamed the panic-stricken USCT division for the defeat.[84]

Combatants—particularly those who were not professional soldiers but until recently civilians—in any war must overcome the willingness to take human life, particularly at close range.[85] Yet for a number of Confederate soldiers at the Crater, the revulsion was less about killing their foes in hand-to-hand combat than about *whom* they were fighting. Shot in the leg as he charged into the fray, Capt. P. M. Vance fell onto the black soldier who wounded him. They wrestled on the ground, where Vance's foe attempted to stab him with a knife. "I had to inhale an odor equaled only by the skunk," Vance recalled. After what seemed to Vance an eternity, several of his soldiers came to his assistance, "plunged their bayonets through the negro's body" and smashed his head with a rifle butt.[86] Vance was carried off by litter bearers, clinging to his opponent's knife as a trophy. The captain's account could be compared to an account of a group hunting expedition in which a dangerous bear was only dispatched after nearly mauling one of the party, and the trophy knife could be analogized to a deer's antlers or a bear's tooth. If it can be helpful for soldiers to dehumanize their foe in order to kill on the battlefield, Vance and other rebels already saw African Americans as less than human, perhaps as animals—hence the skunk reference—which rendered their use by the Union as soldiers even more repellent and evil.

Artillery officer and Petersburg resident William Pegram noted that the "ever ready Mahone was carried down to retake the line with his fine troops, which he did, with . . . great loss to the enemy. I never saw such a sight as . . . on that portion of the line. For a good distance in the trenches the Yankees, white and black, principally the latter, were killed two or three or four deep." Pegram claimed that the black soldiers "threw down their arms to surrender, but were not allowed to do so." This no quarter practice "was perfectly right, as a matter of policy." While it "seems cruel to murder them in cold blood . . . I think the men who did it had very good cause for doing so." Pegram long "wished the enemy would bring some negroes against this army. I am convinced, since Saturday's fight, that it has a splendid effect on our men."[87] Pegram believed that evil actions against soldiers attempting to surrender must be perpetrated for a good outcome: the Union's abandonment of the experiment in employing black soldiers.

Civilians in Petersburg concurred with Pegram's assessment of the situation. "Our brave boys took them at their word and gave them what they had so loudly called or—'*no quarter*,'" a Petersburg newspaper proclaimed.[88] The Petersburg natives among Mahone's men believed they were not simply protecting a few muddy feet of Virginian soil; they were defending their mothers, wives, sweethearts, and sisters from a fate worse than death at the hands of black "savages."

In the weeks after the massacre of black soldiers and would-be prisoners, Confederate soldiers defending other parts of the Petersburg lines demonstrated great anxiety about facing African Americans. If the soldiers on both sides—sharpshooters excepted—had settled into a "live and let live" situation between major offensives, this was decidedly not the case when rebel soldiers confronted black soldiers in the opposite trenches. A regiment of North Carolinians heard a rumor that a USCT regiment now faced them. They sallied forth to determine the truth of this rumor and "one morning attacked their skirmish line and found out they were regular 'blue coats,'" not black soldiers.[89] Thirty of the regiment were wounded or killed in this pointless action; those bent on venting their racial anger were done in by their prejudice.

Although only a fifth of the Union force that charged into the crater, the eight regiments of USCTs suffered 40 percent of the casualties, a testament to their bravery as well as their foes' determination to eliminate them.[90] "White Southerners, both in the ranks and on the home front, confronted the manifestation of their worst fears" at the Battle of the Crater. According to historian Kevin Levin, the "armed black men who, in aiding the Union cause, worked toward the destruction of the Confederacy as well as a way of life built around slavery," posed an existential threat to everything Virginians sought to defend when they agreed to secede.[91] If UCSTs were not slaughtered wherever and whenever encountered, they would bring hell on earth to rebel men and women. Whether Forrest's cavalrymen or Mahone's infantrymen, Confederate soldiers committed war crimes to stave off this supposedly diabolical future of black freedom and white slavery.

Sherman's March to the Sea and Beyond

During the last full year of the war, women and African Americans found themselves the target of armed foes in ways unheard of in the previous two years of the war, as Union and Confederate soldiers found new ways to "fight like the devil" in what now amounted to a total war. At the heart of much of this darkness was William Tecumseh Sherman, who when not condoning violence toward rebel civilians in the path of his army certainly used violent language to threaten the destruction of Confederate cities by hellish fire as he moved on Atlanta and then marched to the sea. He even threatened sexual violence against women.

Sherman minced few words. He wrote to a Confederate leader in early 1864, "The war which now prevails in our land is essentially a war of races." By this he meant the difference between "the Southern people" and "We of the North." Sherman declared that Union leaders should banish traitors and destroy the planter class. He also maintained that the Union would fight forever. "If they want eternal war, well and good; we accept the issue, and will dispossess them and put our friends in their place." After freeing the slaves, Sherman followed with this threat: the Union military and government would liberate southern whites from their ownership of the land. Sherman reasoned that this was all appropriate because it was how God treated Satan. "Satan and the rebellious saints of Heaven were allowed a continuous existence in hell merely to swell their just punishment. To such as would rebel against a Government so mild and just as ours was in peace, a punishment equal would not be unjust."[92]

Sherman's vitriolic language and his wartime realism unnerved Confederates and even some Unionists. He lectured the mayor of Atlanta, "War is cruelty, and you cannot refine it."[93] Some northern Democrats who fought to preserve the Union still dissented from emancipation and Sherman's war without restraint. One of Sherman's veteran foot soldiers, William Standard of Illinois, was tired of African Americans *and* Republicans—combining the

two in the derogatory term "Black Republicans." As he marched toward Atlanta, he told his wife for the umpteenth time about "this infernal war that
the Black Republicans brought on this once happy country." He said that his
ethnically German and Republican-leaning brother-in-law may "kiss my [ass]
and if mine is not black enough I will bring him a nigger wench when I come
home and he can kiss" hers.[94] Indeed, the implementation of the Emancipation Proclamation encouraged Standard to abandon the Union war effort. "It
is more honorable to desert than to stay in this abolition war to free the niggers and [e]nslave the white man."[95] The new war aim meant for him that all
Union soldiers wore "Lincoln's clothes and Lincoln caps," rendering volunteers who enlisted to save the Union nothing but "Lincoln hireling's," or even
demons in human flesh. His fellow soldiers were transformed into beings "as
wicked as the bad one [Satan, who] would be willing to receive them, and I
believe the present administration at Washington is doing more [to] make
men wicked than all classes of Infidels put together, for they might take some
steps to have this *monstrous war* brought to a close."[96]

While his regiment besieged Atlanta in August 1864, Standard hoped that
the Republicans would lose the upcoming elections. "I stand today as I always did," he replied to his wife's query about his political views. Lincoln "says
that he will not agree to any terms of peace without the abolition of slavery.
I do not agree with him. I am for any man for the next president that will use
his influence to put a stop to this unholy war." He feared that if Lincoln won,
"this war will be continued for the next four years, but it seems that the people
are getting their eyes open and will not sell all their liberties for the sake of
the *nigger*."[97] A few weeks later he felt vindicated to report that General
McClellan won the Democratic presidential nomination. "That is what I desired they should do. I think he will give us some peace if he is Elected."[98]
Standard failed to note the recent fall of Atlanta and what it meant for
McClellan's chances. In November, Lincoln won convincingly.

Race war aside, pro-Confederate women and white Union soldiers clashed
in a gender war as Sherman's army marched through Georgia and South Carolina in late 1864 and early 1865. The women of Georgia and South Carolina
believed they faced a fate worse than death from Sherman's soldiers, even as
they endured the fiery destruction of their homes. They looked to their men-
folk to fend off the Yankee scourge, but the Confederate army failed to keep
away what Grace Elmore of Columbia called this "race of liars and murderers

with not a single natural quality that excites respect."[99] If not subjected to the widespread rape that often accompanied military occupation in other wars, rebel women did endure the indignity of foreign men violating their homes and carrying off their possessions. The abject failure of (male) armed resistance to Sherman's army only hardened the resolve of these women in the postwar decades to resist Reconstruction and racial reforms, and to construct a "Lost Cause" narrative about the war's purpose.[100]

In late 1864 and the first months of 1865, Sherman's soldiers demonstrated that not only could they "fight like the devil," but—in the minds of pro-Confederate white women—they might resort to the demonic violence of sexual crime to inflict upon vulnerable women and girls a fate worse than death. Sherman's promise to "make Georgia howl" when he marched to the sea bid fair to be translated and multiplied into the screams of South Carolina's violated female population. Devout women in South Carolina lamented that the Yankees were now teaching them "how impotent is the weakness and helplessness of women," threatening "to wreak [upon us] their vengeance by the most frightful and wicked of crimes" excused by generals like Butler and Sherman who now appeared "but as arch fiends." Grace Elmore vacillated between "death and dishonor," or whether her faith—which held that suicide was an unforgivable sin—would allow her to end her own life if she were sexually assaulted. She feared the violent theft by Yankee soldiers of "what [women value] more than all things, the loss of which would be living death." Suicide must be justified in such a case. "God will, God must justify the deed" in such a situation, Elmore concluded.[101] Another South Carolinian viewed the invaders as "a hard set of demons in the shape of human beings some of them look to me as I imagine the imps of Satan would look."[102]

Even in North Carolina—treated with kid gloves by comparison with its southern sister—rebel women despised and feared Sherman's army. One confessed to her husband, "While I have no personal feeling towards any one of them I hate the nation from the bottom of my soul, Even as I hate Satan, and all things low, mean and hateful" for violating the sanctity of her home and bedroom.[103] This Manichaean gender conflict was not soothed by the fact that many Union soldiers returned the favor, viewing Confederate civilians—and particularly women—as demonic. "Our enemies have shown themselves *devils* in the spirit which ever began this most unprovoked and inexcusable rebellion," one of Sherman's staff officers wrote home. Due to pro-secessionist women's undiminished defiance, "there is nothing for it but 'to fight the devil with fire.'"[104]

The chaplain of the Fifty-eighth Indiana in Sherman's army battled immorality—alcoholism, swearing, brawling, prostitution, and other vices—in his regiment even as he viewed the war as a crusade to end the immorality of slavery. "Sometimes it seems to me that His Satanic Majesty is in full control of our Regiment, and that his emissaries are especially engaged in creating trouble in camp," John Hight noted in October a month before the army marched on Savannah.[105] While operating in Kentucky the previous year, Hight recognized that if most white Kentuckians supported the Union, they "love slavery better than the National Government," and believed that God would judge them for their idolatry. "Slavery is a sin against man—against God. It is one of the most vile of all crimes. It is not only a sin itself, but hinders all virtue and breeds all vice," rendering it "the great crime of America."[106]

At the beginning of the march the chaplain drew attention to the dismantling of a large railroad bridge—the first of many bridges and miles of railroad tracks to be destroyed over the next month. The destruction interrupted his religious services on a Sunday. As teams of men worked, the "whole mass threatens to fall into the stream. It shakes like an aspen leaf; it trembles like Belshaazer of old," until finally, "the timbers begin to tumble, like men in battle; they dash madly against each other, and amid flashing fire and splashing waters, the bridge comes thundering down, like Satan and his hosts, when hurled from Heaven to hell."[107]

The chaplain of another Indiana regiment serving in Sherman's Twentieth Corps was hardened toward the suffering of rebel civilians by the time he reached Savannah. Acknowledging his wife's concern for noncombatants in the army's path, G. S. Bradley recalled the words of a Georgia woman who confessed that "We hate you, but you have the power in your own hands, and sooner or later we must come under." "So far as the women are concerned, we might as well spare our pity," Bradley advised, "for they are the worst secessionists, and why should they not suffer?"[108]

For all the later infamy Sherman's reputation would suffer for this campaign and the burning of Atlanta that inaugurated it, and despite the punitive nature he intended from its inception, the general was concerned about his honor. Sherman met privately with a rebel chaplain in September following the evacuation and destruction of Atlanta. Henry Lay noted that Sherman was sensitive to claims that he was either "brutal or inhuman," and the general insisted that once the war was over, "the past would be quickly forgotten and both parties would love and respect each other."[109] The women of the Carolinas would ensure that this romantic tale of harmonious sectional reunion would exclude Sherman and his army. For instance, Eliza Tillinghast of North Carolina deplored the "scores of falsehoods" Yankees told about the Confederacy, "enough to make Satan grin with delight." She was particularly incensed that the Union lauded "Sherman the foul fiend who *cursed the women* and *children* of [her] native place."[110]

South Carolinian women like Grace Elmore had months to contemplate the advent of Sherman's army after the fall of Atlanta. "When I think of the Yankee march through Georgia unopposed and unimpeded, feeding upon the best in the land," Elmore despaired of the manhood of Confederate soldiers who were marched off to war in 1861 to defend southern women. "I ask myself is this the way, we intend to gain our independence; to feed our enemies, when they hunger & give them drink when they thirst."[111] Ironically, Elmore denied the teachings of Jesus Christ as applicable to Yankees, who must be devils to be resisted rather than fellow human beings to be loved. She feared for the loss of Richmond in far-off Virginia, for if the capital fell, "where will the government fly." She counted her own "suffering is as nothing when compared with the magnitude of this public evil, that hangs over us, and it is not the loss of home, not fear of poverty that haunts me and fills my heart with gloom, but tis the fear of our own men failing, of their being worn out in their struggle and giving up at last, of their lazzly resting upon what they have and leaving to God the rest."[112]

"There is no God in war," a surgeon from Illinois commented from near Savannah. "It is merciless, cruel, vindictive, un-christian, savage, relentless. It is all that devils could wish for."[113] While Sherman presented the city of Savannah as a Christmas present to Lincoln, he and his army did not stop there. After the New Year, the army trudged onward to the Carolinas, with a final stop anticipated in Richmond, Virginia. South Carolina was to see the full force of the wrath of Sherman's veterans, who blamed that state for starting the war and keeping them from their homes for three years and counting. One veteran looked forward with anticipation to the march through "that detested State," confessing to his father that South Carolinians should beware for "the Hell Hounds of Yankeedom are on your track to burn your Cotton and destroy your crops. . . . We will be Wild Tigers let loose."[114] A major from Illinois wrote his wife of his excitement to begin the "chastisement" of the state by fire. "If we don't purify South Carolina, it will be because we *can't get a light*."[115]

A town of less than ten thousand before the war, the capital of South Carolina had ballooned to 24,000 by the time Sherman's army arrived as a result of the arrival of refugees fleeing Union occupation.[116] If started by re-treating Confederate soldiers, the Union vanguard did nothing to stem the fires in Columbia. The first invaders were from the Fifteenth Corps, Sher-man's best western troops, who delighted in the abusing rebel property. As one of them told Grace Elmore, when Sherman put them in front, "we know it means fire and pillage."[117] One of Elmore's fellow Columbians noted that if these troops, these "tigers" were in the van, Sherman "intends to do his worst. He says he would not be afraid to go to [hell] with this [corps] in the lead."[118] "The wind was raging," a third woman of Columbia noted. "The ele-ments conspired with man to remind us of the scenes in which demons de-light."[119] Lily Logan observed Union soldiers in her yard filling the air with "fierce yells of demoniac delight [even as] their forms shone out hideously in numbers on all sides in the light of our flaming home." In other words, Sher-man's soldiers were transfigured into "demons in human shape" in the flick-ering light of their arson.[120]

"Such an army of villains, low bad scoundrels may God keep me from meeting again," Grace Elmore lamented, as the arson began again, for "they seemed to wish to frighten by committing their hellish deeds at night." They went into a neighbor's house "and played on the piano, sang and danced, and even while the fire was burning we could see their dark figures running around to enjoy the sight whilst the band played lively tunes." Words almost failed her, for the "very devils from hell could not rouse greater feelings of disgust and abhorrence than those cowardly wretches did in us."[121] "As the houses burnt down one after another the terrified women & children rushed into the [Ladies'] Asylum for safety surrounded by these yelling devils," Mary Maxcy Leverett recorded, "who tore open their trunks & gave [the contents] to negroes or tore to atoms." The asylum proved a meager sanctuary for five hundred Columbian women, for soldiers followed them in, "the fiends raged curseing, screaming up and down . . . swearing they were going to blow up the Asylum that night."[122]

Given the aggravated harassment of hundreds of Columbia's women recorded by Mary Leverett and Lily Logan, one would not be surprised to find
that the Confederate soldiers of South Carolina's capital returned home to
scenes like that depicted in Adalbert J. Volck's drawing *Tracks of the Armies*. A
Bavarian-born artist and supporter of the Confederacy, Volck resided in Baltimore by the outbreak of civil war. At least a year before Sherman's marches,
he drew a lurid cartoon of a veteran returning to his home to find the residence blasted apart, domestic animals and his wife dead, with vultures sur-
veying the destruction. Not only was the woman left behind to die—presumably
due to Union military action—but she was naked. The viewer was left to infer
that the gallant defenders of the Union raped and murdered her. Fires set by
Confederate negligence and Yankee malice devastated much property in the
Carolinas, but deadly assault on rebel women's honor and lives was rare.

A young resident of Columbia summarized these depredations—even
without the widespread rape and murder of defenseless white women depicted
in Volck's drawing—as the responsibility of "Satan Sherman and his imps."[123]
"The very devils from hell could not rouse greater feelings of disgust and abhorrence than those cowardly wretches did in us," wrote Grace Elmore.[124]
Even slaves, who otherwise viewed Sherman's troops as liberators, thought
they went too far in South Carolina. One former bondman criticized the soldiers for "things they ought not to have done" and for leaving undone "things
they ought to have done." The war waged by Sherman seemed more "bout
stealin" than a "Holy War for de liberation of de poor african slave people."[125]

Even the departure of Sherman's army gave Columbians little relief. "The
sight of that army [on the march] was enough to make the weak faint,
they were so robust, so splendidly equipped," Grace Elmore noted. "There they
passed in thousands yes in tens of thousands, four abreast, by our gate, a huge
serpent trailing its mighty length throughout our land, the maker of famine
and desolation wherever it goes." The analogy to the serpent of the Garden of
Eden was obvious. Elmore's "whole soul rose against them as they passed, a
band of highway robbers, the slayers of women and children. My whole nature is changed, I feel so hard so pitiless, gladly would I witness the death of
each of those wretches, God hear the curses poured upon their heads, God
grant they may suffer in their homes," and their wives and children suffer the
evils Elmore's neighbors endured.[126] The devout Christian named "Grace"

cursed Sherman's "Hell hounds," for she was powerless to inflict any earthly wounds.

Sherman's enemies understood precisely what he wanted them to experience: the force of demons in human and military form. By the end of the war, devilry had become a Union strategy. Fighting the war as Christians or in a just fashion had been tossed aside. When Sherman remarked years later that war "is all hell," he knew from experience and expertise what he meant. He and many other Americans had made it that way.

In 1861 Abraham Lincoln ended his first inaugural address by hoping that the "better angels of our nature" would keep the nation from war. They didn't, and the next four years witnessed Americans turning to another set of angels— fallen ones who went to hell and then tempted and terrorized humanity. Four years later, after winning his second election over General McClellan, who had prioritized "Christian" warfare and respecting the property rights of slaveholders, Lincoln once again invoked the sacred. This time, he was trying to come to grips with the massive devastation of the previous four years and cast a vision for the future. In his second inaugural address, he wondered how those who read the same Bible could disagree so disastrously. He quoted from Christian scriptures, and in his conclusion hoped that the people would follow the biblical mandate to care for widows and orphans.

Just as was the case with his prewar "House Divided" speech, Lincoln did not mention the devil, demons, or hell explicitly in this address. He did mention the curse from Genesis when God told Adam that he would obtain his bread "by the sweat of his brow." The basis for Lincoln's second inaugural, however, relied upon the devil. Just as had been the case with this "House Divided" speech before the war where the title main theme invoked the devil but he did not specifically mention evil, now in 1865, Lincoln did not explicitly mention demons, but they played a role in his creative imagination.

In May 1864, almost one year before his second inaugural, he met with several Baptists. He drafted a letter that made several of the key points he would later use in his inaugural. He wondered how southern white ministers during the war had asked other nations to help the Confederate cause. He wrote, "When, a year or two ago, those professedly holy men of the South, met in the semblance of prayer and devotion, and, in the name of Him who said

'As you would all men should do unto you, do ye even so unto them' and appealed to the Christian world to aid them in doing to a whole race of men, as they would have no man do unto themselves, to my thinking, they contemned and insulted God and His Church, far more than did Satan when he tempted the Saviour with the Kingdoms of the earth." Lincoln furthered his comparison between the South and Satan: "The devils attempt was no more false, and far less hypocritical. But let me forbear, remembering it is also written 'Judge not, lest ye be judged.'"[127]

When it came time for his second inaugural, Lincoln eliminated these references to the devil and softened his tone in other ways as well. He kept and modified, for instance, the final biblical phrase: "Judge not, lest *ye* be judged." With a few slight changes he transformed the accusatory tone of this verse to a unifying one when he spoke in March 1865. It now became "Judge not, that *we* be not judged." American theologians and historians who fell in love with Lincoln's second inaugural after World War II did not know that underneath it were thoughts about devils and Satan.

Lincoln would not live long past his address, however, for one man who certainly stood in judgment was John Wilkes Booth. Six years earlier, in 1859, Booth had been performing in Richmond when John Brown raided Harpers Ferry. The actor traveled to Charlestown, Virginia, to help guard the jail and was then present at Brown's execution. He admired Brown's single-minded conviction but not his cause.[128] Little did Booth realize that he would become like Brown: an actor in the extralegal violence known as guerrilla warfare, a type of fighting that Brown made infamous in Bleeding Kansas in the mid-1850s and then at Harpers Ferry. For Booth, the action would be assassination. His target would be the president. As had happened so often in the war, those who saw demons all around them determined to become like devils themselves.

CHAPTER 5

Hell Let Loose

One month after Abraham Lincoln rhetorically exorcised the devil from his second inaugural address, he became another casualty of a type of violence many labeled demonic: guerrilla warfare. It began indirectly with an order the president may or may not have issued and as part of an attempt to free emaciated prisoners of war. The ambitious young cavalry general Judson Kilpatrick—ominously nicknamed "Kill-Cavalry" for his earlier recklessness at Gettysburg—proposed in February 1864 a daring scheme to liberate the 10,000 Union prisoners held in Richmond. With fewer than 4,000 troops, Kilpatrick, who boasted that his cavalry could "fight anywhere except at sea" and was unsurprisingly dismissed as "a hell of a damned fool," plotted to free three times his force's numbers and somehow lead the malnourished men to safety.[1]

Kilpatrick's main force abandoned the mission at the first hint of Confederate opposition, but his second in command, Ulric Dahlgren, continued toward the rebel capital. He was gunned down as his force attempted to evade Richmond's swarming defenders. Allegedly, the Confederates apprehended written orders on his body easily interpreted as sanctioning the execution of Davis and his cabinet. Lincoln and his administration denied that the orders were authentic, but the incident ignited Confederate indignation. It inspired a Confederate spy ring in Washington to plot Lincoln's abduction and later his assassination.

John Wilkes Booth became the tool. For months, he had sought to aid the Confederacy from within the Union under the guise of the Shakespearean actor he was. He was also volatile and voluble on the subject of northern aggression and any effort to free the slaves or provide citizenship to African Americans.

Son and brother of actors, Booth quarreled with his elder brother Edwin—both a Unionist and a more prominent actor—about the causes and proper outcome of the war. In late August 1864 they had a final falling out.[2] Shortly after leaving his brother's New York home for the last time, Booth traveled to Franklin, Pennsylvania, where he wrapped up his oil investments. Almost shooting a black man, Caleb Marshall, during a verbal altercation after Marshall failed to remove his hat upon entering a barbershop, Booth left town on September 29, 1864.[3] Locals noted that Booth was a changed man on this final visit, and when they asked where he was off to now, Booth replied, "I am going to Hell."[4]

Making contact with Confederate spies residing in the Union capital, Booth concocted a plan to kidnap the president and spirit him to Richmond to be used as a bargaining chip.[5] Booth went so far as to study Lincoln's movements and security in and around Washington, including the president's frequent summertime visits to the Soldiers' Home. Booth's initial plan to kidnap Lincoln was certainly in line with the actions of more orthodox guerrillas, who often grabbed civilians (or soldiers) for ransom or to use as human shields while they made a quick getaway under armed pursuit. After Lincoln mentioned the injustice of some men voting (white men) and others not (black men), Booth darkly declared to his comrades, "That means nigger citizenship. Now, by God, I will put him through. That will be the last speech he will ever make."[6]

Everything changed when Lee's army surrendered at Appomattox in early April 1865. Booth drew inspiration from Colonel Dahlgren's alleged attempt to behead the Confederate government by uniformed men. Instead, Booth would conduct an ununiformed operation against Lincoln and his cabinet once Richmond fell.[7]

His plan was choreographed to maximize surprise and confusion. Booth planned the assassination with theatrical meticulousness, including a dramatic leap from the presidential balcony onto the stage, and a shouted Virginia motto ("sic semper tyrannis") meant to invoke the patriotic assassination of the tyrant Julius Caesar. Last but not least—like any good guerrilla—Booth arranged for a horse to be held nearby on which to ride off into the night. Relying on the mask of a famed theater actor to get him into Ford's Theatre and past any wary guards, Booth did not need the volume of fire of six or twelve revolver chambers to get to his target. However, he did emulate guerrilla operations by striding up to the president—who was unaware, like so many victims of guerrilla violence—to use his derringer. He was not quite face-to-face, but certainly at close range.

Booth and his co-conspirators had bounties placed on their heads. Regular soldiers were not targeted in this way; criminals and guerrillas were. From Booth's plan to his eventual killing, the entire episode smacked of a distinct form of war that many questioned as moral or just: guerrilla warfare.

Although Booth succeeded in murdering the president and his co-conspirator maimed Secretary of State William Seward, this extralegal violence failed to achieve its desired outcome. It did not inspire a Confederate resurgence. It did not confuse the Union government. It did not disunite the Union. In fact, it united Unionists in the conviction that there could only be one power behind Booth's actions: the devil.

Lithographer John L. Magee made the connection graphically with *Satan tempting Booth to the murder of the President*. Magee took a drawing of Booth featured on the cover of *Harper's Weekly* from April 29, 1865, and added supernatural elements. Like artists throughout the war, he formed the visible to draw attention to the invisible. He placed a horned, emaciated devil behind Booth. With his left hand gesturing toward Abraham Lincoln in the background and his right hand pointing to a derringer held by Booth, the devil tempted Booth to the crime. For this image, Magee's additions mixed the material and immaterial. Not only did he materialize the immaterial devil, but he also added Booth's pistol, a weapon that was not in the original drawing.[8]

Booth's actions and the responses to them fit in a line of guerrilla warfare that began before the war and continued after it. As editors of a recent study of Civil War guerrilla warfare have made clear, no single irregular war stretched from Arkansas in the west to Virginia in the east. Instead, guerrillas "fought in many localized conflicts, motivated by diverse issues, with an influence at the county, regional, state, and national levels."[9] Yet northern policy makers—generals and secretaries of war—saw one single problem, and sought one single policy to define these irregular combatants and then suppress them. Guerrilla warriors became the most convenient villains of the war, then and since, however much they are sometimes romanticized as American Robin Hoods.

When approaching guerrillas and guerrilla warfare, most historians have depicted them as a bipolar hybrid, or, as one recent scholar has put it "a demon and a hero." In most scholarship, the guerrilla "has been imagined as an outlaw-in-training and as a social bandit; he was thought of as a valiant soldier of the Confederacy and as a bloody opportunist."[10] Historian Harry Stout maintained that while Lincoln and other Unionist leaders used emancipation as their moral lever to justify harsher tactics against Confederate soldiers, threats of southern guerrilla war created the rationale to attack nonmilitary targets. Denouncing the actions of enemies as extralegal, Unionists could then expand the ways they pursued their ends.[11]

The deadly violence meted out by and against guerrillas called into question the nebulous boundaries of justifiable homicide in combat and murder in warfare. This begs the questions of the morality of either side sanctioning the use of guerrillas in this war, whether the Civil War was a just war, and if so whether guerrillas can be employed in a just war. Just war theory is at least two millennia old and involves a debate among intellectuals, theologians, and leaders (political and military) over the rules of war. "These rules first govern whether a people are right to declare war," writes Harry Stout. "Once war is declared, they provide guidelines for how that war should be fought, with a view toward minimizing the violence and destruction of war and prompting a peaceful future of coexistence."[12]

Since the fifth century and Augustine of Hippo, early just war theorists argued that a just war must by definition be a defensive war, or at least a war in which the righteous side has been invaded. Guerrillas, who often wore no uniform or appropriated the uniforms of enemy soldiers, and who frequently engaged in ambushes of unsuspecting opponents before blending back into the civilian population, were problematic in an attempt to wage war according to the precepts of just war theory.

Conceptions of and references to the demonic and hell played pivotal roles in the defining of guerrilla or extralegal violence. Before Americans jousted over the justness of guerrilla warfare and brought conceptions of the devil to bear upon them during the Civil War, they had long logged certain forms of warfare in demonic registers. For two centuries before the outbreak of this civil war, Protestant North Americans had a strong view of the alleged "savagery" of Native American war practices. Supposedly unlike European and then American Protestants, Indians targeted women and children as well as men, and took trophies—scalps—from their victims. Even those who survived an initial attack were often subject to torture and a painful, lingering death. Puritan narratives such as Mary Rowlandson's detailed the cruelties Native Americans inflicted upon the women and children they dragged into captivity. Of course, white Americans targeted Native American property, women, and children too. They also committed heinous acts, including the massacre of two hundred unsuspecting Cheyenne and Arapahos by a Union (Colorado) militia in 1865 at Sand Creek.[13] These perspectives on immoral Native American warfare played a significant role in how Americans performed and responded to guerrilla warfare in the 1860s.

During and after the war, Americans brought concepts of evil to bear on their definitions of guerrilla warfare and the actions of combatants. When Union strategists and rationalists encountered examples of violence they disliked or could not contain, they created a new category to render it illegal. Central to their definition was the notion that this type of war was somehow evil, constitutionally and spiritually worse than other forms of violence. During the same years, some combatants relished the seeming wildness of irregular war. They chose to become more like devils, and sometimes took upon themselves the moniker of devil, to advance their aims, however complex they may have been. Once again, considerations of evil became central to how Americans defined and pursued the war.

Defying and Defining Wartime Authority

If one counts extralegal violence as warfare, then it is hard to determine the beginning of the Civil War. While most place it in April 1861 with the firing on Fort Sumter, Americans had been turning to violence and coordinated militant efforts for decades. In many ways, the Civil War's guerrilla warfare began before the battle of rival governments did. It was at least present when the territory of Kansas exploded in 1856, and in Virginia in 1859 when John Brown and his men took the arsenal at Harpers Ferry. According to Brown, however, he did not initiate violence. Slavery itself was a system of violence, so the uprisings of African American slaves, such as the Nat Turner revolt of 1830, could be defined as retaliatory warfare.

Many Americans who participated in or paid close attention to these extralegal forms of militarism did so again in the Civil War. During the first five years of the 1860s, both nation-states took an active role in trying to define regular and irregular war. They did so because Americans attacked one another with such ferocity that each government moved to justify the actions of its side and oppose those of its enemies. This set the stage for two developments involving conceptions of evil. First, to denounce particular forms of violence as unjust, many Americans turned to demonization of the enemies' tactics and tacticians. Second, as Americans applauded the concept of fighting like devils as a positive good, some embraced the identity of devils in human disguise. The most infamous of these men would become leaders of vigilante violence after the war.

Well before the Confederate Congress enacted the Partisan Ranger Act in April 1862, which authorized Jefferson Davis to commission officers who in turn would form "bands of partisan rangers" paid by the Confederacy and subject to "the same regulations as other soldiers," guerrillas had attacked Unionists.[14] While professional soldiers resisted major military action, irregular forces in Appalachia—western Virginia, eastern Kentucky and Tennessee— and Missouri leapt into action. This eagerness to use deadly force by individuals or small bands may be partially explained by the chaos of civil war, which enabled guerrillas to redress prewar grudges with neighbors via murder and theft with little fear of legal consequence.

Elijah White led one of the earliest guerrilla forces in Virginia. Now part of the DC metropolitan area, Loudoun County was then in the contested borderland between the Union and the Confederacy in northern Virginia. As locals joined pro- and anti-Union forces, neighbors stood in direct opposition. White had moved from Maryland to Loudoun in 1857 after battling antislavery settlers in "Bleeding Kansas." He had also helped suppress John Brown's raid in 1859.

White joined a cavalry regiment in 1861 and before the end of the year received permission from Secretary of War Judah P. Benjamin to raise an independent company for "ranging service" in the county. During the winter of 1861–62, White's partisans reported to Gen. A. P. Hill.[15]

Inspired by the Comanche nation's ability to fend off incursions by Mexico, Texas, and the United States, White's unit appropriated their name. Comanche Indians relied on horses not only to avoid the diseases that decimated other Native Americans, but also to launch lightning-fast hit-and-run raids that prevented European empires and their postcolonial descendants (the Mexican and American republics) from conquering them. Indeed, the

Comanches were able to maintain an empire of their own in the face of Mexican and US expansion well into the 1840s.[16]

One of White's "Comanches" viewed Union operations in Virginia as "the abolition crusade upon the South."[17] Following multiple ambushes on Union regular forces by White's band, a Unionist force, the Loudoun Rangers, was formed to combat White in May 1862.[18] Union Gen. John D. Stevenson called one of White's more bloody subordinates a "villain" leading "a gang of murderers," while a Unionist miller in the county compared the force's operations to Satan "going up and down the earth seeking whom" he might "devour."[19]

Like White, Virginian John Mosby began as a Confederate cavalryman. A University of Virginia dropout (he had attempted to murder an older bully) Mosby operated as a scout, but felt constrained and desired more independence. J. E. B. Stuart, who considered Mosby a protégé, warned the young man to avoid the nicknames of "ranger" or "guerrilla" once he won command of a partisan ranger company. "It is in bad repute" to be known as a ranger. "Call your command 'Mosby's Regulars'" instead, Stuart counseled in a fascinating form of doublespeak, since there was nothing regular about their behaviors.[20]

The chaos of war and occupation enabled violent resolution of peacetime disputes between neighbors with little or no interference from state or federal authorities.[21] Champ Ferguson was a poster child for this blend of patriotic service and criminal opportunism. He hailed from the borderland between Tennessee and Kentucky, and at least one of his brothers was an active Unionist.[22] Ferguson had already been accused of murder in the 1850s, and took full advantage of the war to plunder and murder at will. He accompanied John Hunt Morgan's rebel cavalry units but found the restrictions of army life overly constricting. Tiring of regular service, Ferguson recruited a band of fellow desperadoes and waged a largely private war, or as his most recent biographer puts it, by the end of 1862 Ferguson was a "regular soldier when convenient, Confederate partisan when otherwise."[23] By the summer of 1862, a Louisville newspaper deemed Ferguson enough of a fiend to (incorrectly) report his death at the hands of Unionist militia (or guerrillas, depending on who was telling the story), and claim that Ferguson had now "met his desserts in the dominions of his Satanic Majesty."[24]

Union political and military leaders struggled with how to deal with this scourge. As they attempted to conduct the Civil War in a civil way, they

endeavored to define that which violated the proper conduct of war. Over-
seeing the Union occupation of Missouri from St. Louis, Maj. Gen. Henry W.
Halleck found his biggest challenge to be rebel irregular forces rather than
the organized Confederate army. At the beginning of 1862 he wrote one of
his subordinates in response to a series of bridge burnings. "This is not usually done by armed and open enemies, but by pretended quiet citizens, living on their farms." Halleck opined to Gen. Thomas Ewing, "A bridge or
building is set on fire, and the culprit an hour after is quietly plowing or
working in his field." The Union army in Missouri "is almost as much in a
hostile country as it was when in Mexico."[25] Matters grew worse when ar-
sonists turned into snipers and ambushers. In March 1862 he issued an order to the effect that "every man who enlists in [a guerrilla outfit], forfeits his
life and becomes an outlaw." Halleck wanted it to be clear that no Missou-
rian in his right mind should take part in an insurgency. "All persons are
hereby warned that if they join any guerrilla band they will not, if captured,
be treated as ordinary prisoners of war, but will be hung as robbers and
murderers."[26]

Unionists in Missouri concurred with Halleck as to the severity of the
problem and the importance of draconian measures to combat it. Civilians
in the central part of the state complained to Gen. John Schofield in July that
their rebellious neighbors could not be reasoned with. "Experience teaches
us that so soon as a man turns against his Government, then he becomes a
liar, deceiver, defrauder, and murderer." Only "a summary and terrifying
punishment" could bring bridge burners and bushwhackers to bay. "Disarm
them entirely . . . leave them destitute. . . . Let them feel the force of the law
& the power of the government," and even though "some innocent men must
suffer" by such blanket measures, the army should do everything necessary
to root out the devils in human garb than too little.[27]

Generals like Halleck worried and complained about how to deal with
guerrillas, but soldiers like Henry Crawford had to fight them. Residents of
Warsaw, Missouri, Crawford and his father wrote that their pro-Confederate
neighbors "seem to have gone to sleep and forgot that there was any war."
Yet the guerrillas among them were pretending. "There is one kind of people
that is asleep with one eye open and only wait an opportunity to murder loyal
people without mercy and these men are the ones that walk up to a federal
soldier," smiling and offering his hand "and say they have always stayed at

home and never done anything." These deceitful combatants were "ten times meaner" than openly Confederate soldiers. Having talked to most of the men in the town, Crawford found that "all but two or three are the stay at home type and don't like the draft because they don't want to take any part in the war," but he did not buy their stories. Rather, Crawford looked forward to the time when they would be unmasked as rebel demons and executed. "Hell will be full of such men before this war is over."[28]

Counterinsurgency operations carried out by Union soldiers aimed not only to root out guerrilla cells but also to protect Unionist civilians in border states like Missouri, Kentucky, and Tennessee. Unionist civilians—their erstwhile neighbors—were after all a major target of many rebel guerrillas. Col. John McNeil sought to avenge the abduction and presumed murder of Unionist Andrew Allsman, who was supposedly an informer to Union forces. McNeil executed fifteen guerrillas after a drumhead trial and was criticized by the northern press, including the *New York Times*. One of McNeil's colleagues leapt to his defense. "Had one half the severity practiced by rebels on the Union men of Tennessee, Arkansas, and Missouri been meted out in return to them," wrote Col. William R. Strachan, "every trace of treason would ere this have been abolished from our land." The guerrillas threatened loyal Unionists, and their "long list of crimes . . . would make even fiends in hell shudder."[29]

In the summer of 1862, Halleck was promoted to general in chief and transferred to Washington to coordinate the Union armies. Finding that Virginia, like Missouri, was rife with irregular forces, Halleck selected a Columbia College professor to draft a code of ethics for this unprecedentedly vast civil war, and to focus particularly on how to deal with guerrillas. Halleck met Francis Lieber sixteen years before the war at the US Army installation on Governors Island near New York, where the two discussed Charles Sumner's pacifism. Halleck was no stranger to the application of law to war, having recently authored the lengthy book *International Law; Or, Rules Regulating the Intercourse of States in Peace and War.*[30]

Halleck's 1861 book argued that "partisan and guerrilla troops" fighting without "commissions or enlistments" operated outside the law, yet if "authorized and employed by the state . . . they become a portion of its troops."[31] From Virginia to Arkansas, armed men fighting for the Confederacy without proper uniforms were attacking Union soldiers and civilians, and should they be summarily executed upon capture, Confederate generals threatened

to similarly kill Union soldiers. Those generals claimed the second part of
Halleck's assessment; they had authorized guerrillas to act.

Halleck looked to the works and theories of Francis Lieber. Lieber's first
memory was of Napoleon's army marching by following their epic 1806 defeat of Frederick the Great's Prussian army. Nine years later the seventeen-
year-old joined a Prussian regiment, fought at Ligny, and was wounded twice
in the pursuit of Napoleon's army into France following Waterloo.[32] Lieber
arrived in the United States in 1827, and eight years later took up a post as
professor of history and political economics at South Carolina College. He
moved to New York only in 1856, and one of his grown sons now fought for
the Confederacy while two others joined the Union army.[33] "Behold in me,"
Lieber wrote a friend, "a symbol of civil war."[34]

Halleck was drawn to Lieber not only by past acquaintance; in the fall of
1861 the professor inaugurated a course for the new law school titled The Laws
and Usages of War, which drew virtually every law student.[35] A week after Halleck asked for a formal memorandum on the international laws of war to
determine Union policy on guerrillas—and still mourning the loss of his
Confederate son, Oscar, near Williamsburg—Lieber delivered. *Guerrilla Parties Considered with Reference to the Laws and Usages of War* found favor with
Halleck, who ordered 5,000 copies to be distributed to the armies.[36] Lieber
made clear that in his judgment—founded upon historical analysis of the irregular war in Spain waged against Napoleon and other conflicts that devolved
into indiscriminate slaughter of noncombatants and prisoners—guerrillas
who operated without governmental restraint were "evil."[37] Lieber followed
this 6,000-word essay a year later with a book at the behest of Gen. Halleck and
Secretary of War Edwin Stanton. *Instructions for the Government of Armies of
the United States, in the Field* may have been written as a legal text, but it had a
moral disclaimer. "Men who take up arms against one another in public war,
do not cease on this account to be moral beings, responsible to one another and
to God," noted an early article.[38] Yet could the laws of war be applied to guerrillas like those in Arkansas's Franklin County who captured a small Union
force? These irregulars did not simply execute their prisoners, but rather proceeded to "the most cruel tortures and inhuman barbarities ever practiced
upon prisoners in this or any age," such as cutting off their ears and noses before stripping and castrating them."[39] Lieber explicitly condemned torture as
inherently cruel, the infliction of "pain for the sake of pain," even if the torture

was aimed at extracting key military information. He endorsed retribution in response to violations of the laws of war by "a reckless enemy" who must be persuaded to avoid "the repetition of a barbarous outrage," yet there must be limits to such reprisals.[40] As Lieber wrote to Halleck privately, "If Indians slowly roast our men, we cannot and must not roast them in turn."[41]

Lieber raised Native Americans in the abstract to discuss with Halleck what was for them the go-to exemplar of uncivilized and demonic warfare. By mapping derogatory conceptions of Native American violence onto the struggle between the Union and Confederacy, Lieber demonstrated how far the Civil War altered the connections among religion, race, and society. In this case, white men became like Indians and in so doing could only be understood in terms of demonic evil. In order to discredit their enemies, Union officials like Lieber, Halleck, and others connected Confederate guerrilla warfare with evil via Native Americans.

The Regularity of Irregular War

Regardless of Union efforts to suppress guerrilla warfare by casting it as diabolical, irregular warfare was widely popular. Even some clergymen wanted in on the action. Virginian W. W. Morison, now a Presbyterian minister in Alabama, proposed a plan "to take 'special care' of the [Union] gunboats operating on the Mississippi River by raising a band of sharpshooting guerrillas to "kill the pilots." If Confederate authorities doubted the military competence of a cleric, Morison noted his military training at Washington College and his acquaintance with Lexington's John Letcher, now governor of Virginia.[42]

A few Unionist clergy exhibited a similar bloodthirstiness. Secessionist civilians were outraged to read of a Methodist minister who proposed upon first meeting a Confederate soldier, "I will discharge the contents of my musket through him, and while the blood is weltering from his veins, I will kneel down by his side, and pray God to pardon his sins."[43]

Crucial to guerrilla operations—whether John Mosby's in northern Virginia or William Quantrill's on the plains of Kansas and Missouri—was the horse. Starting off with their own farm horses but quickly adding the mounts of captured or killed enemy cavalrymen, guerrillas utilized horses

to execute hit-and-run raids, some of them with the express purpose of
acquiring more horses. Fighting on horseback enabled guerrillas to cultivate
a romantic, Walter Scott atmosphere while "riding like the devil" pursuing
infantry. Yet the loss of horses could be fatal. William Quantrill saw the loss
of his favorite horse as a bad omen, and his fatal wounding occurred shortly
thereafter. As Quantrill knew, "without a horse, a man could not be a guerrilla, and in the brush a man who was not a guerrilla was as good as dead."[44]

When considering the importance of horses to the war generally or guerrillas specifically, Bible-literate Americans need only think of the four
horsemen of the Apocalypse in the book of Revelation. The scourges of humanity embodied as War, Famine, Plague, and Death overtook their victims
mounted on steeds. Unwary foot soldiers were particularly vulnerable to the
wrath of well-mounted and well-armed guerrillas, many of whom were more
interested in sowing death and terror while reaping plunder than bestowing
mercy or taking prisoners.

One of the deadliest guerrilla operations was the massacre at and burning of Lawrence, Kansas, on August 21, 1863, by William Quantrill's guerrilla band, which included Jesse James. The murder of more than 150 Unionist
men and boys in front of their families inflamed Kansans into a genocidal
rage against Missouri's Border Ruffians, Lieber's code be damned.[45] One of
the few adult male survivors of the raid was, unsurprisingly, a pastor. Reverend Richard Cordley called Quantrill's attack "the most perfect realization
of . . . 'Hell let loose,' that could ever be imagined." The raiders looked like
wild beasts, "rough in dress, and coarse in speech and brutal in conduct,"
and the people of Lawrence could hardly believe that men could act "like
fiends incarnate."[46] Kansas Senator James Lane—an antislavery veteran of the
1856 Kansas civil war—disregarded the law in order to share with Union Gen.
John M. Schofield his belief in "the necessity . . . of making a large portion of
Western Missouri a desert waste, in order that Kansas might be secure against
future invasion." The conservative Schofield prevented this irregular operation by placing guards along the border. Yet many northern newspapers endorsed Lane's proposed ethnic cleansing of proslavery Missourians. "Hands
off! Let no Copperhead or pro-Slavery General [meaning Schofield] interfere
with him. There will be fire and death along that Border, until the great revenge of Kansas is attained. We may not be Christian in these utterances,
[but] we are human."[47]

While the infantry on both sides were issued single-shot muzzle-loading rifle-muskets—prescribing semi-aimed fire at the direction of officers while deployed in close ranks—guerrillas did their killing at close range, fighting on their own hook. Historian Joseph Beilein emphasizes that if many guerrillas initially rode off to war with shotguns or rifles or carbines, they realized in the brush that volume of fire was crucial to survival and victory when springing an ambush or escaping one. Six-shot revolvers were far superior to muskets or carbines in rate of fire. Their ease of use rendered them superior to repeating carbines and rifles at close range. Also, they could be more effectively fired from horseback than any long arm. And guerrillas carried more than one.[48] A survivor of Quantrill's raid on Lawrence noted that the guerrillas wielded "from two to six revolvers apiece."[49]

Striking without warning, well-mounted, and armed to the teeth, guerrillas fought without a uniform to mark them as combatants, let alone soldiers. Or, more demonic in the eyes of their regular opponents, they wore the uniforms of their enemies in order to disguise their true nature of devils in angels' clothing. For instance, at Baxter Springs in southeastern Kansas in October 1863, several hundred men of Quantrill's band surprised and massacred a smaller Union force escorting Maj. Gen. James Blunt to a new command in Arkansas. Blunt's escort was taken unawares as Quantrill's men were wearing blue uniforms. This and other similar actions earned Quantrill's command the derogatory nicknames of "fiends incarnate," "demons," and "devils from hell." Even some of their regular Confederate allies were disgusted at their antics. Gen. Henry McCulloch, commanding Confederate soldiers in northern Texas, appreciated the utility of Quantrill's raiders, "but certainly we cannot, as a Christian people, sanction a savage, inhuman warfare, in which men are shot down like dogs."[50]

From generals to private soldiers, Union forces grew tired of the depredations and seemingly random murders committed by guerrillas against lone sentries and isolated garrisons. They also tired of irregulars and the communities that sheltered them. En route to Huntsville, Alabama, Lt. Col. John Beatty's train was ambushed. Beatty informed the residents of the nearest town "that this bushwhacking must cease," set fire to the town, and resumed his journey with three hostages from Paint Rock. Beatty saw no place for guerrillas in this war. "If they wanted to fight they should enter the army, meet us like honorable men, and not, assassin-like, fire at us from the woods and run." He pledged to hold local citizens responsible for future ambushes, "mak[ing] them more uncomfortable than they would be in hell."[51] Soldiers garrisoned in Kansas fought mosquitoes and guerrillas. A lieutenant in the Third Wisconsin Cavalry noted the hours spent "desperately fighting flies and mosquitoes which continually bit[e] and sting us day and night, and remind us that the Devils dominions are located at this place, or his imps in miniature form are on a tour of inspection." Beset by two elusive foes, the officer recorded the opinion "that every foot of hell is here exhibited and we have free tickets."[52]

"We are in a country of guerrillas," a brigade staff officer from Massachusetts wrote his wife in July 1862 from near the Blue Ridge Mountains in central Virginia. "They are continually picking [off] our men. At a farm house some five miles off, they urgently pressed two men to stay for tea; they waited some time and then concluded they must go. A little way from the house they were fired on; one shot wounded both of them," another brought down one of their horses, but they both mounted the remaining horse and fled. Henry Bruce Scott noted that the house was quickly "surrounded and 15 men taken prisoners; one of them had a pistol, one barrel of which had been discharged and the ball which lodged in the boot of the wounded man just fitted that barrel. This would be evidence enough to hang him under Gen. Pope's last order," but he feared that the guerrilla would just be administered an oath of allegiance and let go.[53] Dozens of such frustrating brushes with death led volunteer officers to order or just turn a blind eye to soldiers' justice of shooting guerrillas out of hand, sometimes recorded later as killed "while trying to escape." In this policy northern volunteers were supported by professional soldiers reluctant to treat captured guerrillas as anything other than armed criminals, particularly when operating far from Washington and Lieber's legal analysis. Among those skeptical generals was William Tecumseh Sherman.[54]

The Gen. John Pope mentioned by Henry Scott learned the hard way in Missouri in 1861 that guerrillas could severely curtail military efforts to maintain order, and the lesson he learned was to hold local civilians responsible for bridge burnings and sentry slayings. Yet his draconian methods, sanctioned by the new secretary of war, Edwin Stanton, involved in Virginia the imposition of loyalty oaths to civilian men of military age on pain of exile and confiscation of property, and the execution of spies and guerrillas.[55] As staff officer Henry Scott noted, guerrilla operations were a community affair, and the fifteen men captured in the counterinsurgency operation after the

ambush of two of soldiers were a mixture of guerrillas and their (wholly) civilian allies. Pope sought to combat the insurgency by tearing out its commu-
nal roots that fed and sheltered it. Yet Pope's decrees resulted in unprecedented
efforts by the Confederate government to rein in his "hard war" policies, as
will be discussed below.

While his military mentor, William Sherman, advanced on Atlanta in the
summer of 1864, Gen. Stephen Burbridge acted to wipe out the guerrilla
scourge in his native Kentucky. On July 16 he issued an order declaring that
in retribution for the murder of a single unarmed Union citizen, "four guerrillas will be selected from prison and publicly shot to death at the most convenient place near the scene of the outrages."[56] "I would prefer, and will
insist, that no regular guerrillas be sent in as prisoners; direct your command
to deal with characters in a speedy and summary manner," Burbridge ordered
one of his subordinates. Although Sherman believed that even "the veriest
demon" should have a fair hearing before execution, he chose not to interfere with Burbridge's command.[57]

Next door to Burbridge's draconian occupation of Kentucky, the similarly
vindictive Gen. Robert Milroy asked Grant how he should deal with a gang
of Tennessee guerrillas in 1865. The list of their depredations was long: murder of two of his scouts, robbery and shooting of several Unionists, gang rape
of a Unionist woman, and attempted rape of a teenage girl "in the same room
with the corpse of her cousin" killed by them. Could such "demons incarnate" be allowed to surrender under Grant's generous terms of surrender?
Milroy's was a rhetorical question, and Grant's response was in the negative.[58]

West of the Mississippi in the Ozarks, pro- and anti-Union guerrillas
clashed in Missouri and Arkansas. Although from 1863 onward regular combat was absent from this region because northern supremacy had been decided by major Union victories in 1862, the local population descended into
irregular warfare. Irregular rebels self-identified as "guerrillas" while their
opponents—whom they termed "jayhawkers"—called them "bushwhackers."[59] While many of the mutual depredations in this region were in the form
of theft, deadly violence did occur. In September 1862 thirty rebels commanded by Dave Hilliard visited Union sympathizer Jacob Aleshire in Christian County. After robbing the house they rode away with Thomas Budd, who
was visiting the Aleshires. Three days later Budd's burned corpse was found.
Budd had been shot and his ears and nose cut off.[60] Alfred Bolin led a band of

guerrillas who specialized in sniping at Union soldiers traveling home on fur-lough, and operated from a rocky hill in Taney County appropriately nick-named "Murder Rock."[61] That Bolin was an opportunistic murderer at least as much as he was a patriotic Confederate may be seen in that one of his victims was twelve-year-old Bill Willis and another was an eighty-year-old man killed by a ferry on the White River.[62] Unionists in the Ozarks would mobilize dur-ing Reconstruction—and after—as masked "Bald Knobbers" to restore order by way of vigilante violence against supporters of the Confederacy.

Guerrilla war was a two-way street, and uniformed soldiers could adopt guerrilla methods to thieve and terrify. If not as romanticized or numerous as rebel guerrillas, Unionist irregulars inflicted their share of suffering and death on their neighbors, even as uniformed northern soldiers took out their frustrations on rebellious civilians, as seen in the last chapter. Yet Union sol-diers, their officers, and politicians "routinely denied that they waged irreg-ular war on the Southern home front." Historian Lisa Tendrich Frank recently established the argument that "Union soldiers routinely broke what were . . . understood as the stated and unstated rules of war" when invading the homes and bedrooms of southern women.[63] Although sexual violence inflicted on white women was not routine, physical threats and theft were commonplace. Frank argues that Sherman's "regular" soldiers used "irregular" methods as they "violated gender norms that governed peacetime interactions" between middle class men and women.[64] These actions also skirted the bounds of the Lieber Code, which specified that "wanton violence committed against per-sons in the invaded country, all destruction of property not commanded by the authorized officer, all robbery, all pillage or sacking, all rape, wounding, maiming, or killing" of civilians was to be punished with death.[65]

Sexual violence—or at least the threat of it—was certainly inflicted upon white Unionist women in Appalachia. Northern newspapers trumpeted the torture of the "women of loyal men" by rebel guerrillas in efforts to find their husbands' hideouts in eastern Tennessee via whipping, hanging by the thumbs, stripping, and repeated rape threats.[66] In 1864, more irregulars in east Tennes-see "committed a series of acts which the demons inhabiting the lowest hell could not surpass in cruelty," torturing a Unionist woman and threatening to rape her, while actually sexually assaulting two enslaved women.[67] However successful he was as a raider before 1864, John Hunt Morgan vociferously de-fended himself against those who "stigmatized" his "brave army" as a "band of guerrillas and marauders," claiming instead that his command "come to not molest peaceful individuals or destroy private property" but to defend southern independence.[68] Soldiers on both sides sought new shoes, food, and money on battlefields and farms, but sexual assault was beyond the pale for honorable commands and commanders. In their last great—and largely unsuccessful—raid in 1864, Morgan's troopers were accused of pillage *and* attempted rape, which no doubt threatened to downgrade the reputation of his cavalry force from the status of regulars to guerrillas.[69]

Of course, not everyone who claimed to be a guerrilla was one. A Kentuckian wrote to a resident of Louisville that robbers pretending to be members of John Hunt Morgan's command of mounted raiders rode "in about twenty strong, and acted more like devils than humans. They robbed Mr. James Rankin of his money and watch and then beat him over the head and shoulders, with their pistols, cutting one of his ears in two, and finally shot him in the neck."[70] Rankin was still alive, but left in a critical state. Whether in the guise of Confederate cavalry or guerrillas, common thieves, deserters, and even opportunistic guerrillas took advantage of assumed identities and costumes to pilfer money, avenge prewar grudges, or simply survive.

When Lee's army fled west from Petersburg and was cornered at Appomattox, a number of diehard Confederates—particularly the cavalrymen among them—proposed that the army be broken up into one vast guerrilla band that would continue the war. At the top of the list of these proponents was Lee's cavalry chief and nephew, Fitzhugh Lee.[71] Slightly lower down on the list was Lee's artillery chief, Edward Porter Alexander, who actually formulated a plan for widespread guerrilla warfare conducted by Lee's erstwhile regular soldiers. Ironically—given that artillery was rather less mobile than cavalry—Alexander proposed that "the army may be ordered to scatter in the woods & bushes & either to rally upon Gen. Johnston in North Carolina, or to make their way, each man to his own state, with his arms, & to report to his governor."[72] Still a young man, not yet thirty, Alexander of Georgia suggested to the war-aged Lee that the army disperse into multiple guerrilla bands to continue the war by irregular means.

Guerrilla war was a young man's game, and Lee was not willing to countenance it, not least because it would result in years of further death and destruction to his beloved Virginia. Lee appealed to Alexander's faith, claiming that "as Christian men," they must "consider only the effect which our action will have upon the country at large," lest guerrilla war only encourage the Union armies to act like devils against all white southerners. Lee also gave a practical rebuttal to Alexander's plan, noting that only 15,000 of the troops who made it to Appomattox were now armed. "Suppose two thirds, say 10,000, got away. Divided among the states, their numbers would be too insignificant to accomplish the least good." Even if Lee took up Alexander's plan, the men "would have no rations & they would be under no discipline," having already been "demoralized by four years of war. They would have to rob & plunder to procure subsistence. The country would be full of lawless bands in every part." Lee did not fail to note how this situation would encourage Union forces to drop all restraint. The enemy's cavalry "would pursue in the hopes of catching the principal officers, & wherever they went there would be fresh rapine & destruction."[73]

If Gen. Alexander accepted his commander's reasoning, Virginian John "Ham" Chamberlayne, one of Alexander's subordinate artillery officers, fled the scene of Lee's surrender. An artillerist and graduate of the University of Virginia, Chamberlayne refused "to attend the funeral at Appomattox C.H." and rode to join the army under Joseph E. Johnston in North Carolina. "I am not conquered by any means & shall not be while alive," however sad he was to leave his "beloved Virginia."[74] When he learned that Johnston had surrendered, he continued west, until he realized somewhere between Charlotte, North Carolina, and Athens, Georgia, that his nation no longer existed, but neither could he accept defeat in order to return home quickly.[75]

Wade Hampton III, Lee's most recent cavalry chief, did not want to surrender either. He was the nephew of South Carolina senator, serial niece abuser, and "cotton is king" speechifier James Henry Hammond, and his family owned hundreds of slaves. Hampton demonstrated his allegiance to the proslavery cause by raising his own legion—horse, artillery, and foot—in 1861.[76] In 1864 he succeeded the fallen J. E. B. Stuart at the head of the mounted arm of the Army of Northern Virginia. Now he did not want to surrender. Recruiting duty in South Carolina kept him from the final campaign in Virginia, leaving him to lay down his sword with Johnston's army at Durham. He nearly got into a swordfight or brawl with Sherman's cavalry chief, "Kill-Cavalry" Kilpatrick—encountered in the last chapter—over Napoleon's views on the honor of soldiers who accepted surrender over death until Johnston and Sherman personally intervened.[77]

Presbyterian theologian and Stonewall Jackson's former chief of staff Robert Dabney lamented the theft of his horses—for "Yankees *sometimes* stole people's things"—which kept him from departing Virginia for what was left of the Confederacy, let alone to checking in on his aged mother. He was "surrounded with absolute want, and with no horses to flee from it" in the summer of 1865.[78] The want of horses kept former preacher-officers like Dabney from evading Union occupation, let alone mounting continued resistance to it.

"The army of the Confederacy is the South," Gen. Sherman wrote the Republican senator from Ohio who was also his brother in late 1863. "I am not going to bother myself about guerrillas and citizens. If they can't do our main arteries harm, is all I aim at."[79] Three weeks later he told one of his subordinates why he paid "but little attention to guerrillas": they never threatened any important post, "and are chiefly engaged in harassing their own people."[80] In 1864 and 1865 Sherman's army outdid the depredations of the guerrillas in a large swath of Georgia and South Carolina and certainly harassed the people of those states. Like Lee, Sherman discounted the military value of guerrillas, even as he took inspiration from the physical and psychological terror inflicted by their tactics to devastate southern civilians.

Robert E. Lee understood what recent historians who overemphasize the impact of Civil War irregular warfare miss: "the Confederacy had no chance of gaining its independence by continuing the struggle by waging a sustained guerrilla warfare against the armies of the North."[81] At least in Virginia, guerrillas could not be the decisive factor in a final Confederate victory. As early as August 1862, a West Point graduate and Union general saw the increase in guerrilla activity in northern Virginia as evidence that "the resources of the south are about played out," and smugly commented that "their guerilla warfare will in the end hurt themselves more than us."[82] Guerrillas were both hometown heroes and turbulent terrorists, often within the same communities. Yet if guerrillas could not win the war for the Confederacy, they could play a crucial role in winning the peace by eroding and overturning the revolutionary reforms of Reconstruction by targeted acts of arson and assassination.

Nathan Bedford Forrest earned the nickname "that devil Forrest" the hard way. He refused to surrender his cavalry regiment to Grant's army at Fort Donelson. Finding himself charging Sherman's infantry alone in the aftermath of Shiloh, Forrest refused to surrender but instead grabbed one of the blue soldiers, yanked him onto his horse, and used him as a human shield until he reached safety. Forrest killed at least one of his own officers, a Lt. Andrew Gould, fatally stabbed by the general after he shot Forrest in the hip in an altercation over the lieutenant's transfer. He bedeviled isolated Union garrisons, supply lines, and forces sent to destroy him, continually frustrating Grant and Sherman. "That devil Forrest must be hunted down and killed if it costs ten thousand lives and bankrupts the Federal Treasury," Sherman erupted as he prepared to march to the sea.[83] Forrest of course was not hunted down and slain.

If there was a hybrid guerrilla-soldier in the Civil War, it was Forrest. Historians go back and forth as to whether or not he should be classified as a guerrilla in regular uniform or a trooper who used unorthodox, guerrilla-like tactics.[84] Forrest's class-crossing background—poor yeoman and overseer turned slave trader turned planter—enabled him to bestride a twofold Confederate legacy of honorable cavalier and dastardly guerrilla.[85] Like his fellow cavalrymen Fitzhugh Lee and Wade Hampton, Forrest attempted to avoid surrender and headed west after Joseph E. Johnston's army capitulated at Durham Station, but finally gave up in Alabama in early May. He used the threat of the massacre of a defeated garrison on several occasions to intimidate isolated posts into surrender, and this take-no-prisoners threat paid bloody dividends at Fort Pillow when combined with the racial implications of the post's black defenders to Forrest's troopers. Forrest will return in the next chapter, because regardless of whether he considered himself a guerrilla, his irregular tactics and reliance of firepower and shock at close range was used by Confederate veterans to win the Reconstruction. To Klansmen and other white southerners resisting Reconstruction, Forrest was the postwar founder of a voluntary association of terrorists crusading to restore the rights of white men over former slaves. Imprisoned by their antebellum racial views, they could not accept the freedom and civil rights being exercised by former slaves.

A month after Lee's surrender, half of a unit of Texas Rangers stationed west of the Mississippi pledged to "fight the incarnate fiend, so long as we have an organized force, and a kind Providence will give us strength and power to wield a sword or aim a rifle."[86] The other half refused to cross the Mississippi in a quixotic effort to liberate the eight eastern Confederate states. Yet while a few diehard rebels fled the scene of Appomattox and Durham

Station, and an odd Confederate general or two wound up in the service of Egypt rather than surrender, most rebel veterans acknowledged that they had been beaten on the battlefield.[87] Yet if the war could be lost, the peace could also be won—perhaps by the mounted, cloak-and-dagger tactics of guerrillas and by unorthodox costumes like those donned by Lincoln and Davis or the stage clothing of John Wilkes Booth—and so the Ku Klux Klan was born on horseback. And its members were dressed to look like demons.

CHAPTER 6

The God of This World

In 1865 as the Civil War ground to its close, Satan arrived at a masquerade ball in Washington, DC. He described his attire in a letter to his wife. He wore black shorts with red tights underneath. Along with a red velvet cape, he had "two upright feathers, for horns." His black shoes had "pointed toes upturned." A handsome belt and a black silk mask completed his costume.[1] His real name was George Armstrong Custer, and for fun he had disguised himself as the prince of darkness. Barely in his mid-twenties and already a brigadier general, Custer paraded as the chief rebel in Christian tradition. For Custer, his mounted soldiers, and the rebel cavalry and guerrillas they chased, playfulness with clothing was nothing new. During the war, some irregulars wore feathered hats and capes, while Custer distinguished his men from others with flamboyant custom uniforms.[2] After the war, Custer brought his brash style against Native Americans in the West. It ended for him as it supposedly had for the biblical Lucifer: Custer fell.

Custer made himself appear like the devil as part of a burlesque gag. Following the traditions of European folklore that visualized Satan with these cues, Custer performed evil for play. He wanted to draw attention to himself, to shock his friends, and to make them laugh. He intended no part of his performance to be considered real or genuine. During Reconstruction, however, a group of southern white men dressed in similar fashion but with dramatically different hopes. What Custer did for comedy, these white men did for horror. Clothing became key to performances of evil as white men in the South dressed as demons to intimidate and harm newly free men, women, and children, along with any whites who would help them. The Ku Klux Klan built upon and redirected the place of devils in American society, politics, racism, and relationships among the federal government, state governments, and local communities. In so doing, it became an enduring symbol of the failures of Reconstruction.

Beginning around 1868, a set of southern whites decided to put evil into operation by dressing and performing as devils. In various towns and hamlets throughout the South, white men purposefully mimicked demons in order to terrorize African Americans and their white supporters. Collectively known as the Ku Klux Klan, these whites enacted evil to dissuade blacks from voting, whites from teaching them, and anyone interested in opposing white supremacy from doing so. The Ku Klux Klan became the physical manifestation of evil in the United States, the despicable fruit of slavery and Confederate failure. When Republicans in the federal government set out to destroy the Klan, their demonic culture became a pivotal political, legal, and jurisdictional issue to create some of the most expansive laws in American history.

The white men who wore clothing to look like demons became precisely what some African Americans called them before it: devils in human form. By donning the attire of demons, southern white men expanded the role of evil. They endeavored to weaponize hell as a tactic to subvert the emancipatory gains of the Civil War. While they succeeded in some ways, their masquerade also gave the federal government leeway to expand once again after the Civil War to attack devils in their midst.

Personifying and performing the demonic, the Klan took to extremes several important trends of Reconstruction. The devil, hell, and Satan played vital roles in perpetuating the schisms and conflicts wrought by slavery and the Civil War. During the late 1860s and the beginning of the 1870s, many Americans tied their political and social agendas to conceptions of evil. Notions of the demonic, in particular, often fueled various forms of antagonism. Sometimes racial, sometimes political, sometimes sectional, demonization kept the nation fractured and unable to move toward reconciliation and justice. During the first few years of Reconstruction, Americans in the North and the South aired their anger and hurts from the wartime years by accentuating the evils that happened during the war and by using them to further their aims for the postwar period. Evil became so widespread that it stretched to encompass the most memorable clothing of the postwar era. As one writer put it at the end of Reconstruction, the devil had become "the god of this world."

Continuing Antagonisms

There was no absolute end to the Civil War. Often historians date it to April 9, 1865, when Robert E. Lee surrendered his remaining troops to the Union forces led by Ulysses S. Grant. Others push the end to the summer as Confederates farther to the South and toward Texas ended their militancy. Still others maintain that the Civil War truly never ended. One date for the conclusion could be April 14, 1865, Good Friday, when John Wilkes Booth shot Abraham Lincoln. Since Lincoln's election precipitated the first wave of secession, his death seemed to end an era. For many in the North, Lincoln's demise heralded a new moment to determine what the war meant and how to move forward.

On the weekend of Easter, Christian ministers throughout the North used the occasion to discuss their feelings on the war and the future for Reconstruction. The moment became an opportunity for some Americans to reflect on the place of evil among them. In Brooklyn at the First Presbyterian Church, Charles Robinson discussed the many faces of evil during the war. First, he connected the devil to the assassination. "With a recoil of feeling so violent that it wearies my will, and shocks my very being, with uttermost loathing for an offence so abominable; seeing in it that keen, fine relish of depravity that marks it not only as devilish, but one of the master works of the prince of devils, I stand simply appalled—wondering, with unspeakable wonder, how it can be accepted by any creature wearing the form of civilized humanity!"

In his confusion and anger, Robinson emphasized differences between northerners and southerners. For him, the only way to comprehend and explain the distinction between the two groups was with biblical history. "Talk to me no more of the same race, educated at the same colleges, born of the same blood," Robinson fumed. "Satan was of the same race as Gabriel, and educated at the same celestial school of love and grace," he continued and then borrowed words from the Gospel of Luke and connected them to guerrilla warfare to accentuate the differences between Unionists and Confederates: "But one became a rebel, and between them ever thereafter was 'a great gulf fixed.' He cannot be brother of mine, he belongs to no race of mine, who, in the foul cause of human bondage, fights with a rural massacre, makes war with midnight arson."

The assassination exposed other evils that sprang from slavery and the war. He opined that southern whites had become wicked through "the essential iniquity and barbarism there is in any system of human oppression." The devil's fruits included wartime prisons: "And these murders in the prisons are, every one of them, just so much the more diabolical, as starvation slowly is more horrible than the quicker death of the bullet." Even southern women became corrupted. After hearing reports that southern women cheered when they heard of Lincoln's death, Robinson declared: "Hence it is that a deed combining so much of execrable meanness with so much of hellish cruelty, finds women unsexed enough to applaud it! Home on the diabolical system it represents."

Robinson ended his sermon with political punch. The only appropriate action for the government would be to treat Confederates as devils. Robinson saw in the biblical past a political program for the present. "When there was rebellion in heaven, the rebels were punished. God sent the fallen angels to hell. We are not to find fault with that kind of administration."[3]

Although rarely as sustained or full of vitriol as Robinson, many other Americans continued to regard and treat one another as devils in human form or servants of Satan. Two days after the last guards and medical staff at Andersonville abandoned the prison in early May 1865, Union officers arrested its leader, Henry Wirz, in front of his wife and daughters.[4] Gen. Lew Wallace, who later wrote *Ben-Hur* (the only novel of the century to rival *Uncle Tom's Cabin* in sales) presided over Wirz's trial in the US Capitol, and he was hardly an unbiased judge. Wallace described Wirz's appearance as diabolical, making the officer an obvious choice for his "awful duty" at Andersonville.[5]

Northern public opinion was primed to demonize Wirz as well, as evident by the title of the 1865 book *The Demon of Andersonville*. The title page featured a color illustration of a malevolent-looking Wirz in an oval frame. A winged demon sporting long nails, horns, and a leering grin gripped the frame. Bearing a similarity to the Civil War envelopes where the devil stood behind the seals of Confederate states, this one had the devil somewhat hiding behind Wirz while at the same time holding him up on display for the nation to see.[6]

Resigned to his fate during the trial, Wirz nevertheless refused to forgive the witnesses "who have sworn to these enormous falsehoods." He repaid evil

for evil, confessing that "I have cursed them often, & my curse will I leave
them as my legacy."[7] Despite his withered left shoulder and useless right arm
that seemed to indicate that he could not have been guilty of the alleged personal shooting and beating of prisoners, Wirz was found guilty on all counts
and sentenced to hang. The 12,200 Union soldiers buried at Andersonville
testified to the hellish conditions there, although Wirz was hardly the sole
responsible "demon."[8]

Almost weekly, Americans put the demonic and hellish to work to comprehend their moment. Jefferson Davis fled the Confederate capital in early
April when it appeared that Lee would surrender. Now a refugee, he was
captured on May 10, 1865, wearing his wife's overcoat. Varina Davis recalled the Union cavalry found them before dawn, and "charged our camp
yelling like demons." She "threw over his head a little black shawl which
was around my own shoulders" as he ran off in the hope that "he would not
be recognized."[9]

Davis in disguise became a joke in the North, a way to symbolize the overall defeat and emasculation of the Confederacy. The rumor ran rampant
that Davis had dressed entirely as a woman. Newspaper and magazines
printed depictions of him this way, and several lithographers presented him
in a full dress.[10]

One of the images combined Davis's supposed feminine disguise with
hellish connections in order to both feminize and demonize him. Oscar Harpel, a German immigrant and typographer, created and distributed a lithograph titled *A Proper Family Re-Union*. It featured Benedict Arnold on the
left, Satan in the center, and Jefferson Davis on the right dressed in a woman's
gown. While Arnold welcomed Davis to reside with "thy father," the devil
expressed how "proud" he felt of his "American sons." Davis acknowledged
that he has finally found his "home."

Together, the three stirred a cauldron of "Treason Toddy." The devil
dropped miniature black humans into the boiling liquid, and underneath it
there were skulls and snakes. One of the skulls bore the label "Libby" and
the other "Andersonville." Davis's gown, in fact, was marked by several images of snakes.

Harpel's title signaled that this print was far more than mockery of Davis
or anger toward traitors and prisons. The image had a political point: supporters of the Union should think long and hard about what "Re-Union" would

mean. Alive, Lincoln had hoped for a quick reuniting of the rebellious states in order to discourage militarism. Others, especially in Congress and after Lincoln's assassination, felt less inclined toward an easy reunion. The only "proper" one for the moment was Davis in hell with the two grand traitors: Benedict Arnold and Satan himself.[11]

Near the end of 1865, one minister in Massachusetts warned his congregation that the war had been won, "yet not finished. Our great curse and crime and shame has been dragged in chains, the old Serpent still, foaming in the rage of baffled ambition, and writhing with the torture of humiliating pride,— dragged to the mouth of hell, but not yet cast into those bottomless depths, whence is no resurrection. Not yet cast, but will be."[12] For some Republicans in Congress, this pastor's words seemed to epitomize their approach to legislating the reconstructing South.

During the first years of Reconstruction, Republicans made the rhetoric of evil a regular feature of their politics. They referred to their Democratic opponents as the party of "Dixie, Davis, and the devil."[13] Perhaps no one deployed the language of evil more often or more effectively than Thaddeus Stevens. A longtime Republican Congressman from Pennsylvania, he championed loyalty and hated disloyalty. This led him to call for the inclusion of African Americans as full members of society and to banish southern whites to second-class citizenship. Stevens believed simply that treason should be punished and fidelity rewarded. For this reason, southern whites should be stripped of their possessions and African Americans should be given repayment for their years of stolen labor.

Stevens repeatedly threatened his opponents with hell. When Andrew Johnson ascended to the presidency after Lincoln's death and echoed a common Democratic line that the nation was a "white man's Government," Stevens exploded by comparing these words to the majority decision in the *Dred Scott* case of 1857 where Supreme Court Chief Justice Roger Taney maintained that African Americans were not citizens of the nation and therefore whites did not need to respect any of their rights. "Sir, this doctrine of a white man's Government is as atrocious as the infamous sentiment that damned the late Chief Justice to everlasting fame," Stevens lectured Johnson, "and, I fear, to everlasting flame."[14]

Once again, political and legal positions seemed to dictate eternal rewards. Just as Stonewall Jackson had assumed that John Brown would be cast into hell because of his attack on Harpers Ferry before the Civil War, and just as Unionists found in Milton's interpretation of Satan's rebellion against God a theological approach to war against secession, Stevens now maintained that the political and legal opinions of the president and the chief justice of the Supreme Court came from hell and meant that the two would eventually reside there.

In 1867 when Stevens justified many of his political points before Congress, he explained that he based his concept of the law upon notions of heaven and hell. "The same law which condemns or acquits an African should condemn or acquit a white man. The same law which gives a verdict in a white man's favor on the same state of facts. Such is the law of God and such ought to be the law of man." At the same time, he asked those who would oppose equality before the law a rhetorical question about their ultimate future: "I would say to those above referred to, who admit the justice of human equality before the law but doubt its policy: 'Do you believe in hell?'"[15]

Stevens made it clear that his mixing of religion and politics came from genuine faith. After being accused of lacking true Christianity because of his strong support for civil rights for African Americans, he responded, "I have always been a firm believer in the Bible. He is a fool who disbelieves the existence of God as you say is charged on me. I also believe in the existence of a hell for the especial benefit of this slander. . . . I make no pretension to piety (the more pity), but I would not be thought to be an infidel. I was raised a Baptist and adhere to their belief."[16]

There were some Unionists who opposed this approach. Near the end of 1867, John C. Underwood of Virginia wrote to Horace Greeley begging him to tone down his denunciations of southerners. Underwood was one of a small number of southern whites who had actively opposed the Confederacy and supported rights for African Americans. He hoped to build a "Union party" in Virginia and wrote to Greeley, "Indeed God only knows the hardship of a live union [party] in this den of rebellious" men and women. He acknowledged that around him remained "infuriate demons are these even in form + shape," but hoped for himself, Greeley, and other Unionists, "May we learn to return good for their evil, blessings for their cursing + try to imitate the glorious example of our divine Lord + Saviour."[17]

Throughout the South, whites responded to the events in a variety of ways. A few expressed the belief that the devil, rather than God, reigned in the land.

One Confederate colonel wrote, "I shall never believe that it was Providence but the devil that defeated us." Presbyterian minister and Confederate chaplain Robert Lewis Dabney agreed when he concluded, "the devil is apparently triumphant." Another southern white asserted that God was omnipotent, but "it was Satan that ruled the hour."[18]

They sometimes accused northerners of being devils. When Sidney Andrews toured the South, he recorded hearing one bitter southern white remark, "Hell's the place for Yankees, and I want 'em all to go thar as soon's possible, and take the niggers 'long with 'em..'"[19] One decade later when some northern and southern whites discussed the possibility of reuniting their church denominations, a writer for the *Atlanta Constitution* denounced it. He called northern Christians "imposters who brought the country to grief, and who were most appropriately named the 'hell-hounds of Zion.'"[20]

Some southern whites blamed abolitionists and northern whites for using the heated language of hell and called upon northern whites to cease. In late April 1865, a Presbyterian writer to the *Free Christian Commonwealth* of Kentucky opined that abolitionists brought on the war. It was they who "denounced the Federal Constitution as a 'covenant with hell and an agreement with death' because it recognized and protected slave property." There was more, he complained. "A preacher, closing a sermon on the war, and speaking of the Secessionists, exclaimed, 'Kill the devils! kill the devils!'"[21]

African Americans who experienced the highs and lows of Reconstruction—the new opportunities and laws and the violent terrorism from southern whites—had a difficult time making sense of the moment. Henry Turner wrote in the summer of 1866 about one of his colleagues who "had been severely cut and beaten nearly to death. Four white citizens broke into his room at midnight, and beat and stabbed him till he appeared, when I met him, like a lump of curdled blood. . . . The miscreants told him that no d—d negro schools should be taught there, nor should any negro preacher remain there." Turner wondered, "Where is our civilization? Is this Christendom, or is it hell? Pray for us."[22]

Similarly in 1866, at the Illinois State Convention of Colored Men, one speaker connected slavery to any form of oppression and rendered both demonic. "In the midst of its empire," he intoned, slavery "set up its idol Moloch, and made reverence for it the price of admission to the blood-stained privileges of its realm." Following the demon of war, Moloch, slaveholders created tools of exploitation: "The lash was its stern ukase—the manacle the sacred symbol of its power, while incest and adultery were at once among its means of commerce and the hand-maidens of its pleasures." Ultimately, this speaker denounced this society as one beholden to demons: "The deity of its worship was the demon of injustice and oppression, while it exultingly trampled beneath its sacrilegious feet the mandates of the God of the universe!"[23]

Altogether, the initial months and the first year after the war seemed similar to those preceding it. Northern and southern whites attacked one another as friends of the devil, while African Americans depicted violence against them and exploitation of them as spawns of satanic structures. What was most assuredly different after the war was what a collection of white men did: they operationalized the demonic as no other Americans had by dressing up as devils, claiming to be them, and seeking to use terror to achieve their political, economic, social, and racial ends. Rather than accuse others of evil, they became devils for one end: white supremacy.

The Ku Klux Klan

In the late 1860s in various southern locales, white men turned to secretive intimidation against black Americans and their allies. The effort was to curtail African American political gains, especially manhood suffrage, to hold back black economic and social development, and to demolish any attempts at genuine interracial coordination. Although there were many different white men who participated and created distinct groups, the name Ku Klux Klan became a catchall for these behaviors. These individuals and groups remade white supremacy into a weapon for the post-emancipation nation. They did so in secret; and they did so with various claims to the demonic. Their approach to devils and hell came from European folklore and it appeared that these whites hoped to prey upon African Americans' supposed beliefs in supernatural invasions of this world. Their plans hinged upon at least some African Americans believing that the agents of hell had come to the land of the living. When the federal government endeavored to destroy Klan organizations, they used the devilish cultures of these white men to expose them. President Ulysses S. Grant made it clear that when the federal government determined to strike against the Klan, the goal was "to correct these evils."[24]

Although the Klan endeavored to act in secret, their behaviors became widely known through intensive newspaper coverage and then a federal investigation. After the presidential election of 1868, which highlighted the importance of black male voters who almost unanimously cast their lots for the Republican candidate, Ulysses S. Grant, violence against African Americans and whites who labored to help them grew in number and ferocity. As the federal government passed legislation trying to compel states to protect the rights of their people and as southern states and counties did little to bring law, order, or justice for African Americans, the federal government decided to intervene. Congress commissioned an inquiry into violence in the South. It sent representatives into southern states to convene hearings, and the evidentiary results were massive.[25]

The investigation uncovered demons running amok in southern society. Many witnesses mentioned that the Klansmen claimed to be Confederate soldiers returned from hell. A judge from Alabama, for instance, reported the story of a black man named James Webb. "They took him out and told him that they were the spirits of confederate soldiers just from hell." Their goal was simple: "to run every damned radical out of the country, and for him to give notice to the negroes that they must not too many work for one man; that they must scatter out so that all could have some—that is, some of their labor. They hit him two or three licks, but only one that hurt."[26] Other Klansmen offered more particularity. One black Alabaman reported that those who visited him "said they came from hell; that they died at Shiloh" and fought at "Bull Run."[27]

At least one Klansmen geographically rendered himself in "Hell Town, Ga." when he wrote to a black legislator in Alabama. Demanding that the man withdraw from political life, the author explained "we swear by the powers of both *Light and Darkness* that no other Negro shall ever enter the Legislative Halls of the South." In this case, the author did not claim to be from hell but that hell was now a place, a town no less, within the state of Georgia.[28]

For some of these white men, hell was both an origin and a destination. When Klansmen attacked Mary Elder in Alabama, dragging her almost without clothing into the woods, "They asked where the nearest grave-yard was; and that they said they would have us in hell before next night."[29] When more than twenty men attacked John Gill for failing to give his horse to a white man earlier, the night terrorists told him that "they wanted him for a charger to ride to hell." According to Gill, these men "said they had couriers come from hell nine times a day, and they wanted that horse."[30] Another black man reported that when asked from where they came, one group of Klansmen explained, 'Hell! and we must be back before day.'"[31]

On another occasion, an Alabama man terrorized by the Klan had a theological discussion related to these hell claims. When Klan members came to his door, they maintained "we are just from hell" and then demanded that he "get up and open the door." The black man responded, "No one who goes to hell ever returns back again." The terrorist shouted back, "we have come out of the moon to-night, and are come to kill you." At this point, the debate ended. The men tried to burst through the door, but the man fled.[32]

These claims to come from hell or to return to hell gave the Klan an ethereal sense, of being both here and there, close and distant. This allowed the white men to perform heinous acts and be members of the community. Connections to hell played into a point that historian Elaine Parsons has recognized. In her examination of the Klan, she asserted that these white men constructed identities defined by "being from elsewhere." By mixing and matching a variety of cultural expressions, Klansmen refused easy categorizing and thus were difficult to comprehend, let alone thwart. Other than their threatening militarism toward African Americans and their allies, Klan members presented themselves as material and ethereal, white and hidden, human and demonic.[33]

Klansmen not only claimed to be devils, they dressed the part. When they did, they borrowed from European folklore that presented the demonic as horned, tailed, and somehow animalistic.[34] One black Alabaman explained, "Some of them had something like horns. They were not all disguised alike. One had one kind of thing, and another had another thing. Some had on something that stuck away out in front like a sheep's head, and some stuck away up high."[35] John Gill mentioned that, "Some of them had horns about as long as my finger, and made black." From Atlanta, Georgia, E. H. Chambers told the members that those who visited him, "Some had great horns sticking up on the side of their faces."[36]

Clothing became central in the fight for white supremacy and the struggle against it. White terror in the form of the Klan followed a time when clothing and apparel changes were ripe with military and political meaning. The Civil War wrought a change in clothing for many Americans. Men who had previously dressed as farmers, laborers, bankers, or riverboat workers now wore uniforms that classified them into particular types of soldiers and ranks. No longer defining profession, clothing now indicated military position. Pants, coats, buttons, and medals became primary identifiers of identity and status.[37]

On occasion, clothing became a lightning rod for political commentary. In 1861 when President-elect Abraham Lincoln arrived in his new capital in the dead of night, he did so in disguise. Correspondent Joseph Howard Jr. of the *New York Times* noted that Lincoln, fearful of an assassination attempt, arrived in Washington by train wearing "a Scotch plaid cap and a very long military cloak, so that he was entirely unrecognizable."[38] Published in a Republican newspaper, this damaging account inspired rebel artist Adalbert Volck to emphasize Lincoln's unfitness to office and moral cowardice in the 1863 cartoon *Passage Through Baltimore*. In it, Lincoln cowered behind a railroad car door, his face showing fear while his gown showed weakness.[39] Similarly, when the war ended, Confederate President Jefferson Davis suffered similar public shame when rumors flew of his dressing in women's clothing in order to escape capture. For some southern whites of the postwar era, clothing became means of distraction and identification. First, their garb hid their individual identities. Second, it paired them one by one and collectively with powerful forces of evil. Men who had lost at war in human uniforms now hoped to win through terrorism in demonic dress.

Some Klansmen joined animalistic behavior to their demonic regalia. In Mississippi, one teacher reported that the men who visited him had horns on their heads and "shook their heads and horns at me, and acted like cows." He described some of the horns as almost two feet in length. They were "curled horns like sheep's horns." The horns themselves associated these white men with Satan and with various animals.[40]

Along with the disguises and behaviors, some white terrorists constructed physical contraptions to prove they were spirits from hell. They did this through water. On one occasion, Klansmen in Alabama visited one man and "said they were just from hell; that they had had no water for three or four days at a time." The witness then tried to explain that "they had some false thing put in around them somewhere, so they would keep drinking, to make us blacks believe that they hadn't any since they come from the devil." The device did not seem to impact this informant, who told the committee that he knew "better than that."[41]

This collective testimony suggests that while white men hoped to cast fear into the hearts of southern blacks with claims to affiliation with hell and the demonic, African Americans paid little heed to the supposedly supernatural connections of the terrorists. Black men and women discussed feeling terrified by the physical threats, the shouting, the pounding on their doors, the grabbing of their bodies, and the shots fired at them. When testifying, however, African Americans expressed no fear that these men actually came from hell or were real demons. They saw through the disguises and recognized humans in demonic form.

When narrating the events, African American and white witnesses rarely expressed fears of the outfits. Sarah Allen, a white teacher in Mississippi, felt threatened by Klansmen who wore long robes and "had long horns on their head." Although they did not attack her, she "concluded that they were savages—demons."[42] When most others described the elaborate costumes and horns of the terrorists, the witnesses often did so in ways that mocked the white men. Witnesses routinely likened the clothes to "lady's dress." Other times, they tried to describe the various pieces that made up the costumes.

At times, tales of the demonic took bizarre turns and likely to become silly local legends rather than accounts of violence. This seemed the case in tales of a "Ku-Klux baby." According to one story told to congressional representatives, a southern woman gave birth "to a child that was a perfect representation and fac-simile of a disguised Ku-Klux." Describing the alleged baby, one individual reported, "At two points near the temples were two gristly horns . . . projecting from the forehead." Along with horns, the "eyes and mouth were of scarlet red." According to hearsay, local whites demanded to see the baby even though it was stillborn. This informant maintained that the look of this child corresponded to their Klan disguises.[43]

The testimony indicated that southern white men and women put significant work into their demonic designs. They sewed gowns together (or borrowed them from their wives); they constructed elaborate horns that could be visible at night; they painted feed sacks red and black. Their disguises showed planning and premeditation. They were not simply acting in a hellish manner. They conscientiously and purposefully brought demons into their world— onto their bodies—to oppose rights and uplift for African Americans.

Klansmen and their supporters even reworked attempts to expose them into demonic presentations of themselves. After a federal general captured two white men acting suspiciously near Huntsville, Alabama, he confiscated their weapons and disguises. They escaped incarceration, but the general determined to document his efforts to stop unlawful behavior. Two other men put on the disguises and a local photographer took a picture of them. The image became nationally known in December 1868 when *Harper's Weekly* featured a drawing of it.

Nothing in the original photograph suggested devils or demons. The feed sacks the men wore over their heads, for instance, lacked horns. Yet as Americans modified the original image they brought new meanings to bear. The artists for *Harper's Weekly* drew a much longer firearm in the hand of one of them to emphasize their militarism.

In another instance, a photographer in the South manipulated negatives to create a haunting image that other southerners used to threaten African Americans and their white allies. This rendering reversed the light and dark so the men now looked like ghosts with ominous headdresses. When an anti-black southerner mailed a copy of this photograph to African Americans, he made the link to evil explicit. "Hell is gasping," the author threatened, "and the Eyes of the Grand Cyclops are upon you."[44]

African Americans discussed the Klan, its actions, and its supporters in terms of the devil. While they did not fear the literal manifestation of devils who would drag them to hell, these black writers and speakers nonetheless used the rhetoric of evil to make their points in a bid for protection and social justice. They tried to leverage the evil performances into calls for governmental action against white supremacists. James Harris, a member of the North Carolina legislature, supported federal action to intervene and did so by calling the Democratic Party "the machinery of the devil."[45] He mocked the idea that justice could come from southern juries. "How could you expect to get a conviction, how could you expect to get justice," he asked other elected officials. He took the concept of evil used by southern whites and turned it into a rationale to distrust them. "I tell you, gentlemen you might as well arraign the devil before his angels—you might as well descend to the lower regions and arraign Lucifer the prince of devils and swear his imps on the jury with more prospect of obtaining justice then to swear those bloodthirsty murderous and unprincipled, damnable imps of hell on a jury to try their compeers in assassination, bloodshed, and destruction."[46]

Northern representations of the Klan linked it to previous examples of southern white militant treason and the demonic. Just a few weeks before the election of 1868, *Harper's Weekly* printed Thomas Nast's drawing titled *The Democratic Hell-Broth*. Similar to the print of Jefferson Davis in hell, this one borrowed Shakespeare's "Song of the Witches" from *Macbeth* as its inspiration. It featured the members of the Democratic presidential ticket, Horatio Seymour and Francis Blair, along with South Carolinian Wade Hampton. Nast made Seymour appear the most demonic, with hair fashioned to look like horns, and a serpent crawling up his leg. The accompanying poem by W. A. Croffut connected various evils: copperheads, Robert E. Lee, planters, Fort Pillow, John Wilkes Booth, and Nathan Bedford Forrest, and culminated with Seymour stirring the brew "with a weird and hissing sound."[47]

Historians have brilliantly analyzed the cultural and social meanings of these various white supremacist disguises. The demonic associations also had important political, governmental, and ultimately legislative import. Congressmen investigating Klan activities needed to prove conspiracies that crossed county and state borders. Only by showing that southern locales and states could not adequately respond to the violence and terrorism could Republicans justify federal intervention. This was the primary reason legislators keyed in on the disguises of the Klansmen.

The legislators questioning the witnesses routinely asked about the connections to the demonic. Congressmen asked about the clothing and other physical accessories of the terrorists. In Georgia, they inquired, "Did they have anything on their heads?"[48] Demonic descriptions of the terrorists were so common that Congressional questioners often asked witnesses, "Any horns or such ornaments on their hats?"[49] On another occasion, although the informant made no reference to demonic behavior or trends, the legislator inquired, "Were there any horns on their heads?" Disappointingly, this man responded, "No, sir."[50]

The Klan hearings produced fascinating material. Representatives from the federal government went to everyday men and women to hear their experiences. They produced thousands of pages of materials that chronicled widespread and massive terrorism. These investigations also showcased how potent the demonic had become in American society. Throughout the South, from small towns to large cities, white men took the time to fashion outfits to mimic devils. They professed to be spirits returned not from heaven, but from hell. They created an entire white supremacist culture premised upon behaving like demons. And what they used as a scare tactic became a legislative opportunity for their enemies.

The Klan hearings gave Republicans the ammunition to pass a series of Enforcement Acts. On paper, these laws allowed for widespread governmental intervention when voting and citizenship rights were violated within counties and states. In reality, however, the federal government failed to put teeth into the legislation. Although hundreds of white men and women were implicated in Klan activities, very few were convicted or spent considerable time in prison. The government spent thousands of dollars and hours to identify evil, but when push came to shove, it did little tangibly to exorcise it. Unlike Unionist responses to secession, where the supposed inspiration of Satan led to a massive war, Republican attacks upon white supremacist devilry lacked potency. The evil of governmental separation far outweighed the hellishness of racial terror.[51]

But There Was No Peace

The years after the Klan hearings witnessed Americans of various stripes continuing to deploy notions of hell to understand the postwar environment. As the years passed, however, northern whites turned to these approaches with less frequency. Mostly African Americans continued to accuse southern whites of being in league with the devil. Some northern and southern whites began advocating sectional reconciliation by blaming the devil, rather than themselves, for the earlier discord. In these ways, the postwar years witnessed a racial bifurcation in considerations of evil among Americans. Northern and southern whites put the devil to work as part of their reconciliatory culture, while African Americans continued to rely on these conceptions to draw attention to racism and discrimination.

In the months after the Klan trials and the passage of the Enforcement Acts, several noteworthy Americans continued to liken white violence against African Americans to the demonic. During the 1872 presidential election, when Horace Greeley encouraged northern whites to "clasp hands over the bloody chasm," Thomas Nast mocked him with a political print. In it, Greeley stood along a fence at Andersonville Prison. Within the prison, rows and rows of gravestones marked the landscape. Women, men, and children mourned for their lost loved ones. At the entrance to the prison, beneath a skull and crossbones, Nast created an inscription that modified a line from Dante's *Inferno* by putting it in the past tense: those who entered hell, or in this case Andersonville, "left hope behind."[52]

In Alabama, Judge Richard Busteed presided over several cases in this regard. Although Busteed had been a Democrat before the war and then opposed Ulysses S. Grant and black manhood suffrage during his years as a Republican, he nonetheless refused to allow white Alabamians to let murderers escape justice. In one case that involved the slaying of a white woman and black man for their romantic and sexual relationship, Busteed mocked the weak alibis of the defense. He instructed the jury to remember, "Satan himself was an archangel before he became the devil." Busteed then used the occasion to maintain that events like this proved the need for the Enforcement Acts. He ended his instructions to the jury with a threat: "People who will not, when they may, consign to just punishment those outlaws, deserve to suffer all the horrors their existence produces, and by the poetry of justice the juror who sympathizes with them or their crimes, ought to be their very next victim."[53]

When James Melville Beard, a northern author, attempted to capitalize on the Klan's notoriety in his book *K.K.K. Sketches, Humorous and Didactic*, he linked their disguises to their designs. He exclaimed that for their "Satanic designs" they "prescribed the regalia and mask." Their clothing showed so much "expansiveness of detail that" it "must have affected the cotton-market." To Beard, the ultimate goal of these white men was "rendering the State a revolutionary hell."[54]

In the years after the Klan trials, however, national reunion became more pronounced than antagonism. Together, some northern and southern whites came to agree upon the actions of the devil in their domain. While some continued to discuss slavery as hell on earth or war as all hell, an increasing number of whites labeled societal discord—not slavery or secession—the ultimate design of the devil.[55]

After the yellow fever epidemic of 1878 ravaged many southern communities and northerners responded with compassion and care, one southern doctor described the past as dead and buried: "The hideous phantoms and weird ghosts of past differences and animosities are of the buried past; the demon of discord and contention among the dead and the dying, with one hand upon the dead husband and the other soothing the gurgling death-rattles of a dying wife, *the North and the South have shaken hands over the bloody chasm;* and may the God of heaven and earth decree that it be closed forever!"[56]

A judge in Mississippi, J. F. Simmons, made a similar point in a poem he published in 1881 titled "The Welded Link." He described the years before the Civil War as a time when Satan found a home in the United States:

And here the serpent came to rend the ties
Approved of Him who rules the earth and skies,
Sowed seeds of discord o'er the smiling land,
Till brother's blood was shed by brother's hand."[57]

While these southern and northern whites endeavored to reach across the bloody chasm by repositioning the devil, African Americans and their white allies cried out against reconciliation without justice. Without doubt, African Americans and whites who supported rights, freedom, and protection for them continued to regard violations of civil rights as demonic. One black man in Mississippi wrote to a governor revealing the bitter hatred felt by many African Americans: "The wrath of God is now let loose upon the South for all their wickedness . . . , the southern people are whiskey-drinking, Tobacco-chewing, constant-spitting, Negro-hating, Negro-killing, red-handed, ignorant, uneducated, uncivilized set of devils."[58]

In 1880, Norvel Blair published an autobiographical pamphlet where he urged in his final prayer: "Lord, their is a great army against us, and we are in sore distress: yea, we are compassed about by legions of devils, and, from the depths of despair, we cry, Help! Lord, help, yes, help us Lord, and we will sing praises unto Thee as long as Thou permittest our breath to last. We are in the great, dark valley, but come."[59] White missionary Martha Schofield advocated more than prayers; she called for militant action: "I wish every colored man in the South had gone to the polls with knives in his belt and pistols in his boots. Yes, I <u>do</u>—I would sooner <u>die</u> than kill—but if liberty is worth having, it is worth dying for—and such miserable white demons ought to die—and will."[60]

Unlike what had happened in earlier years, voices like Schofield's and others were unable to mobilize the government or its citizens. In the middle of the 1870s and then for the rest of the century, African Americans had fewer and fewer white allies in the struggles for justice. By the end of the century, slavery and the Civil War seemed relics of the past, not immediate evils that had to be annihilated. As bondage and disunion seemed more distant, hell itself seemed further away. The devil did not die, but the association of hell and its denizens to these topics went cold.

Hollis Read had seen much of the world, more of it than most Americans including Abraham Lincoln and Jefferson Davis combined. He was born in Vermont, studied in New Jersey, worked in Connecticut, and then traveled to India as a missionary. He merged his globetrotting with his religious convictions. Read believed that he could trace the actions of God in human history, and his forty years before and during the Civil War led him to one conclusion: the God of heaven did not rule on earth. Instead, there was another deity whose power was so "universal and controlling . . . that he is called the 'God of this world.'"[61]

At the end of the Civil War, he published a lengthy book about the "God of this world." He subtitled it "The Footprints of Satan." While Read's earlier works emphasized the power and providence of God, this one focused upon "how a great opposing Power, by usurpation the god of this world, has been allowed to try his hand at the management of the affairs of this lower world." Read sought to accomplish what so many other Americans had: to locate the domains of the devil in American society. He found that Satan saturated the nation. According to Read, the present moment was unique in human history because of Satan's role: "Never before did he come down with so 'great wrath'—never were his acts more determined and daring."[62]

The book went through multiple editions and Read added to it on several occasions in the late 1860s and 1870s. He found Satan at work just about everywhere. He located the devil in alcohol abuse, the theater, the Catholic Church, gambling, new religions, disease, pestilence, political corruption, disruptions of monogamous marriage, and many other aspects of modern life. Of special merit, or rather detriment, Read identified this aspect of life above others: "WAR."[63]

Read despised war for one particular reason. It wasted money. The "*expense* of war" unnerved him. "Our Indian wars," he lamented, could have been avoided if the money spent for violence had instead been used for education.

No war was worse than "the late CIVIL WAR IN AMERICA." Making war cost money; restoring the land cost money; the lack of agricultural production during the war meant a lack of money; and no one should ignore "the tens of millions, if not the hundreds of millions, gone and going in aid of freedmen—an indirect tax on account of the war."[64] Unlike African Americans and abolitionists before the war who saw in slavery a satanic structure or Unionists during the four years of fighting who tied secession to the machinations of Satan, Read now created a Christian pacifism that emphasized the material wastes of war.

When it came to the postwar era, in particular issues of racial violence, Read employed a telling tactic. He attacked violence against African Americans as another form of the diabolical in the nation. He included two cases, one from Kansas and another from Texas, of belligerent whites attacking peaceful African Americans. According to Read, these episodes provided evidence of "the state of society generally," which he understood to be under the dominion of the devil.[65]

Read knew about racial violence and injustice. He traced it as another footprint of Satan. But when it came to selling books to particular markets, he hid it. He included these stories only in editions of the book published in Canada. Versions of *The God of This World* sold in the United States did not contain these stories. They were purposefully omitted, footprints erased so that white Americans would not have to trouble themselves with the moral problems of racial violence.

When it came to the evil and connections to race relations, American readers encountered the devil only in relationship to slavery and the war. Read's unwillingness to confront the devil's place in the nation's racial dynamics became typical. The reluctance to attack white supremacy as demonic set the stage for future generations to detach secession, the Civil War, and even postwar Klan violence from considerations of evil. In the decades after the war, the Klan would be reframed as a Christian organization while slavery and the war were sanitized so that their evil elements could be forgotten.

EPILOGUE

Jefferson Davis didn't go to hell, at least not during the Civil War or right after it, as many northern artists envisioned. Instead, he went to federal prison. After spending only two years there, he received a pardon. In the late 1870s, he determined to write a history of the Confederacy to defend it from its many detractors. The title of his two-volume *Rise and Fall of the Confederate Government* echoed Henry Wilson's *History of the Rise and Fall of the Slave Power in America*. Wilson, a senator from Maine who became vice president under Ulysses S. Grant, wrote American history as an epic and ultimately successful struggle against slavery built by the "slave power." Davis dissented. Long after the war, he still had a political ax to grind. With his first sentence, he maintained that the "object of this work" was to "show that the Southern States had rightfully the power to withdraw" from the Union. With several hundred pages of detail, Davis then walked through the war as one Union action after another in violation of the sovereignty and constitutional rights of southern states. He invoked radical evil on only a few occasions, but when he did, he attached it to the most poignant problems of the war.[1]

When trying to describe the touchstone wrongs of the war, which for Davis were federal government expansion and the destruction of slavery, he turned to religious references. Discussing the beginning of hostilities in the spring and fall of 1861, Davis wrote, "With the slow and sinuous approach of the serpent, the General Government, little by little, gained power over Kentucky."[2]

In the second volume, writing about emancipation, Davis described Lincoln's actions as destroying the harmony of an Edenic South. He described African Americans in the prewar years as happy workers who cared for their owners. "Their strong local and personal attachment secured faithful service to those to whom their service or labor was due. A strong mutual affection was the natural result of this life-long relation, a feeling best if not only understood by those who have grown from childhood under its influence. Never was there happier dependence of labor and capital on each other." But emancipation and especially the arming of African American men devastated this reality. "The tempter came, like the serpent in Eden, and decoyed them with the magic word of 'freedom.'" Davis concluded by asserting that the outcomes were akin to the expulsion from Eden. "Too many were allured by the uncomprehended and unfulfilled promises, until the highways of these wanderers were marked by corpses of infants and the aged. He put arms in their hands, and trained their humble but emotional natures to deeds of violence and bloodshed, and sent them out to devastate their benefactors."[3]

Davis's references to evil mirrored the way many Americans came to describe the war and its impact. Direct links to hell, devils, and demons seemed to diminish in the postwar years. But when Americans articulated their feelings about central aspects of the war, they continued to invoke evil. This was true even for those who opposed Davis and his Confederate government.

Ambrose Bierce stood on the opposite side from Jefferson Davis. He nonetheless also invoked the devil and hell when he remembered it. Back in the 1860s, he enlisted from Indiana and participated actively until receiving a head wound in the summer of 1864. Having fought at Shiloh and several other large battles, Bierce later expressed his understanding of the conflict in ways that resonated profoundly with other Americans. Darkness, death, and the devil became central to his conception of the war and life itself.[4]

After the war, he moved to California and became a journalist. He wrote all types of articles. Some were about politics; others involved social reform; many dealt with the trauma of war. In them, Bierce toyed with readers' expectations and imaginations. In his most famous short story of the war, "An Occurrence at Owl Creek Bridge," the fantasy of life after the war met the reality of death at the end of a rope.[5]

Bierce placed the demonic and hell into several of his short stories. He turned to evil to express powerful psychological experiences of war. In one story, "Chickamauga," a six-year-old boy, the son of a soldier who had earlier fought against Native Americans, now walked on a horrific battlefield. Some men were dead; others lay with streaks of blood across their faces. To the boy, the horror was not horror. It was hilarity. He found it to be a "merry spectacle" because he had been raised amid abuse. His father owned slaves and the desolate scene of human destruction reminded him of "his father's negroes"

who were made to "creep upon their hands and knees for his amusement."
The boy had even treated them as animals and "ridden them so, 'making
believe' they were his horses."

But then, shock overwhelmed the boy. He found that his own house was
on fire. He felt "stupefied by the power of the revelation." He saw a woman,
presumably his mother, her "white face turned upward, the hands thrown out
and clutched full of grass, the clothing deranged, the long dark hair in tan-
gles and full of clotted blood." The child felt no merriment in this. Instead,
with his little hands he made "wild, uncertain gestures." Then he "uttered a
series of inarticulate and indescribable cries—something between the chat-
tering of an ape and the gobbling of a turkey." Bierce described the sound as
"a startling, soulless, unholy sound, the language of the devil." The result was
the destruction of his own body. "The child was a deaf mute." Just as disability and physical immobility led many soldiers during the war to ruminate
on hell in their midst, this short story relied upon disability and the demonic
to comprehend what seemed to be incomprehensible about the war.[6]

The devil and hell also became central to Bierce's comedy. Beginning in
the 1880s and continuing until his death in the early twentieth century, he
created a series of comical definitions for words commonly used in the United
States. He endeavored to reveal the real meanings of the words in order to
expose the nation's and people's true nature. Although originally titled *The
Cynic's Word Book*, shortly before his death Bierce gave it the title he preferred:
The Devil's Dictionary.

Several of the words directly referenced slavery, race, the Civil War, and
sectional rivalries. "Debt," he wrote, was an "ingenious substitute for the
chain and whip of the slave-driver." For the word "Yankee," Bierce jokingly
claimed, "In the Southern States the word is unknown. (See DAMNYANK)."
To extend the joke, the word "DAMNYANK" had no listing in the dictionary.
Of "African," he noted it meant "A nigger that votes our way." Of "Negro," he
maintained: "The *pièce de résistance* in the American political problem. Representing him by the letter n, the Republicans begin to build their equation
thus: 'Let n = the white man.' This, however, appears to give an unsatisfac-
tory solution."[7] In *The Devil's Dictionary*, Satan, slavery, sectionalism, and
race became playthings, not profound political, social, or economic problems
that needed to be addressed. While Bierce could joke about slavery and race,

those who experienced enslavement, whose bodies were abused, family members sold, and dignities deprived found nothing laughable. Instead, for many African Americans who lived through the age, hell could be a symbol, a metaphor, and an analogy. Many of them refused the shift in emphasis of evil from slavery to the Civil War. In the decades after the war, many recalled their past as one of literal hell that continued to influence their approach to the United States, their lives, and existence after death. Hell stood as a perennial and continued critique of the past and present, a reminder of how bad life had been and how vilely whites could behave. As African Americans discussed the hellishness of experiences in slavery and the behaviors of whites, they called into question the unjust nation that emerged from the war, defined by racial segregation and violent terrorism.

These African Americans refused to hold nostalgic views of years gone by. With slavery now an institution of the past, hell became a historical time period in some memories. In a series of interviews in the 1930s, one former slave in Alabama remarked, "If you's want to know 'bout slavery time, it was Hell."[8] The white interviewer who spoke to Delia Garlic of Montgomery, Alabama, found her to be an anomaly. "Unlike many of the old Negroes of the South, she has no good words for slavery days or the old masters." Instead, Garlic remembered how the whipping, the taking of children from their mothers, and the feeling of being treated "lak cattle" meant that the whites owned "you soul an' body." She told her interviewers, "Dem days wuz hell."[9] One minister told Clifton Johnson, a black sociologist from Fisk University, "Yes, in them days it was hell without fires. This is one reason why I believe in a hell. I don't believe a just God is going to take no such man as that into his kingdom."[10]

The conviction continued for some that slaveholders and evil whites would never make it to heaven. According to one southern article in 1897, former slaves believed there would be "no white people in Heaven."[11] A song during the Great Depression from Louisiana rang out:

My ole mistress promised me
Before she died she would set me free. . . .
Now she's dead and gone to hell,
I hope the devil will burn her well.[12]

Perhaps the most poignant story of demonic whites and hopes for justice in hell came from Mary Armstrong. She was born in St. Louis and claimed to be 91 when interviewed in Houston, Texas in 1937. She remembered her mistress "old Polly Cleveland." To Armstrong, her owners were "the meanest two while folks what ever lived." One day, "old Polly, she was a Polly devil if there ever was one, and she whipped my little sister what was only nine months old and jes' a baby to death." Armstrong recounted how the mistress whipped and whipped her baby sister until "the blood jes' ran." The baby was killed, Armstrong fumed, "'cause she cry like all babies do." That memory lived with Mary Armstrong for her entire life, and she hoped Mr. and Mrs. Cleveland "is burnin' in torment now."[13]

Mary Armstrong followed a long line of Americans thinking that decisions made on earth that related to slavery would determine life after death. Before the war, Frederick Douglass had maintained that African Americans knew enough of Christian theology to believe that all slaveholders went to hell. Before he became "Stonewall," Thomas Jackson had wondered what the everlasting fate of John Brown would be after he was captured trying to put an end to slavery. During the war itself, men believed they experienced hell and then cheered one another as they tried to make hell on earth. Songwriters and cartoonists imagined hell with the rival presidents, Abraham Lincoln and Jefferson Davis, living there.

Eventually in the decades after the war, the wish from Abraham Lincoln's first inaugural address came true. Northern and southern whites became "friends." The "mystic chords of memory" came from the war itself, as whites from the Union and the Confederacy cheered one another. Whites accomplished this in large part by agreeing that African Americans would be, at best, second-class citizens in the nation. At worst, they would be terrorized into submission through lynching and threats of it.

The legacies of slavery and the failure of the nation to live up to the promises of the Civil War left many African Americans feeling as Mary Armstrong did: the whites involved would certainly be in hell. As these Americans waited for the real world to become a place of justice, they had to hold onto another realm where justice already existed—hell. Satan seemed present in slavery, the American Civil War, and after. Neither his footprints nor his presence have been erased or exorcised, in part because of the massive shift in considerations of evil during the war. When the continuity of the nation-state became more important than destroying the racial injustices of slavery, only one devil was defeated. When Satan became the architect of secession, many white Americans seemed to forget what African Americans and abolitionists had long insisted: the real evil was slavery and its all-too-human, white supremacist legions.

NOTES

Preface

1. C. R. Milne, "A Dream Caused by the Perusal of Mrs. H. Beecher Stowe's Popular Work Uncle Tom's Cabin" (Louisville, KY: J. C. Frost and G. W. Hall, 1853). https://www.loc.gov/item/2004665375/.

2. Bartolomé de Las Casas, *A Brief Account of the Destruction of the Indies* (New York: Echo Library, 2007), 20.

3. Quoted in Elizabeth Reis, *Damned Women: Sinners and Witches in Puritan New England* (Ithaca, NY: Cornell University Press, 1997), xvi.

4. Frances Hill, ed., *The Salem Witch Trials Reader* (Da Capo Press, 2000).

5. Thomas S. Kidd, *God of Liberty: A Religious History of the American Revolution* (New York: Basic Books, 2010), chapter 3.

6. W. Scott Poole, *Satan in America: The Devil We Know* (Lanham, MD: Rowman and Littlefield, 2009), 56.

Introduction

1. Lacon, *The Devil in America: A Dramatic Satire* (Philadelphia: J. P. Lippincott, 1860), 7, 16.

2. Lacon, *The Devil in America*, 7

3. Lacon, *The Devil in America*, 26, 39.

4. Lacon, *The Devil in America*, 121, 72, 70.

5. Lacon, *The Devil in America*, 122, 128, 139–140.

6. Lacon, *The Devil in America*, 120.

7. Elizabeth R. Varon, *Disunion! The Coming of the American Civil War, 1789–1859* (Chapel Hill: University of North Carolina Press, 2010); Jason Phillips, *Looming Civil War: How Nineteenth-Century Americans Imagined the Future* (New York: Oxford University Press, 2018).

8. George C. Rable, *God's Almost Chosen Peoples: A Religious History of the American Civil War* (Chapel Hill: University of North Carolina Press, 2015); Nicholas Guyatt, *Providence and the Invention of the United States, 1607–1876* (New York: Cambridge University Press, 2007).

9. Randall Balmer, *God in the White House: A History* (New York: HarperOne, 2008); Stephen R. Prothero, *American Jesus: How the Son of God Became a National Icon* (New York: Farrar, Straus and Giroux, 2003); *God in America*, six-part series, aired October 11, 2010, on PBS, https://www.pbs.org/godinamerica/view/.

10. Rable, *God's Almost Chosen Peoples*; Harry S. Stout, *Upon the Altar of the Nation: A Moral History of the Civil War* (New York: Viking, 2007); Drew Gilpin Faust, *This Republic of Suffering* (New York: Alfred A. Knopf, 2008).

11. W. Scott Poole, *Satan in America: The Devil We Know* (Lanham, MD: Rowman and Littlefield, 2009); Kathryn Gin Lum, *Damned Nation: Hell in American from the Revolution to Reconstruction* (New York: Oxford University Press, 2014).

12. Mark A. Noll, *America's God: From Jonathan Edwards to Abraham Lincoln* (New York: Oxford University Press, 2002), 3; Philip Goff, Arthur E. Farnsley II, and Peter J. Thuesen, eds., *The Bible in American Life* (New York: Oxford University Press, 2017).

13. Jeffrey Burton Russell, *Mephistopheles: The Devil in the Modern World* (Ithaca, NY: Cornell University Press, 1986).

14. Charles Taylor, *A Secular Age* (Cambridge, MA: Belknap Press of Harvard University Press, 2007).

15. Megan Kate Nelson, *Ruin Nation: Destruction and the American Civil War* (Athens: University of Georgia Press, 2012); Lisa M. Brady, *War Upon the Land: Military Strategy and the Transformation of Southern Landscapes During the American Civil War* (Athens: University of Georgia Press, 2012).

16. Leonard L. Richards, *Who Freed the Slaves? The Fight over the Thirteenth Amendment* (Chicago: University of Chicago Press, 2015).

17. Harold Holzer, Edna G. Medford, and Frank J. Williams, *The Emancipation Proclamation: Three Views* (Baton Rouge: Louisiana State University Press, 2006).

18. Carter Jackson, "Texas Narratives," vol. 16, part 2, p.180, in *Born in Slavery: Slave Narratives from the Federal Writers' Project, 1936–1938*, Library of Congress, http://memory.loc.gov/ammem/snhtml/.

19. Delia Garlic, "Alabama Narratives," vol. 1, pp. 129–131, in *Born in Slavery.*

20. Clifton H. Johnson, ed., *God Struck Me Dead: Voices of Ex-Slaves* (1969; reprint, Cleveland, OH: Pilgrim Press, 1993), 161.

Chapter 1

1. G. W. Henry, *Tell Tale Rag, and Popular Sins of the Day* (Oneida, Madison Co., NY: published and bound by the author, 1861), 30; Charles B. Dew, *Apostles of Disunion: Southern Secession Commissioners and the Causes of the Civil War* (Charlottesville: University Press of Virginia, 2001); Kenneth M. Stampp, *And the War Came: The North and the Secession Crisis* (1950; reprint, Baton Rouge: Louisiana State University Press, 1970).

2. Henry, *Tell Tale Rag*, 30–35.

3. George W. Henry, *Trials and Triumphs (for half a century) in the life of G. W. Henry* (New York: published for the author, 1853), 122, 343.

4. W. Scott Poole, *Satan in America: The Devil We Know* (Lanham, MD.: Rowman and Littlefield, 2009), 65–75.

5. John Rogers, *The Slave Auction*, sculpture, 1859, New-York Historical Society, http://www.nyhistory.org/exhibit/slave-auction.

6. *A Narrative of the Uncommong Sufferings, and Surprizing Deliverance of Briton Hammon, a Negro Man* (Boston: Green and Russell, 1760); *The Interesting Narrative of the Life of Olaudah Equiano, or Gustavus Vassa, the African, Written by Himself,* vol. 2 (London, 1789), 148. *The Interesting Narrative of the Life of Olaudah Equiano, or Gustavus Vassa, The African, Written by Himself,* vol. 1 (London, 1789); *Collections of the Massachusetts Historical Society,* vol. 3, 5th series (Boston: The Society, 1878) 432–437.

7. Thomas Jefferson, *Notes on the State of Virginia* (Philadelphia: Prichard and Hall, 1788), 96.

8. James Monroe to John Mason, August 31, 1829, quoted in "Highland and Slavery," http://highland.org/james-monroe-and-slavery/; John P. Kaminski, ed., *A Necessary Evil? Slavery and the Debate of the Constitution* (Lanham, MD.: Rowman and Littlefield, 1995).

9. David Walker, *Walker's Appeal, in Four Articles; Together With a Preamble, to the Coloured Citizens of the World, But in Particular, and Very Expressly, to Those of the United States of America* (Boston: revised and published by David Walker, 1830), 14, 20, 25, 32, 35, 37, 40.

10. Charles Stearns, *Narrative of Henry Box Brown, Who Escaped from Slavery in a Box 3 Feet Long and 2 Wide* (Boston: Brown and Stearns, 1849), 47; Gilbert Osofsky, ed., *Puttin' On Ole Massa: The Slave Narratives of Henry Bibb, William Wells Brown, and Solomon Northup* (New York: Harper and Row, 1969), 243; William J. Anderson, *Life and Narrative of William J. Anderson, Twenty-four Years a Slave; Sold Eight Times! In Jail Sixty Times!! Whipped Three Hundred Times!!!* (Chicago: Daily Tribune Book and Job Printing Office, 1857), 17, 22, 50; Harriet A. Jacobs, *Incidents in the Life of a Slave Girl* (Boston: published for the author, 1861), 63; John Greenleaf Whittier, "Slaves of Martinique," in *Poems of John Greenleaf Whittier* (London: George Routledge, 1857), 78.

11. Thomas S. Gaines, ed., *Buried Alive (Behind Prison Walls) for a Quarter of a Century: Life of William Walker* (Saginaw, MI: Friedman and Hynan, 1892), 14.

12. Lewis Garrard Clarke, *Narrative of the Sufferings of Lewis Clark, During a Captivity of More than Twenty-Five Years, Among the Algerines of Kentucky, One of the So Called Christian States of North America* (Boston: David H. Ela, 1845), 11–12, 58.

13. *Narrative of the Life of Frederick Douglass, An American Slave,* edited by Benjamin Quarles (Cambridge: Belknap Press of Harvard University Press, 1980), 93..

14. Stearns, *Narrative of Henry Box Brown,* 18–19, 47; Frederick Douglass, *My Bondage and My Freedom* (1855; reprint, New York: Arno Press and the New York Times, 1968), 68, 90, 195.

15. Nathan O. Hatch, *The Democratization of American Christianity* (New Haven, CT: Yale University Press, 1989).

16. Charles Taylor, *A Secular Age* (Cambridge, MA: Belknap Press of Harvard University Press, 2007).

17. Frank Luther Mott, *A History of American Magazines, 1850–1865* (Cambridge, MA: Harvard University Press, 1938), 288.

18. "The Fugitive Slave Law," *The North Star,* October 24, 1850.

19. Donald Yacovone, *A Covenant with Death and an Agreement with Hell,* broadside, 1854, Massachusetts Historical Society, Object of the Month (July 2005), http://www.masshist.org/object-of-the-month/objects/a-covenant-with-death-and-an-agreement-with-hell-2005-07-01.

20. David Boocker, "Garrison, Milton, and the Abolitionist Rhetoric of Demonization," *American Periodicals* 9 (1999):15–26.

21. Henry Mayer, *All on Fire: William Lloyd Garrison and the Abolition of Slavery* (New York: W. W. Norton, 1998).

22. Lydia Maria Child to E. Carpenter, March 20, 1838, in *Letters of Lydia Maria Child with a Biographical Introduction* (Boston: Houghton, Mifflin, 1883), 27.

23. Kenneth S. Greenberg, ed., *The Confessions of Nat Turner and Related Documents* (Boston: Bedford Books of St. Martin's Press, 1996), 41, 84.

24. Quoted in Scot French, *The Rebellious Slave: Nat Turner in American Memory* (New York: Houghton Mifflin, 2004), 90.

25. Harriet Beecher Stowe, *Uncle Tom's Cabin* (Boston: John P. Jewett, 1852), 86, 200.

26. *Henry Ward Beecher, and his principal supporters*, ca. 1860, print, Brooklyn Historical Society.

27. Abraham Smith to Abraham Lincoln, July 20, 1858, Abraham Lincoln Papers, Library of Congress.

28. Edward J. Blum, "The Kingdom of Satan in America: Weaving the Wicked Web of Antebellum Religion and Politics," *Common-Place* 15, no. 3 (Spring 2015), http://www.common -place-archives.org/vol-15/no-03/blum.

29. *Cong. Globe*, 30th Cong., 1st Sess. 905 (1848).

30. *Cong. Globe*, 35th Cong., 1st Sess. 425–426 (1858).

31. *Cong. Globe*, 34th Cong., 1st Sess. 534 (1856).

32. R. J. M. Blackett, *The Captive's Quest for Freedom: Fugitive Slaves, the 1850 Fugitive Slave Law, and the Politics of Slavery* (New York: Cambridge University Press, 2018).

33. Tony Horowitz, *Midnight Rising: John Brown and the Raid that Sparked the Civil War* (New York: Henry Holt, 2011).

34. John Brown to My Dear Friend E. B. of R.I., Charleston, VA, November 1, 1859, in Zoe Trodd and John Stauffer, eds., *Meteor of War: The John Brown Story* (Maplecrest, NY: Brandywine Press, 2004), 139.

35. Trodd and Stauffer, eds., *Meteor of War*, 80, 123–124.

36. Thomas J. Jackson, letter to wife, December 2, 1859, in Trodd and Stauffer, eds., *Meteor of War*, 165.

37. Gin Lum, *Damned Nation*, 2.

38. Jackson to wife, December 2, 1859, in Trodd and Stauffer, eds., *Meteor of War*, 165.

39. *Cong. Globe*, June 4, 1860, 2590.

40. Quoted in Elizabeth Fox-Genovese and Eugene D. Genovese, *The Mind of the Master Class: History and Faith in the Southern Slaveholders' Worldview* (Cambridge: Cambridge University Press, 2005), 646.

41. March 23, 1861, in James I. Robertson Jr., ed., *Soldier of Southwestern Virginia: The Civil War Letters of Captain John Preston Sheffey* (Baton Rouge: Louisiana State University Press, 2007), 18.

42. *Proceedings of the Mississippi State Convention* (Jackson, MS: Power and Cadwallades, 1861), 14, 81; Ernest William Winkler, ed., *Journal of the Secession Convention of Texas* (1861; Austin, TX: Austin Printing Company, 1912); *The History and the Debates of the Convention of the People of Alabama* (Montgomery, AL: White Pfister and Company, 1861).

43. See online Google Books Ngram Viewer search for "Black Republicans."

44. Quoted in Andrew Ward, *The Slaves' War: The Civil War in the Words of Former Slaves* (Boston: Houghton Mifflin, 2008), 17.

45. Sarah H. Bradford, *Scenes in the Life of Harriet Tubman* (Auburn, NY: W. J. Moses, 1869), 40; Ward, *The Slaves' War*, 44–46.

46. Wendell Phillips, quoted in Adam Goodheart, *1861: The Civil War Awakening* (New York: Alfred A. Knopf, 2011), 75.

47. Jupiter Hesser to Abraham Lincoln, March 31, 1861, Abraham Lincoln Papers, Library of Congress, https://www.loc.gov/resource/mal.0851800/.

48. *Brownlow's Knoxville Whig*, October 13, 1860, 2.

49. *Cincinnati Daily Commercial*, April 5, 1862, quoted in Ellis Merton Coulter, *William G. Brownlow: Fighting Parson of the Southern Highlands* (1937; reprint Chapel Hill: University of North Carolina Press, 2018), 214–15.

50. William G. Brownlow, *Sketches of the Rise, Progress, and Decline of Secession; with a Narrative of Personal Adventures Among the Rebels* (Philadelphia: George W. Childs, 1862), 437–440, quoted in Coulter, *William G. Brownlow,* 220.

51. James W. Hunnicutt, *The Conspiracy Unveiled: The South Sacrificed; or, the Horrors of Secession* (Philadelphia: J. B. Lippincott, 1863), 165, 177, 310, 368.

52. James Russell Lowell, "E Pluribus Unum," *Atlantic Monthly* 7, no. 40 (February 1861): 235–246; Elliott C. Cowdin quoted in "Foreign Intelligence," *Sacramento Daily Union* 21, no. 3203 (July 3, 1861): 5–6.

53. Frank Moore, *The Rebellion Record: A Diary of American Events,* vol. 2 (New York: G. P. Putnam, 1862), 800.

54. William Tell Barnitz, letter to the editor, *Pennsylvania Daily Telegraph,* March 27, 1863, William Tell Barnitz Papers, Valley of the Shadow Civil War Project, http://valley.lib.virginia .edu/papers/FN0000.

55. G. S. Hillard, *Fifth Reader: For the Use of Public and Private Schools* (Boston: Brewer and Tileston, 1863), 372; Robert R. Raymond, ed., *The Patriotic Speaker: Consisting of Specimens of Modern Eloquence, together with poetical extracts adapted for recitation, and dramatic pieces for exhibitions* (New York: A. S. Barnes and Burr, 1864), 183; John D. Philbrick, *The American Union Speaker: Containing Standard and Recent Selections in Prose and Poetry, for Recitation and Dec-lamation, in Schools, Academies and Colleges* (Boston: Taggard and Thompson, 1869), 420.

56. Charles Hodge, "The State of the Country," *Princeton Review* (January 1861); Samuel T. Spear, "Obedience to the Civil Authority," in Moore, *The Rebellion Record,* 122–123.; "God and Man," in Horatio W. Dresser, ed., *The Quimby Manuscripts* (New York: Thomas Y. Crowell, 1921), 337.

57. "Report of the Postmaster General," Appendix, *Cong. Globe,* vol. 4, 37th Cong., 2d Sess. 7 (1861).

58. Steven R. Boyd, *Patriotic Envelopes of the Civil War: The Iconography of Union and Confederate Covers* (Baton Rouge: Louisiana State University Press, 2010).

59. *Florida,* patriotic envelope collection, series 1: Civil War envelopes, 1861–1865, New-York Historical Society, http://digitalcollections.nyhistory.org/islandora/object/islandora%3A32846.

60. *Louisiana,* patriotic envelope collection, series 1: Civil War envelopes, 1861–1865, New-York Historical Society, http://digitalcollections.nyhistory.org/islandora/object /islandora%3A32727.

61. Samuel C. Upham, *The Root of Treason,* patriotic envelope collection, series 1: Civil War envelopes, 1861–1865, New-York Historical Society, http://digitalcollections.nyhistory.org /islandora/object/islandora%3A32745.

62. Samuel C. Upham, *Uncle Sam Cutting Down the "Secession Tree,"* patriotic envelope collection, series 1: Civil War envelopes, 1861–1865, New-York Historical Society, http:// digitalcollections.nyhistory.org/islandora/object/islandora%3A32745.

63. Stephen Mihm, *Nation of Counterfeiters: Capitalists, Con Men, and the Making of the United States* (Cambridge, MA: Harvard University Press, 2007), 324.

64. Edward J. Blum, "'The First Secessionist Was Satan': Secession and the Religious Pol-itics of Evil in Civil War America," *Civil War History* 60, no. 3 (September 2014): 234-269.

65. Blum, "The First Secessionist Was Satan."

66. Rev. Hollis Read, A.M., *The God of This World; The Footprints of Satan: Or, the Devil in History* (Toronto: Maclear, 1875), 29.

67. For more on animality, see Steve Baker, *Picturing the Beast: Animals, Identity, and Representation* (Champaign: University of Illinois Press, 2001).

68. Harriet Beecher Stowe, *The Key to Uncle Tom's Cabin* (1854; reprint, New York: Arno Press, 1968), 42.

69. Anthony B. Pinn, *Terror and Triumph: The Nature of Black Religion* (Minneapolis, MN: Fortress Press, 2003); Mia Bay, *The White Image in the Black Mind: African-American Ideas About White People, 1830–1925* (New York: Oxford University Press, 2000), chap. 4.

70. *An Eminent Southern Clergyman, envelope,* 1860, Wisconsin Historical Society, https://www.wisconsinhistory.org/Records/Image/IM76530.

71. Gary W. Gallagher, *The Union War* (Cambridge, MA: Harvard University Press, 2011).

72. R. Laurence Moore, *Selling God: American Religion in the Marketplace of Culture* (New York: Oxford University Press, 1994); Amanda Porterfield, *Corporate Spirit: Religion and the Rise of the Modern Corporation* (New York: Oxford University Press, 2018).

73. Charles N. Tenney to Adelaide E. Case, July 26, 1862, Corinne Carr Nettleton Civil War Collection, Letters of Charles Tenney, collection 11616, box 11336, folder 1862 July–Dec, 7, University of Virginia Special Collections Library, Charlottesville, VA.

Chapter 2

1. "The Reunion," *Sacramento Daily Record-Union* 11, no. 151 (August 12, 1880): 2.

2. William Tecumseh Sherman to John Sherman, January 25, 1863, quoted in Rachel Sherman Thorndike, ed., *The Sherman Letters: Correspondence Between General and Senator Sherman from 1837 to 1891* (New York: Charles Scribner's Sons, 1894), 185.

3. Versions of Sherman's quotation traveled far and wide. For uses, see "Meissoniers," *Fort Worth Daily Gazette*, August 4, 1886, 2; "Workingmen and War," *Magnolia Gazette* 5, no. 8 (April 14, 1882): 4; "An Old Newspaper Relic," *Perrysburg Journal* 36, no. 17 (July 20, 1888): 2.

4. Charles Taylor, *A Secular Age* (Cambridge, MA: Belknap Press of Harvard University Press, 2007); W. Clark Gilpin, *Religion Around Emily Dickinson* (University Park: Penn State University Press, 2014).

5. Edward G. Lengel, *Inventing George Washington: America's Founder, in Myth and Memory* (New York: HarperCollins, 2012); Joseph F. Stoltz III, *A Bloodless Victory: The Battle of New Orleans in American Historical Memory* (Baltimore: Johns Hopkins University Press, 2017); Catherine L. Albanese, *Sons of the Fathers: The Civil Religion of the American Revolution* (Philadelphia: Temple University Press, 1976).

6. John O'Sullivan, "Annexation," *The United States Magazine and Democratic Review*, 17 (New York: 1845), 5.

7. Marli F. Weiner, ed., *A Heritage of Woe: The Civil War Diary of Grace Brown Elmore, 1861–1868* (Athens: University of Georgia Press, 1997), 11.

8. Charles F. Johnson to Mary Johnson, March 24, March 31, 1862, in Fred Pelka, ed., *The Civil War Letters of Colonel Charles F. Johnson*, 101, 103.

9. John S. Collier and Bonnie B. Collier, eds., *Yours for the Union: The Civil War Letters of John W. Chase, First Massachusetts Light Artillery* (New York: Fordham University Press, 2004), 8, 10.

10. Pelka, ed., *The Civil War Letters of Colonel Charles F. Johnson*, 94.

11. George B. McClellan to Abraham Lincoln, July 7, 1862; George B. McClellan, General Order No. 154, August 9, 1862, *OR*, ser. 1, 11, part 3, 364.

12. Marsena Rudolph Patrick diary, July 21, 1862, Marsena Rudolph Patrick Papers, Library of Congress.

13. Warren B. Armstrong, *For Courageous Fighting and Confident Dying: Union Chaplains in the Civil War* (Lawrence: University Press of Kansas, 1998), 1–3; and Ronit Stahl, *Enlisting Faith: How the Military Chaplaincy Shaped Religion and State in Modern America* (Cambridge, MA: Harvard University Press, 2017), 9.

14. William Clegg diary, January 1, 1862, Gilder Lehrman Collection, New-York Historical Society, quoted in Robert E. Bonner, *The Soldier's Pen: Firsthand Impressions of the Civil War* (New York: Hill and Wang, 2006), 150–151.

15. Edward J. Hagerty, *Collis' Zouaves: The 114th Pennsylvania Volunteers in the Civil War* (Baton Rouge: Louisiana State University Press, 1997), 23.

16. Anthony Battillo, "The Red-Legged Devils from Brooklyn," *Civil War Times Illustrated* 10, no. 10 (February 1972): 11–12.

17. "The South and the North," Civil War Song Sheets, Library of Congress.

18. Jane Isabella Watt White diary, October 1861, Jane Isabella Watt White Papers, James G. Leyburn Library, Washington and Lee University, Lexington, VA (hereafter cited as WLU).

19. White diary, May 5, 1862 , White Papers, WLU.

20. Sara S. Frear, "'You My Brother Will be Glad with Me': The Letters of Augusta Jane Evans to Walter Clopton Harriss, January 29, 1856, to October 29, 185[8?], *Alabama Review* 60 (April 2007): 121, quoted in George C. Rable, *God's Almost Chosen Peoples: A Religious History of the American Civil War* (Chapel Hill: University of North Carolina Press, 2010), 68.

21. Benjamin Brooke journal, March 12, 1862, Benjamin Brooke Papers, Bell Archives, Handley Library, Winchester, VA.

22. Robert Taylor Scott to Fanny Scott, December 31, 1862, Keith Family Papers, Virginia Museum of History and Culture (hereafter cited as VMHC), Richmond.

23. James I. Robertson Jr., ed., *Soldier of Southwestern Virginia: The Civil War Letters of Captain John Preston Sheffey* (Baton Rouge: Louisiana State University Press, 2007), 182–183.

24. Jeremiah T. Boyle to Abraham Lincoln, Sunday, August 31, 1862, Abraham Lincoln Papers, Library of Congress.

25. Lydia Smith to Abraham Lincoln, October 4, 1862, Abraham Lincoln Papers, Library of Congress.

26. Max Langenschwartz, "Antietam," 1863, America Singing: Nineteenth-Century Song Sheets, Library of Congress.

27. Collier and Collier, eds., *Yours for the Union*, 8, 10, 63, 93, 132.

28. Charles F. Smith, quoted in James Lee McDonough, *William Tecumseh Sherman: In the Service of My Country* (New York: W. W. Norton, 2016), 314–315.

29. Benjamin F. Butler, *Autobiography and Personal Reminiscences of Major-General Benj. F. Butler* (Boston: A. M. Thayer, 1892), 438–440.

30. Thomas Williams, "Letters of General Thomas Williams, 1862," *American Historical Review* 14 (January 1909): 310–314.

31. *OR*, series 1, vol. 15, 426; available online at http://www.civilwarhome.com/butlerorder.htm (last accessed June 11, 2018).

32. "Gen. Butler Defends the Woman Order," *New York Times*, July 16, 1862.

33. "The Evidences of Southern Civilization," *New York Times*, April 7, 1862.

34. James M. McPherson, *Embattled Rebel: Jefferson Davis as Commander in Chief* (New York: Penguin Press, 2014), 120; and Chester G. Hearn, *When the Devil Came Down to Dixie: Ben Butler in New Orleans* (Baton Rouge: Louisiana State University Press, 1997), 107.

35. Quoted in Frederick S. Daniel, ed., *The Richmond Examiner During the War, or, the Writings of John M. Daniel* (New York: printed by the author, 1868), 54–55, 67.

36. Mary Boykin Chesnut, May 21, 1862, in *Mary Chesnut's Civil War*, ed. C. Vann Woodward (New Haven, CT: Yale University Press, 1981), 343.

37. A New Yorker, quoted in Hearn, *When the Devil Came Down to Dixie*, 221. On Butler's explosive wealth growth during the war, see James Ford Rhodes, *History of the United States from the Compromise of 1850 to the Final Restoration of Home Rule in the South*, 8 vols. (New York: Macmillan, 1902–19), 5: 312, and Hearn, 223.

38. Mildred Bullitt letter, November 1864, Bullitt Family Papers, folder 303, Filson Historical Society, Louisville, KY.

39. Abraham Lincoln, *Oration of Abraham Lincoln at the Dedication of the Gettysburg National Military Cemetery* (November 19, 1863), https://www.loc.gov/item/scsm001032/.

40. *Address of Hon. Edward Everett, at the Consecration of the National Cemetery at Gettysburg, 19th November, 1863* (Boston: Little, Brown, 1864).

41. Michael C. C. Adams, *Living Hell: The Dark Side of the Civil War* (Baltimore: Johns Hopkins University Press, 2016).

42. Collier and Collier, eds., *Yours for the Union*, 114.

43. William Lewis Nugent to Eleanor Smith Nugent, August 1861, quoted in William M. Cash and Lucy Somerville Howorth, eds., *My Dear Nellie: The Civil War Letters of William L. Nugent to Eleanor Smith Nugent* (Jackson: University Press of Mississippi, 1977), 46.

44. Kent T. Dollar, *Soldiers of the Cross: Confederate Soldier-Christians and the Impact of War on Their Faith* (Macon, GA: Mercer University Press, 2005), 17; Nugent to Nugent, May 1862, quoted in *My Dear Nellie*, 74.

45. David Coe, ed., *Mine Eyes Have Seen the Glory: Combat Diaries of Union Sergeant Hamlin Alexander Coe* (Cranbury, NJ: Fairleigh Dickinson University Press, 1975), 154.

46. Annie Starling, Sunday night, November 10, 1861, Ellen Wallace and Annie Starling diaries, Kentucky Historical Society.

47. Sunday, September 1, 1861, John F. Lanneau Papers, Z. Smith Reynolds Library, Special Collections, Wake Forest University, Winston-Salem, NC.

48. Ted Genoways and Hugh H. Genoways, eds., *A Perfect Picture of Hell: Eyewitness Accounts by Civil War Prisoners from the 12th Iowa* (Iowa City: University of Iowa Press, 2001), 76.

49. Charles Johnson to Mary Johnson, May 16, 1862, in Fred Pelka, ed., *The Civil War Letters of Colonel Charles F. Johnson: Invalid Corps* (Amherst: University of Massachusetts Press, 2004), 114.

50. Olynthus B. Clark, ed., *Downing's Civil War* (Des Moines: Historical Department of Iowa, 1916), 140n1.

51. Collier and Collier, eds., *Yours for the Union*, 43.

52. Elliott Ashkenazi, ed., *The Civil War Diary of Clara Solomon: Growing Up in New Orleans, 1861–1862* (Baton Rouge: Louisiana State University Press, 1995), 349–351, 377.

53. Pelka, ed., *The Civil War Letters of Colonel Charles F. Johnson*, 125.

54. Quoted in Mark Michael Smith, *Listening to Nineteenth-Century America* (Chapel Hill: University of North Carolina Press, 2001), 202.

55. Charles East, ed., *The Civil War Diary of Sarah Morgan* (Athens: University of Georgia Press, 1991), 151.

56. Craig A. Warren, *The Rebel Yell: A Cultural History* (Tuscaloosa: University of Alabama Press, 2014), 56.

57. Paul Fatout, ed., *Letters of a Civil War Surgeon* (West Lafayette, IN: Purdue University Press, 1996), 93.

58. Warren, *The Rebel Yell*, 29.

59. Judith Lee Hallock, ed., *The Civil War Letters of Joshua Calloway* (Athens: University of Georgia Press, 1997), 136.

60. John Lewis Thomson, *History of the Second War Between the United States and Great Britain* (Philadelphia, 1848), 424.

61. Mark Olcott and David Lear, eds., *The Civil War Letters of Lewis Bissell: A Curriculum* (Washington, DC: Field School Educational Foundation Press, 1981), 8–9.

62. Olcott and Lear, ed., *The Civil War Letters of Lewis Bissell*, 17, 9, 10, 285.

63. Olcott and Lear, ed., *The Civil War Letters of Lewis Bissell*, 30, 48–49.

64. Olcott and Lear, ed., *The Civil War Letters of Lewis Bissell*, 62.

65. Olcott and Lear, ed., *The Civil War Letters of Lewis Bissell*, 76, 247–248.

66. Olcott and Lear, ed., *The Civil War Letters of Lewis Bissell*, 250.

67. William Hopkins, *Plan of Fort Sedgwick generally known as Fort Hell*, c. 1903, Library of Congress, http://hdl.loc.gov/loc.gmd/g3884f.cw0543000/.

68. Thomas P. Beals, "In a Charge Near Fort Hell, Petersburg, April 2, 1865," *War Papers: Read Before the Commandery of the State of Maine, Military Order of the Loyal Legion of the United States,* 4 vols. (Portland, ME: Lefavor-Tower, 1902), 2:106.

69. Quoted in Shirley Samuels, *Facing America: Iconography and the Civil War* (New York: Oxford University Press, 2004), 81.

70. Collier and Collier, eds., *Yours for the Union*, 301, 379.

71. Richard Lowe, ed., *A Texas Cavalry Officer's Civil War: The Diary and Letters of James C. Bates* (Baton Rouge: Louisiana State University Press, 1999), 202.

72. "The Note Book of John F. Lanneau," 98 in John F. Lanneau Papers.

73. Hallock, ed., *The Civil War Letters of Joshua Calloway,* 154.

74. Charles Johnson diary, August 27, 1862, Charles F. Johnson Papers, 1846–1866, Bancroft Library, University of California, Berkeley.

75. Pelka, ed., *The Civil War Letters of Colonel Charles F. Johnson*, 129.

76. Don E. Fehrenbacher and Virginia Fehrenbacher, eds., *Recollected Words of Abraham Lincoln* (Stanford: Stanford University Press, 1996), 106.

77. Charles W. Sanders Jr., *While in the Hands of the Enemy: Military Prisons of the Civil War* (Baton Rouge: Louisiana State University Press, 2005).

78. William D. Wilkins, August 31, 1862, "My Libby Prison Diary," William D. Wilkins Papers, Library of Congress.

79. Alexander G. Downing, December 3, 1864, in Clark, ed., *Downing's Civil War*, 234; Kenyon diary, W. S. Hoole Special Collections Library, University of Alabama, Tuscaloosa; Lessel Long, *Twelve Months in Andersonville* (Washington, DC: Lessel Long and Thad Butler, 1886), 58.

80. Quoted in Lonnie Speer, *Portals to Hell: Military Prisons of the Civil War* (Mechanicsburg, PA: Stackpole Books, 1997), 16.

81. *William Dolphin's Civil War Diary* (Ossining, NY: Ossining Historical Society, 991), 20.

82. William B. Hesseltine, ed., *Civil War Prisons* (Kent, OH: Kent State University Press, 1997), 88–89.

83. John McElroy, *Andersonville: A Story of Rebel Military Prisons, Fifteen Months a Guest of the So-Called Southern Confederacy* (Toledo, OH: D. R. Locke, 1879), 125, 292.

84. Henry Kyd Douglas, *I Rode with Stonewall* (Chapel Hill, NC: University of North Carolina Press, 1940), 280.

85. Quoted in Genoways and Genoways, eds., *A Perfect Picture of Hell*, 212–213.

86. McElroy, *Andersonville*, 67.

87. Quoted in W. Fitzhugh Brundage, *Civilizing Torture: An American Tradition* (Cambridge, MA: Belknap Press of Harvard University Press, 2018), 149.

88. Genoways and Genoways, eds., *A Perfect Picture of Hell*, 136.

89. Hesseltine, ed., *Civil War Prisons*, 124.

90. Ezra Hoyt Ripple, *Dancing Along the Deadline: The Andersonville Memoir of a Prisoner of the Confederacy,* ed. Mark A. Snell (Novato, CA: Presidio Press, 1996), 117.

91. McElroy, *Andersonville*, 125–127.

92. Mrs. K. B. Yale to Abraham Lincoln, December 20, 1864, Abraham Lincoln Papers, Library of Congress.

93. Genoways and Genoways, eds., *A Perfect Picture of Hell*, 56.

94. U.S. Sanitary Commission, *Narrative of Privations and Sufferings of United States Officers and Soldiers While Prisoners of War in the Hands of the Rebel Authorities* (Philadelphia: King and Baird, 1864), quoted in Brundage, *Civilizing Torture*, 146.

95. McElroy, *Andersonville*, 153.

96. Ripple, *Dancing Along the Deadline*, 78.

97. Genoways and Genoways, eds., *A Perfect Picture of Hell*, 243–244.

98. Genoways and Genoways, eds., *A Perfect Picture of Hell*, 109.

99. Genoways and Genoways, eds., *A Perfect Picture of Hell*, 184.

100. Samuel J. Gibson diary, August 26, 1864, Library of Congress.

101. McElroy, *Andersonville*, ix–xi.

102. Ripple, *Dancing Along the Deadline*, 45.

103. Orvey S. Barrett, *Reminiscences, Incidents, Battles, Marches and Camp Life of the Old 4th Michigan Infantry in War of Rebellion, 1861 to 1864* (Detroit: W. S. Ostler, 1888), 17.

104. Quoted in Victor E. Taylor, *The Religious Pray, the Profane Swear: A Civil War Memoir* (Aurora, CO: Davies Group, 2002), 48.

105. McElroy, *Andersonville*, 292.

106. Ripple, *Dancing Along the Deadline*, 19–20.

107. Walt Whitman, *Specimen Days and Collect* (Philadelphia: Rees Welsh, 1882–83), 55, 80–81.

Chapter 3

1. George N. Barnard, *Photographic Views of Sherman's Campaign* (New York: Press of Wynkoop and Hallenbeck, 1866), no. 27.

2. "Photographic Views of Sherman's March," *Harper's Weekly* 10 (December 8, 1866): 771.

3. Joshua Brown, "Toward a Meeting of the Minds: Historians and Art Historians," *American Art* 17, no. 2 (Summer 2003): 4–9; James W. Cook, "Seeing the Visual in U.S. History," *Journal of American History* (September 2008): 432–441; Maurie D. McInnis, *Slaves Waiting for Sale: Abolitionist Art and the American Slave Trade* (Chicago: University of Chicago Press, 2011); Alan Trachtenberg, "Albums of War: On Reading Civil War Photographs," *Representations* 9 (Winter 1985): 1–32; Harold Holzer, "Picturing Freedom: The Emancipation Proclamation in Art, Iconography, and Memory" in Holzer, Medford, and Williams, *The Emancipation*

Proclamation; Kirk Savage, *Standing Soldiers, Kneeling Slaves: Race, War, and Monument in Nineteenth-Century America* (Princeton, NJ: Princeton University Press, 1997).

4. John Lossing Benson, *The Pictorial Field-Book of the Revolution,* vol. 1 (New York: Harper and Brothers, 1851), 508; David Copeland, "'Join, or Die': America's Press During the French and Indian War," *Journalism History* 24, no. 3 (Autumn 1998): 112–121; Lester C. Olson, *Benjamin Franklin's Vision of American Community: A Study in Rhetorical Iconology* (Columbia: University of South Carolina Press, 2004).

5. John Lossing Benson, *The Pictorial Field-Book of the Revolution,* vol. 2 (New York: Harper and Brothers, 1852), 505n 2.

6. Schuyler Hamilton, *The History of the National Flag of the United States of America* (Philadelphia: Lippincott, Grambo,1853), 74; Marc Leepson, *Flag: An American Biography* (New York: Thomas Dunne Books, 2005), 12–13.

7. J. B. Elliott, *Scott's Great Snake,* 1861, map, Library of Congress, https://lccn.loc.gov /99447020.

8. *Jeff Davis reaping the harvest,* 1861, wood engraving, Library of Congress Prints and Photographs, https://www.loc.gov/pictures/item/95522073/.

9. Analysis of snakes in the letter envelopes based upon books of hundreds of envelopes at the Filson Historical Society, Louisville, Kentucky. patriotic covers, 1861, and miscellaneous materials, 1861–1889 Miss./ BC A615.

10. *Resist the devil,* patriotic covers, 1861, and miscellaneous materials, 1861–1889 Miss./ BC A615, 4e, Filson Historical Society, Louisville, Kentucky.

11. Patriotic covers, 1861, and miscellaneous materials, 1861–1889 Miss./ BC A615, 13 f, Filson Historical Society, Louisville, Kentucky.

12. *The Game of Secession or Sketches of the Rebellion,* wood engraving, 1862, Library Company of Philadelphia, https://digital.librarycompany.org/islandora/object/digitool%3A129781.

13. Jeff Wants to Get Away, 1864, sheet music, Civil War Sheet Music Collection, Library of Congress, https://www.loc.gov/resource/ihas.200001461.0?st=gallery.

14. "Lincoln on Snakes," Franklin *Repository,* June 20, 1860, *Valley of the Shadow Project,* Franklin County 1857–April 1861.

15. Alfred West to unknown. August 22, 1861, folder 5, Alfred West Papers, Kentucky Historical Society, Frankfort.

16. Mrs. M. V. Victor, *The Unionist's Daughter: A Tale of the Rebellion in Tennessee* (New York: Beadle and Company, 1861), 123.

17. For more on the song, see John Stauffer and Benjamin Soskis, *The Battle Hymn of the Republic: A Biography of the Song That Marches On* (New York: Oxford University Press, 2013).

18. "Proclamation Calling Militia and Convening Congress," April 15, 1861, in *Collected Works of Abraham Lincoln,* vol. 4 (New Brunswick, NJ: Rutgers University Press, 1953), 331–333; Abraham Lincoln to Erastus Corning and Others, June 12, 1863, in *Collected Works of Abraham Lincoln:* vol. 6 (New Brunswick, NJ: Rutgers University Press, 1953), 261–269.

19. "Statues at Large, 37th Congress, 2nd Session," in *A Century of Lawmaking for a New Nation: U.S. Congressional Documents and Debates, 1774–1875,* 597–600, https://memory.loc .gov/ammem/amlaw/lawhome.html.

20. Patriotic covers, 1861, and miscellaneous materials, 1861–1889 Miss./ BC A615, 37c, Filson Historical Society, Louisville, Kentucky.

21. Quoted in James M. McPherson, *For Cause and Comrades: Why Men Fought in the Civil War* (New York: Oxford University Press, 1997), 51.

22. Edward McPherson, *The Political History of the United States of America During the Great Rebellion* (Washington, DC: Philip and Solomons, 1864), 547.

23. "Philosophy of Crushing the Rebellion Vindicated," *New York Times*, Oct. 20, 1862.

24. David Gilmour Blythe, *Lincoln Crushing the Dragon of Rebellion*, oil on canvas, 1862, Museum of Fine Arts, Boston, https://www.mfa.org/collections/object/lincoln-crushing-the -dragon-of-rebellion-33167.

25. https://www.mfa.org/collections/object/lincoln-crushing-the-dragon-of-rebellion -33167.

26. Thomas Prentice Kettell, *History of the Great Rebellion, from its Commencement to Its Close* (Cincinnati: L. Stebbins, 1865), 113.

27. Frances B. Wallace, ed., *Memorial of the Patriotism of Schuylkill County in the American Slaveholder's Rebellion* (Pottsville, PA: Benjamin Bannan, 1865), vii, 547.

28. Jennifer L. Weber, *Copperheads: The Rise and Fall of Lincoln's Opponents* (New York: Oxford University Press, 2008), 18; C. S. Rafinesque, "Natural History of the Scytalus Cupreus, or Copper-head Snake," in *The American Journal of Science, More Especially of Mineralogy, Geology, and the Other Branches of Natural History* 1 (New York: J. Eastburn and Co., 1819): 84–86.

29. Charles H. Coleman, "The Use of the Term 'Copperhead' during the Civil War," *Mississippi Valley Historical Review* 25, no. 2 (September 1938): 263–264.

30. Advertisement in *The Assassination and History of the Conspiracy* (New York: J. R. Hawley and Company, 1865).

31. *Ye Book of Copperheads* (Philadelphia: Frederick Leypoldt, 1863).

32. *G. T. Blow-Regard,* illustrated envelope, patriotic envelope collection, series 1, New-York Historical Society, http://digitalcollections.nyhistory.org/islandora/object/islandora %3A32580.

33. J. E. Hayes, *When shall we three meet again, very soon,* illustrated envelope, 1861, Booth Family Center for Special Collections, Georgetown University Library, https://repository .library.georgetown.edu/handle/10822/550482.

34. Benjamin Henry Day, *The Emblem of the Free,* lithograph, 1862 or 1864, Library of Congress. http://www.loc.gov/pictures/item/2004665368/.

35. United States War Department, *The War of the Rebellion: A Compilation of the Official Records of the Union and Confederate Armies* series 1, vol.14 (Washington, DC: Government Printing Office, 1885), 448–449.

36. E. W. T. Nichols, *The Great American What is it? chased by Copper-head*s, lithograph, 1863, Library of Congress, https://www.loc.gov/pictures/item/2008661651/.

37. John Conness to Abraham Lincoln, January 4, 1864, Abraham Lincoln Papers, Library of Congress.

38. J. S. Hastings to Abraham Lincoln, August 9, 1861, Abraham Lincoln Papers, Library of Congress.

39. Currier and Ives, *The Chicago Platform and Candidate,* cartoon, 1864, Library of Congress, https://www.loc.gov/pictures/resource/pga.04752/.

40. *How the Copperheads Obtain their Votes* and *Election-Day* in *Harper's Weekly* (November 12, 1864), 725.

41. Thomas Nast, *Emancipation, wood engraving,* 1865, Library of Congress, https://www .loc.gov/pictures/item/2004665360/.

42. Adalbert Volck, *The Emancipation Proclamation*, in *V. Blada's War Sketches* (London [Baltimore]: 1864); caricature, Library of Congress, https://www.loc.gov/item/90710014/.

43. Alfred Gale, *Pictorial History of the Cause of the Great Rebellion* (Asbury, NJ; 1866), vol. 2.

44. *Masks and Faces, Southern Illustrated News,* November 8, 1862, 8.

45. "Mr. N. B. Browne and Mr. Justice Woodward," *The Press* (Philadelphia), September 8, 1863, 1. Also in *The True Issues Now Involved*, https://archive.org/details/trueissuenowinvo00phil/page/n3.

46. "Lincoln's Fiendish Proclamation," *Staunton Spectator*, October 7, 1862, 2.

47. "John Brown's Entrance into Hell" (Baltimore: C.T.A., 1863), America Singing: Nineteenth Century Song Sheets, Library of Congress.

48. Quoted in Frederic May Holland, *Frederick Douglass: The Colored Orator* (New York: Funk and Wagnalls, 1891), 301.

49. Quoted in Frederick S. Daniel, ed., *The Richmond Examiner During the War, or, the Writings of John M. Daniel* (New York: printed by the author, 1868), 60–61.

50. Nancy D. Baird, ed., "Josie Underwood's Civil War: An Introduction," *Register of the Kentucky Historical Society* 112, no. 3 (Summer 2014): 475, 478.

51. "In for His Second Innings," *Comic News*, December 6, 1864, 240.

52. *Abraham Africanus I: His Secret Life, As Revealed Under the Mesmeric Influence* (New York: J. F. Feeks, 1864).

53. Henry C. Work, "Babylon is Fallen" (Chicago: Root and Cady, 1863). https://library.duke.edu/digitalcollections/hasm_b0984/.

54. Alfred R. Waud, *Infernal machines discovered in the Potomac*, drawing, 1861, Library of Congress, https://www.loc.gov/resource/cph.3g12570/; *Submarine Infernal machine intended to destroy the Minnesota*, wood engraving, 1861, Library of Congress, https://www.loc.gov/resource/cph.3c27603/.

55. *Photographs, Illustrative of Operations in Construction and Transportation* (Boston: Wright and Potter, Printers, 1863).

56. Quoted in John Stauffer, Zoe Trodd, and Celeste-Marie Bernier, *Picturing Frederick Douglass: An Illustrated Biography of the Nineteenth Century's Most Photographed American* (New York: W. W. Norton, 2015), iv; *The Portable Frederick Douglass* (New York: Penguin, 2016), 363.

57. Oliver Wendell Holmes, "Doings of the Sunbeam," *Atlantic Monthly* (July 1863): 1–15.

58. Holmes, "Doings of the Sunbeam," 1–15.

59. "Brady's Photographs; Pictures of the Dead at Antietam," *New York Times,* October 20, 1862.

60. *A Harvest of Death*, in *Gardner's Photographic Sketchbook of the War*, vol. 1 (Washington, DC: Philip and Solomons, 1865).

61. *Antietam Bridge, Maryland*, in *Gardner's Photographic Sketchbook of the War*, vol. 1.

62. *Quarters of Men in Fort Sedgwick, generally known as "Fort Hell,"* in *Gardner's Photographic Sketchbook of the War*, vol. 2 (Washington, DC.: Philip and Solomons, 1866).

63. Frederick Gutekunst, *Political Still Life*, ca. 1865, Nelson-Atkins Museum of Art, https://art.nelson-atkins.org/objects/51095.

64. Julie K. Brown, *Making Culture Visible: The Public Display of Photography at Fairs* (2001; reprint, New York: Routledge, 2019).

65. https://www.wisconsinhistory.org/Records/Image/IM76509.

66. https://www.wisconsinhistory.org/Records/Image/IM76585.

67. https://www.loc.gov/resource/ihas.200001768.0?st=gallery.

68. http://digitalcollections.nyhistory.org/islandora/object/islandora%3A32746.

Chapter 4

1. *Cong. Globe* vol. 4, 3392 (July 16, 1862).

2. See Joanne Freeman, *The Field of Blood: Violence in Congress and the Road to Civil War* (New York: Farrar, Straus and Giroux, 2018), 209, 217.

3. *Cong. Globe*, vol. 4, 3392 (July 16, 1862).

4. Faust, *This Republic of Suffering*.

5. W. Nelson to G. V. Fox, September 25, 1861, in Robert Means Thompson and Richard Wainwright, eds., *Confidential Correspondence of Gustavus Vasa Fox* (New York: De Vinne Press, 1918), 380.

6. C. Vann Woodward and Elisabeth Muhlenfeld, eds., *The Private Mary Chesnut: The Unpublished Civil War Diaries* (New York: Oxford University Press, 1984), 86.

7. Charles East, ed., *The Civil War Diary of Sarah Morgan* (Athens: University of Georgia Press, 1991), 201.

8. *Henry V*, act 3, scene 7.

9. See Charles Winterfield, "Adventures on the Frontier of Texas and Mexico, No. III," in *The American Whig* (November 1845): 514; James Fenimore Cooper, *Wyandotte* (New York: Stringer and Townsend, 1852), 159.

10. "Letter Thirty-Second," Springfield, Missouri, August 10, 1861, in Franc B. Wilkie, *The Iowa First: Letters from the War* (Dubuque, IA: Herald Book and Job Establishment, 1861), 113.

11. Fred Pelka, ed., *The Civil War Letters of Colonel Charles F. Johnson*, 95.

12. Rev. Louis N. Rourdrye, *Historic Records of the Fifth New York Cavalry* (New York: J. Munsell, 1865), 33.

13. DeAnne Blanton and Lauren Cook Wike, *They Fought Like Demons: Women Soldiers in the American Civil War* (Baton Rouge: Louisiana State University Press, 2002).

14. Noah Andre Trudeau, *Like Men of War: Black Troops in the Civil War, 1862–1865* (Boston: Little, Brown, 1998), 44.

15. Quoted in Leon F. Litwack, *Been in the Storm So Long: The Aftermath of Slavery* (New York: Vintage, 1980), 101.

16. Benjamin W. Crowninshield, *A History of the First Regiment of Massachusetts Cavalry Volunteers* (Boston: Houghton, Mifflin, 1891), 225, 263.

17. *War of the Rebellion: A Compilation of the Official Records of the Union and Confederate Armies*, Additions and Corrections to series, vol. 22, 1880–1901 (Washington, DC: Government Printing Office, 1902), 730.

18. "Fight at Liverpool Heights, on the Yazoo River," in Frank Moore, *The Rebellion Record: A Diary of American Events*, vol. 4 (New York: G. P. Putnam, 1865), 418.

19. Abraham Lincoln, "Reply to Emancipation Memorial Presented by Chicago Christians of All Denominations," September 13, 1862, in *The Collected Works of Abraham Lincoln*, ed. Roy W. Basler, 8 vols. (New Brunswick, NJ: Rutgers University Press, 1953), 5: 423.

20. Warren H. Hurd diary, June 23 and July 24, 1864, Historical Society of Schuylkill County, Pottsville, quoted in Earl J. Hess, *In the Trenches at Petersburg: Field Fortifications and Confederate Defeat* (Chapel Hill: University of North Carolina Press, 2009), 54.

21. William T. Sherman to Ellen Sherman, quoted in Brian Steel Wills, "Nathan Bedford Forrest and Guerrilla War," in *The Guerrilla Hunters: Irregular Conflicts During the Civil War*, ed. Brian D. McKnight and Barton A. Myers (Baton Rouge: Louisiana State University Press, 2017), 53.

22. James Lee McDonough, *Sherman: In the Service of My Country* (New York: W. W. Norton, 2016), 500.

23. Lawrence Lee Hewitt, *Port Hudson, Confederate Bastion on the Mississippi* (Baton Rouge: Louisiana State University Press, 1987), 140–149.

24. David W. Blight, "The Shaw Memorial in the Landscape of Civil War Memory," in *Hope and Glory: Essays on the Legacy of the Fifty-Fourth Massachusetts Regiment*, ed. Martin H. Blatt, Thomas J. Brown, and Donald Yacovone (Amherst: University of Massachusetts Press, 2001), 84.

25. Chauncey H. Cooke to mother, July 28, 1863, in *A Badger Boy in Blue: The Civil War Letters of Chauncey H. Cooke*, ed. William H. Mulligan Jr. (Detroit: Wayne State University Press, 2007), 81.

26. John Cimprich, *Fort Pillow, a Civil War Massacre, and Public Memory* (Baton Rouge: Louisiana State University Press, 2005), 70.

27. Cimprich, *Fort Pillow*, 73.

28. Cimprich, *Fort Pillow*, 78.

29. Cimprich, *Fort Pillow*, 72.

30. Cimprich, *Fort Pillow*, 78.

31. George Bodnia, ed., "Fort Pillow 'Massacre': Observations of a Minnesotan," *Minnesota History* 43 (Spring 1973): 188, quoted in Cimprich, *Fort Pillow*, 80.

32. John Cimprich and Robert C. Mainfort Jr., eds., "Fort Pillow Revisited: New Evidence About an Old Controversy," *Civil War History* 28 (December 1982): 301.

33. Cimprich, *Fort Pillow*, 81.

34. Cimprich and Mainfort, "Fort Pillow Revisited," 301.

35. John Allan Wyeth, *That Devil Forrest: Life of General Nathan Bedford Forrest* (Baton Rouge: Louisiana State University Press, 1989), xxi; and Cimprich, *Fort Pillow*, 81.

36. Achilles V. Clark, *Compiled Service Record (20th Tennessee Cavalry)*, record group 109, National Archives, quoted in Cimprich, *Fort Pillow*, 81.

37. Andrew Ward, *River Run Red: The Fort Pillow Massacre in the American Civil War* (New York: Viking, 2005), 211–212.

38. Nathan Bedford Forrest to Jefferson Davis, April 15, 1864, quoted in Cimprich, *Fort Pillow*, 94.

39. Ulysses S. Grant, *Personal Memoirs of U.S. Grant* (London: Sampson Low, 1895), 417.

40. U.S. Navy Department, *Official Records of the Union and Confederate Navies in the War of the Rebellion*, 31 vols. (Washington, DC: Government Printing Office, 1880–1901), 26: 224–225; Cimprich, *Fort Pillow*, 95.

41. Nathan Bedford Forrest to Cadwallader C. Washburn, June 23, 1864, quoted in Wills, "Nathan Bedford Forrest and Guerrilla War," 65.

42. U.S. Congress, *Report of the Joint Committee on the Conduct of the War on the Fort Pillow Massacre and on Returned Prisoners*, 38th Cong., 1st sess., rep. com. 63 and 68 (Washington, DC: Government Printing Office, 1864), 1–4.

43. *St. Louis Missouri Democrat*, April 16, 1864, quoted in Cimprich, *Fort Pillow*, 90.

44. Evander Law, "From the Wilderness to Cold Harbor," in *Battles and Leaders of the Civil War*, ed. Clarence C. Buel and Robert U. Johnson, 4 vols. (New York: Century, 1884–88), 4, 141.

45. Joshua Lawrence Chamberlain, *The Passing of the Armies: An Account of the Final Campaign of the Army of the Potomac, Based Upon Personal Reminiscences of the Fifth Army Corps* (New York: G. P. Putnam, 1915), 2–3.

46. Joan Waugh, *U.S. Grant: American Hero, American Myth* (Chapel Hill: University of North Carolina Press, 2009), 129–136.

47. Mark Grimsley, *And Keep Moving On: The Virginia Campaign, May–June 1864* (Lincoln: University of Nebraska Press, 2002), 175.

48. Gordon C. Rhea, *The Battle of the Wilderness, May 5–6, 1864* (Baton Rouge: Louisiana State University Press, 2004), 171.

49. David J. Fitzpatrick, *Emory Upton: Misunderstood Reformer* (Norman: University of Oklahoma Press, 2017), ch. 3.

50. Gordon C. Rhea, *The Battles for Spotsylvania Court House and the Road to Yellow Tavern, May 7–12, 1864* (Baton Rouge: Louisiana State University Press, 1997), ch. 8.

51. Earl J. Hess, *Trench Warfare Under Grant and Lee: Field Fortifications in the Overland Campaign* (Chapel Hill: University of North Carolina Press, 2007), xv.

52. Stephen W. Sears, *To the Gates of Richmond: The Peninsula Campaign* (New York: Ticknor & Fields, 1992), ch. 9.

53. Reuben Allen Pierson to William H. Pierson, July 11, 1862, in *Brothers in Gray: The Civil War Letters of the Pierson Family*, ed. Thomas W. Cutrer and T. Michael Parrish (Baton Rouge: Louisiana State University Press, 1997), 101.

54. William S. Long to Breckinridge Long, Breckinridge Long Papers, Library of Congress. (See Ernest Furgurson, *Not War But Murder*, p. 128.)

55. Karla Jean Husby, *Under Custer's Command: The Civil War Journal of James Henry Avery*, ed. Eric J. Wittenberg (Washington, DC: Brassey's, 2000), 79.

56. Husby, *Under Custer's Command*, 81.

57. Horace Porter, *Campaigning with Grant* (New York: Century, 1897), 174–175.

58. John D. Billings, *The History of the Tenth Massachusetts Battery of Light Artillery in the War of the Rebellion* (Boston: Arakelyan Press, 1909), 200.

59. "Lieutenant May," quoted in J. W. Jones, *The Story of American Heroism: Thrilling Narratives of Personal Adventures During the Great Civil War as Told by the Medal Winners and Roll of Honor Men* (Springfield, OH: Werner Company, 1897), 413.

60. Frederick W. Mather, *Albany Evening Journal*, October 23, 1895, quoted in Gordon C. Rhea, *Cold Harbor: Grant and Lee, May 26–June 3, 1864* (Baton Rouge: Louisiana State University Press, 2002), 329.

61. Rhea, *Cold Harbor*, 245.

62. The only source for this account was Shelby Foote, *The Civil War: A Narrative*, 3 vols. (New York: Vintage, 1986), 3: 290.

63. Joseph Hume diary, June 3 and 4, 1864, https://collectmedicalantiques.com/gallery/civil-war-medicine-and-the-battle-of-cold-harbor (last accessed December 7, 2018).

64. Lewis Bissell to father, June 2–4, 1864, in *The Civil War Letters of Lewis Bissell: A Curriculum*, ed. Mark Olcutt and David Lear (Washington, DC: Field School Educational Foundation Press, 1981), 245–249.

65. Henry R. Swan to Abbie, June 4, 1864, quoted in Rhea, *Cold Harbor*, 334.

66. Newell M. Smith, "The Story of the 155th New York," 46, quoted in Rhea, *Cold Harbor*, 335.

67. W. I . Hallock, letter to the editor, *American Tribune*, August 24, 1893, quoted in Rhea, *Cold Harbor*, 334.

68. Alanson A. Haines, *Fifteenth Regiment New Jersey Volunteers* (New York: Jenkins and Thomas, 1883), 208.

69. Quoted in Frederic May Holland, *Frederick Douglass: The Colored Orator* (New York: Funk and Wagnalls, 1891), 301.

70. Hess, *In the Trenches at Petersburg*, 45–49.

71. Hess, *In the Trenches at Petersburg*, 87–88.

72. Hess, *In the Trenches at Petersburg*, 97.

73. Paul M. Higginbotham to Aaron Higginbotham, August 1, 1864, Paul M. Higginbotham Papers, Virginia Museum of History and Culture, Richmond (hereafter cited as VMHC).

74. Delevan Bates, January 1891, quoted in George S. Bernard, *War Talks of Confederate Veterans* (Petersburg, VA: Fenn and Owen, 1892), 183.

75. William H. Stewart, "The Charge of the Crater," *Southern Historical Society Papers* 25 (1897): 79–80, quoted in Hess, *In the Trenches at Petersburg*, 99.

76. William H. Stewart, *The Spirit of the South: Orations, Essays and Lectures* (New York: Neale, 1908), 135.

77. William H. Etheredge, "Another Story of the Crater Battle," *Southern Historical Society Papers* 37 (1909): 205, quoted in Hess, *In the Trenches at Petersburg*, 100.

78. Stewart, *The Spirit of the South*, 135.

79. Frank Kenfield, "Captured by Rebels: A Vermonter at Petersburg, 1864," *Vermont History* 36 (1968): 233, quoted in Hess, *In the Trenches at Petersburg*, 100.

80. John F. Schmutz, *The Battle of the Crater: A Complete History* (Jefferson, NC: McFarland and Company, 2009), 291–292.

81. George L. Kilmer, "The Dash into the Crater," *Century Magazine* 34 (1887): 776, quoted in Hess, *In the Trenches at Petersburg*, 102.

82. William L. Hyde, *History of the One Hundred and Twelfth Regiment N.Y. Volunteers* (Fredonia, NY: W. McKinstry, 1866), 94–95.

83. Freeman S. Bowley, "The Petersburg Mine," in *Civil War Papers of the California Commandery and the Oregon Commandery of the Military Order of the Loyal Legion of the United States* (Wilmington, NC: Broadfoot, 1995), 36, quoted in Hess, *In the Trenches at Petersburg*, 100.

84. Kevin M. Levin, *Remembering the Battle of the Crater: War as Murder* (Lexington: University Press of Kentucky, 2012), 23–24.

85. Jonathan M. Steplyk, *Fighting Means Killing: Civil War Soldiers and the Nature of Combat* (Lawrence: University Press of Kansas, 2018), 22.

86. P. M. Vance, "Incidents of the Crater Battle," *Confederate Veteran* 14, no. 4 (1906): 179, quoted in Richard Slotkin, *No Quarter: The Battle of the Crater, 1864* (New York: Random House, 2009), 292.

87. William R. J. Pegram to Jennifer McIntosh, August 1, 1864, Pegram-McIntosh-Johnson Papers, VHMC.

88. *Petersburg Daily Express*, August 1, 1864, quoted in Levin, *Remembering the Battle of the Crater*, 31.

89. Henry Biggs to sister, August 28, 1864, Biggs Family Papers, David M. Rubenstein Rare Book and Manuscript Library, Duke University (hereafter cited as DU), quoted in Peter S.

Carmichael, *The War for the Common Soldier: How Men Thought, Fought, and Survived in Civil War Armies* (Chapel Hill: University of North Carolina Press, 2018), 71.

90. Hess, *In the Trenches at Petersburg*, 104.

91. Levin, *Remembering the Battle of the Crater*, 32.

92. William T. Sherman to R. M. Sawyer, January 31, 1864, quoted in Lisa Tendrich Frank, *The Civilian War: Confederate Women and Union Soldiers During Sherman's March* (Baton Rouge: Louisiana State University Press, 2015), 51. *The War of the Rebellion: A Compilation of the Official Records of the Union and Confederate Armies*, series 1, vol. 32, part 2 (Washington, DC: Government Printing Office, 1891), 278–281.

93. William T. Sherman to James M. Calhoun et al., September 12, 1864, quoted in *Memoirs of Gen. W. T. Sherman*, 2 vols., 4th ed. (New York: Charles L. Webster, 1891), 2:126.

94. William M. Standard to Jane Standard, April 26, 1864, quoted in *"This Infernal War": The Civil War Letters of William and Jane Standard*, ed. Timothy Mason Roberts (Kent, OH: Kent State University Press, 2018), 190.

95. Standard to Standard, February 1, 1863, quoted in Roberts, ed., *"This Infernal War,"* 66.

96. Standard to Standard, February 8, 1863, quoted in Roberts, ed., *"This Infernal War,"* 67–68.

97. Standard to Standard, August 21, 1864, quoted in Roberts, ed., *"This Infernal War,"* 214.

98. Standard to Standard, September 11, 1864, quoted in Roberts, ed., *"This Infernal War,"* 216.

99. Grace Elmore diary, November 20, 1864, in *A Heritage of Woe: The Civil War Diary of Grace Brown Elmore, 1861–1868*, ed. Marli F. Weiner (Athens: University of Georgia Press, 1997), 79.

100. Frank, *The Civilian War*, 136; Gaines M. Foster, *Ghosts of the Confederacy: Defeat, the Lost Cause, and the Emergence of the New South, 1865–1913* (New York: Oxford University Press, 1985), 33.

101. Grace Elmore diary, November 26, 1864, in Weiner, ed., *A Heritage of Woe*, 81–82.

102. Sarah Conner to sister, August 7, 1864, Henry Calvin Conner Papers, South Caroliniana Library, University of South Carolina, Columbia (hereafter cited as USC), quoted in Jason Phillips, *Diehard Rebels: The Confederate Culture of Invincibility* (Athens: University of Georgia Press, 2007), 63.

103. Eliza Tillinghast to David R. Tillinghast, May 3, 1865, Tillinghast Family Papers, DU, quoted in Frank, *The Civilian War*, 139.

104. Henry Hitchcock to Mary Hitchcock, November 4, 1864, Hitchcock Collection, Library of Congress, quoted in Frank, *The Civilian War*, 65.

105. John J. Hight, *History of the Fifty-Eighth Regiment of Indiana Volunteer Infantry* (Princeton, IN: Press of the Clarion, 1895), 382.

106. Hight, *History of the Fifty-Eighth Regiment*, 273.

107. Hight, *History of the Fifty-Eighth Regiment*, 405.

108. G. S. Bradley, *Star Corps, or Notes of an Army Chaplain During Sherman's Famous "March to the Sea"* (Milwaukee: Jermain and Brightman, 1865), 186, 225.

109. Henry Champlin Lay diary, September 28, 1864, North Carolina Division of Archives and History, Raleigh, quoted in Jacqueline Glass Campbell, *When Sherman Marched North from the Sea: Resistance on the Confederate Home Front* (Chapel Hill: University of North Carolina Press, 2003), 23.

110. Eliza Tillinghast to David R. Tillinghast, May 3, 1865, Tillinghast Family Papers, DU, quoted in Frank, *The Civilian War*, 142.

111. Grace Elmore diary, January 4, 1865, in Weiner, ed., *A Heritage of Woe*, 89.

112. Grace Elmore diary, January 4, 1865, in Weiner, ed., *A Heritage of Woe*, 89–90.

113. John L. Hostetter, December 13, 1864, in Edwin W. Payne, *History of the Thirty-Fourth Regiment of Illinois Volunteer Infantry* (Clinton, IA: Allen Printing Company, 1903), 173, quoted in Joseph T. Glatthaar, *The March to the Sea and Beyond: Sherman's Troops in the Savannah and Carolinas Campaigns* (New York: New York University Press, 1985), 174.

114. William Scofield to sister, January 25, 1865, and to father, February 1, 1865, Scofield Family Papers, DU, quoted in Campbell, *When Sherman Marched*, 35.

115. James A. Connolly, *Three Years in the Army of the Cumberland*, ed. Paul M. Angle (Bloomington: Indiana University Press, 1959), 375.

116. Campbell, *When Sherman Marched*, 58.

117. Grace Elmore diary, February 18, 1865, USC, quoted in Campbell, *When Sherman Marched,* 61.

118. Anonymous to "My Dear Gracia," March 3, 1865, in Katherine M. Jones, *When Sherman Came: Southern Women and the "Great March"* (Indianapolis: Bobbs-Merrill, 1964), 176.

119. Mrs. W. K. Bachman to Kate Bachman, March 27, 1865, Bachman Family Papers, USC, quoted in Campbell, *When Sherman Marched*, 61.

120. Lily Logan to "My Precious Brother," March 2, 1865, in Jones, *When Sherman Came*, 194.

121. Grace Elmore diary, February 21, 1865, in Weiner, ed., *A Heritage of Woe*, 102.

122. Mary Maxcy Leverett to Milton Maxcy Leverett, February 24, 1865, in *The Leverett Letters: Correspondence of a South Carolina Family, 1851–1868*, ed. Frances Wallace Taylor, Catherine Taylor Matthews, and J. Tracy Power (Columbia: University of South Carolina Press, 2000), 384–387.

123. Mary Rowe, February 17, 1865, "A Southern Girl's Diary," *Confederate Veteran* 40 (July 1932): 265, quoted in Frank, *The Civilian War*, 14.

124. Grace Elmore diary, February 21, 1865 entry, in Weiner, ed., *A Heritage of Woe*, 102.

125. George P. Rawick, ed., *The American Slave: A Composite Autobiography*, 19 vols. (Westport, CT: Greenwood Press, 1972), 3(3), 26, quoted in Campbell, *When Sherman Marched*, 47.

126. Grace Elmore diary, February 21, 1865, in Weiner, ed., *A Heritage of Woe*, 103.

127. Abraham Lincoln to James R. Doolittle, George B. Ide, and A. Hubbell, Monday, May 30, 1864, Abraham Lincoln Papers, Library of Congress.

128. Edward Steers Jr., *Blood on the Moon: The Assassination of Abraham Lincoln* (Lexington: University Press of Kentucky, 2001), 36.

Chapter 5

1. Emory M. Thomas, "The Kilpatrick-Dahlgren Raid," *Civil War Times Illustrated* (February 1978), 4–5, 8, quoted in Herman Hattaway and Archer Jones, *How the North Won: A Military History of the Civil War* (Urbana: University of Illinois Press, 1983), 505.

2. Terry Alford, *Fortune's Fool: The Life of John Wilkes Booth* (New York: Oxford University Press, 2015), 183.

3. Alford, *Fortune's Fool*, 183–184.

4. Alford, *Fortune's Fool,* 185.

5. Alford, *Fortune's Fool*, 206.

6. Steers, *Blood on the Moon*, 91.

7. Michael W. Kauffman, *American Brutus: John Wilkes Booth and the Lincoln Conspiracies* (New York: Random House, 2004), ch. 8.

8. J. L. Magee, *Satan Tempting Booth to the Murder of the President*, lithograph, 1865, Library of Congress. https://www.loc.gov/pictures/item/2003689283/.

9. *The Guerrilla Hunters: Irregular Conflicts During the Civil War*, ed. Brian D. McKnight and Barton A. Myers (Baton Rouge: Louisiana State University Press, 2017), 4.

10. Joseph M. Beilein Jr., *Bushwhackers: Guerrilla Warfare, Manhood, and the Household in Civil War Missouri* (Kent, OH: Kent State University Press, 2016), 3.

11. Harry S. Stout, *Upon the Altar of the Nation: A Moral History of the Civil War* (New York: Viking, 2006), 381–382.

12. Stout, *Upon the Altar of the Nation*, xiii.

13. Jennifer Graber, *The Gods of Indian Country: Religion and the Struggle for the American West* (New York: Oxford University Press, 2018), 69–70.

14. John Fabian Witt, *Lincoln's Code: The Laws of War in American History* (New York: Free Press, 2012), 190.

15. Scott Thompson, "The Irregular War in Loudoun County, Virginia," in *The Guerrilla Hunters*, ed. McKnight and Myers, 126–127.

16. See Pekka Hämäläinen, *The Comanche Empire* (New Haven, CT: Yale University Press, 2008).

17. Frank M. Myers, *The Comanches: A History of White's Battalion, Virginia Cavalry, Laurel Brig., Hampton Div., A.N.V., C.S.A.* (Baltimore, MD: Kelly, Piet, 1871), 21–22, quoted in Thompson, "The Irregular War in Loudoun County," 127.

18. Thompson, "The Irregular War in Loudoun County," 130.

19. John D. Stevenson to Edwin M. Stanton, March 28, 1865, and Charles P. Janney to Elisha H. Walker, April 2, 1864, Walker Family Papers, Waterford Foundation Archives, Waterford, VA, both quoted in Thompson, "The Irregular War in Loudoun County," 137.

20. J. E. B. Stuart to John S. Mosby, March 25, 1863, Mosby Papers, Library of Congress, quoted in Daniel E. Sutherland, *A Savage Conflict: The Decisive Role of Guerrillas in the American Civil War* (Chapel Hill: University of North Carolina Press, 2009), 166.

21. For European case studies, see Robert Gildea's study of Vichy France in *Marianne in Chains: Daily Life in the Heart of France During the German Occupation* (New York: Metropolitan Books, 2003); and Reynald Secher's account of the civil war in the Vendée during the French Revolution in *A French Genocide: The Vendée*, trans. George Holoch (South Bend, IN: Notre Dame University Press, 2003).

22. Thomas D. Mays, *Cumberland Blood: Champ Ferguson's Civil War* (Carbondale: Southern Illinois University Press, 2008), 29–30.

23. Brian D. McKnight, *Confederate Outlaw: Champ Ferguson and the Civil War in Appalachia* (Baton Rouge: Louisiana State University Press, 2011), 90.

24. *Louisville Courier Journal*, quoted in McKnight, *Confederate Outlaw*, 91–92.

25. Henry W. Halleck to Thomas Ewing, January 1, 1862, quoted in Michael Fellman, *Inside War: The Guerrilla Conflict in Missouri During the American Civil War* (New York: Oxford University Press, 1989), 88.

26. Halleck, General Orders #2, March 13, 1862, quoted in Fellman, *Inside War*, 88.

27. G. O. Yeiser to John M. Schofield, July 19, 1862, Letters Received File 367, Record Group 393, National Archives, quoted in Fellman, *Inside War*, 44.

28. Henry C. and William Crawford to their friends, August 19, 1863, H. C. and W. H. Crawford Letters, Joint Collection, University of Missouri, Western Historical Manuscript Collection-Columbia, State Historical Society of Missouri Manuscripts, quoted in Fellman, 163.

29. *OR*, 1I:22 (1), 860–866, quoted in Sutherland, *A Savage Conflict*, 123–124.

30. Witt, *Lincoln's Code*, 188.

31. Henry W. Halleck, *International Law; or, Rules Regulating the Intercourse of States in Peace and War* (San Francisco: H. H. Bancroft, 1861), 386.

32. Witt, *Lincoln's Code*, 173–174.

33. Witt, *Lincoln's Code,*180.

34. James Childress, "Francis Lieber's Interpretation of the Law of War: General Orders No. 100 in the Context of his Life and Thought," *American Journal of Jurisprudence* 21 (1976), 43.

35. Witt, *Lincoln's Code,*181.

36. Witt, *Lincoln's Code* 193.

37. Francis Lieber, *Guerrilla Parties Considered with Reference to the Laws and Usages of War* (New York: D. Van Nostrand, 1862), 19, 21.

38. Lieber, *Instructions for the Government of Armies of the United States, in the Field* (New York: D. Van Nostrand, 1863), 7.

39. *White Cloud Kansas Chief*, May 19, 1864, 4; *Marysville Big Blue Union*, May 7, 1864, both quoted in W. Fitzhugh Brundage, *Civilizing Torture: An American Tradition* (Cambridge, MA: Belknap Press of Harvard University Press, 2018), 130.

40. Lieber, General Orders No. 100, April 24, 1863, quoted in Brundage, *Civilizing Torture*, 138.

41. Lieber to Halleck, December 21, 1864, quoted in Witt, *Lincoln's Code,* 236.

42. Request of W. W. Morison, May 10, 1862, Letters Received, Confederate Secretary of War, Record Group 109, M-437, roll 60, National Archives and Records Administration, Washington, DC, quoted in Barton A. Myers, "Partisan Ranger Petitions and the Confederacy's Authorized *Petite Guerre* Service," in McKnight and Myers, ed., *The Guerrilla Hunters*, 26–27.

43. John Bell Robinson, *Pictures of Slavery and Anti-Slavery: Advantages of Negro Slavery and the Benefits of Negro Freedom Morally, Socially, and Politically Considered* (Philadelphia: 1330 North Thirteenth Street, 1863), 110, quoted in Jonathan M. Steplyk, *Fighting Means Killing: Civil War Soldiers and the Nature of Combat* (Lawrence: University Press of Kansas, 2018), 193.

44. Beilein, *Bushwhackers*, 123.

45. Aaron Sheehan-Dean, *The Calculus of Violence: How Americans Fought the Civil War* (Cambridge, MA: Harvard University Press, 2018), 211.

46. Reverend Richard Cordley, *A History of Lawrence, Kansas: From the First Settlement to the Close of the Rebellion* (Lawrence, KS: Lawrence Journal Press, 1895), 207, 245, quoted in Beilein, *Bushwhackers*, 27.

47. Matthew J. Clavin, "American Toussaints: Symbol, Subversion, and the Black Atlantic Tradition in the American Civil War," in *African Americans and the Haitian Revolution: Selected Essays and Historical Documents*, ed. Maurice Jackson and Jacqueline Bacon (New York: Routledge, 2010), 115.

48. Beilein, *Bushwhackers*, ch. 7.

49. Cordley, *History of Lawrence*, 207.

50. Sutherland, *A Savage Conflict*, 199.

51. John Beatty diary, May 2, 1862 diary entry, in *The Citizen-Soldier: Or, Memoirs of a Volunteer* (Cincinnati, OH: Wilstatch, Baldwin, 1879), 138–139.

52. Charles W. Porter, *In the Devil's Dominions: A Union Soldier's Adventures in "Bushwhacker Country,"* ed. Patrick Brophy (Nevada, MO: Vernon County Historical Society, 1998), 152–153, quoted in Matthew M. Stith, "Guerilla Warfare and the Environment in the Trans-Mississippi Theater," in McKnight and Myers, ed., *The Guerrilla Hunters*, 203.

53. Henry Bruce Scott to Lizzie Scott, July 27, 1862, Henry Bruce Scott Papers, Massachusetts Historical Society, Boston.

54. Robert R. Mackey, *The Uncivil War: Irregular Warfare in the Upper South, 1861–1865* (Norman: University of Oklahoma Press, 2004), 32–36.

55. Mark Grimsley, *The Hard Hand of War: Union Military Policy Toward Southern Civilians, 1861–1865* (New York: Cambridge University Press, 1995), 88.

56. *War of the Rebellion: Official Records of the Union and Confederate Armies*, Series 1, Volume 39, Part II 2 (Washington, DC: Government Printing Office, 1892), 174.

57. Sutherland, *A Savage Conflict*, 224.

58. Sutherland, *A Savage Conflict*, 274.

59. Matthew J. Hernando, *Faces Like Devils: The Bald Knobber Vigilantes in the Ozarks* (Columbia: University of Missouri Press, 2015), 33–34.

60. Hernando, *Faces Like Devils*, 38.

61. Hernando, *Faces Like Devils*, 39.

62. Hernando, *Faces Like Devils*, 39.

63. Lisa Tendrich Frank, "The Union War on Women," in McKnight and Myers, ed., *The Guerrilla Hunters*, 172–173.

64. Frank, "The Union War on Women," 174.

65. Lieber, *Instructions for the Government of Armies of the United States*, 13–14, quoted in Frank, "The Union War on Women," 184.

66. *Jefferson City State Times*, July 25, 1863, 1; *Cleveland Daily Leader*, April 18, 1863, both quoted in Brundage, *Civilizing Torture*, 129.

67. *Pittsburgh Daily Commercial*, November 16, 1864, 1, quoted in Brundage, *Civilizing Torture*, 130.

68. John Hunt Morgan handbill, 1863, Kentucky Historical Society Library, Frankfort, quoted in Stephen Rockenbach, "Home Rebels, Amnesty, and Antiguerilla Operations in Kentucky in 1864," in McKnight and Myers, ed., *The Guerrilla Hunters*, 88.

69. Mackey, *Uncivil War*, 192.

70. Sue Dixon to Thomas Bullitt, July 15, 1863, Folder 303, Bullitt Family Papers, Filson Historical Society, Louisville, KY.

71. Edward G. Longacre, *Fitz Lee: A Military Biography of Major General Fitzhugh Lee, C.S.A.* (Boston: DaCapo, 2005), 185.

72. E. P. Alexander, *Fighting for the Confederacy: The Personal Recollections of General Edward Porter Alexander*, ed. Gary W. Gallagher (Chapel Hill: University of North Carolina Press, 1989), 531.

73. Alexander, *Fighting for the Confederacy*, 532.

74. John Hampden Chamberlayne to Edward Pye Chamberlayne and Lucy Parke Chamberlayne Bagby, April 12, 1865, Chamberlayne Family Papers, VMHC, Richmond, VA.

75. Peter S. Carmichael, *The Last Generation: Young Virginians in Peace, War, and Reunion* (Chapel Hill: University of North Carolina Press, 2005), 213.

76. Rod Andrew, Jr., *Wade Hampton: Confederate Warrior to Southern Redeemer* (Chapel Hill: University of North Carolina Press, 2008), 59, 69.

77. Samuel J. Martin, *Kill-Cavalry: The Life of Union General Hugh Judson Kilpatrick* (Mechanicsburg, PA: Stackpole Books, 2000), 231–232.

78. Robert Lewis Dabney to Elizabeth Randolph Dabney, July 13, 1865, Dabney Family Papers, VMHC.

79. William Tecumseh Sherman to John Sherman, December 29, 1863, in *Sherman's Civil War: Selected Correspondence of William T. Sherman, 1860–1865*, ed. Brooks D. Simpson and Jean V. Berlin (Chapel Hill: University of North Carolina Press, 1999), 578.

80. Sherman to Nathaniel P. Banks, January 16, 1864, *OR*, 11, 32 9(2), 115, quoted in Earl J. Hess, "Civil War Guerrillas in a Global, Comparative Context," in McKnight and Myers, ed., *The Guerrilla Hunters*, 342.

81. Williamson Murray and Wayne Wei-Siang Hsieh, *A Savage War: A Military History of the Civil War* (Princeton, NJ: Princeton University Press, 2016), 505.

82. John Porter Hatch to Moses Porter Hatch, August 13, 1862, John P. Hatch Papers, Library of Congress.

83. James Pickett Jones, *Yankee Blitzkrieg: Wilson's Raid Through Alabama and Georgia* (Lexington: University Press of Kentucky, 1976), 42.

84. See for instance Paul Ashdown and Edward Caudill, *The Myth of Nathan Bedford Forrest* (Lanham, MD: Rowman and Littlefield Publishers, 2005), 85, 94–95; Mackey, *The Uncivil War*, 6, 122; and Brian Steel Wills, "Nathan Bedford Forrest and Guerrilla War," in McKnight and Myers, ed., *The Guerrilla Hunters*, 54–56.

85. Stephen Deyle, *Carry Me Back: The Domestic Slave Trade in American Life* (New York: Oxford University Press, 2005), 105, 280.

86. William Williston Hearsill Diary, May 13, 1865 entry, in *Fourteen Hundred and 91 Days in the Confederate Army*, ed. Bell I. Wiley (Jackson, MS: McCowat-Mercer, 1954), 233. I am indebted to Jason Phillips for this quotation.

87. Jason Phillips, *Diehard Rebels: The Confederate Culture of Invincibility* (Athens: University of Georgia Press, 2007), ch. 5.

Chapter 6

1. George A. Custer to Elizabeth Bacon Custer, nd, quoted in Evan S. Connell, *Son of the Morning Star: Custer and the Little Bighorn* (New York: North Point Press, 1984), 124.

2. Andrew J. Walker, *Recollections of Quantrill's Guerillas*, ed. Joanne Chiles Eskin (Independence, MO: Two Trails, 1996), 22.

3. Rev. Chas. S. Robinson, *The Martyred President: A Sermon Preached in the First Presbyterian Church, Brooklyn, N.Y.* (New York: John F. Trow, 1865), 15–25.

4. William Marvel, *Andersonville: The Last Depot* (Chapel Hill: University of North Carolina Press, 1994), 241.

5. Lew Wallace to Sarah Wallace, August 21, 1865, Lew Wallace Collection, Indiana Historical Society, Indianapolis, quoted in Marvel, *Andersonville*, 243.

6. James M. Gillispie, *Andersonvilles of the North: The Myths and Realities of Northern Treatment of Civil War Confederate Prisoners* (Denton: University of North Texas Press, 2008), 10.

7. Henry Wirz to Carrie Furlow, October 24, 1865, George W. Dutton Papers, Massachusetts Historical Society, quoted in Marvel, *Andersonville*, 246.

8. Marvel, *Andersonville*, 224.

9. Varina Howell Davis to Francis Preston Blair, June 6, 1865, in Gist Blair, "Annals of Silver Spring," *Records of the Columbia Historical Society* 21 (1918): 172.

10. Nina Silber, *The Romance of Reunion: Northerners and the South, 1865–1900.* (Chapel Hill: University of North Carolina Press, 1993).

11. Oscar Harpel, *A Proper Family Re-Union*, lithograph, 1865, Library of Congress, https://www.loc.gov/item/2008661687/.

12. Rev. F. R. Abbe, *Wisdom Better than Weapons of War: A Discourse, Delivered on the Day of National Thanksgiving, at Abington, Mass. December 7, 1865* (Boston: T. R. Marvin and Son, 1865), 8.

13. Mark Wahlgren Summers, *The Ordeal of the Reunion: A New History of Reconstruction* (Chapel Hill: University of North Carolina Press, 2014), 33.

14. Beverly Wilson Palmer, ed., *The Selected Papers of Thaddeus Stevens, Vol. 2: April 1865–August 1868* (Pittsburgh: University of Pittsburgh Press, 1998), 55.

15. Palmer, ed., *The Selected Papers of Thaddeus Stevens, Vol. 2*, 220.

16. Palmer, ed., *The Selected Papers of Thaddeus Stevens, Vol. 2*, 243.

17. John C. Underwood to Horace Greeley, November 27, 1867, Horace Greeley Papers, New York Public Library, microfilm edition, reel 2, 910–911.

18. Quoted in Charles Reagan Wilson, *Baptized in Blood: The Religion of the Lost Cause, 1865–1920* (Athens: University of Georgia Press, 1980), 66.

19. Sidney Andrews, *The South Since the War as Shown by Fourteen Weeks of Travel and Observation in Georgia and the Carolinas* (Boston: Houghton Mifflin, 1971), 320.

20. Hunter Dickinson Farish, *The Circuit Rider Dismounts: A Social History of Southern Methodism, 1865–1900* (1938; reprint, New York: Da Capo Press, 1969), 90–91.

21. Quoted in Luke E. Harlow, *Religion, Race, and the Making of Confederate Kentucky, 1830–1880* (New York: Cambridge University Press, 2014).

22. Reginald F. Hildebrand, *The Times Were Strange and Stirring: Methodist Preachers and the Crisis of Emancipation* (Durham, NC: Duke University Press, 1995), 47.

23. *Proceedings of the Illinois State Convention of Colored Men, Assembled at Galesburg, October 16th, 17th, and 18th, Containing the State and National Addresses Promulgated by it with a list of the Delegates Composing It*, October 1866, in Philip S. Foner and George E. Walker, eds., *Proceedings of the Black National and State Conventions, 1865–1900, vol. 1* (Philadelphia: Temple University Press, 1986), 263.

24. Ulysses S. Grant to Congress, March 23, 1871, in John Y. Simon, ed., *The Papers of Ulysses S. Grant: November 1, 1870–May 31, 1871* (Carbondale: Southern Illinois University Press, 1998), 246; Elaine Frantz Parsons, *Ku-Klux: The Birth of the Klan During Reconstruction* (Chapel Hill: University of North Carolina Press, 2015).

25. Shawn Leigh Alexander, *Reconstruction Violence and the Ku Klux Klan Hearings* (Boston: Bedford/St. Martin's, 2015).

26. *Testimony Taken by the Joint Select Committee to Inquire into the Condition of Affairs in the Late Insurrectionary States: Alabama,* vol. 1 (Washington, DC: Government Printing Office, 1872), 533, 556.

27. *Testimony Taken by the Joint Select Committee to Inquire into the Condition of Affairs in the Late Insurrectionary States: Alabama,* vol. 2 (Washington, DC: Government Printing Office, 1872), 813–814.

28. *Testimony Taken by the Joint Select Committee to Inquire into the Condition of Affairs in the Late Insurrectionary States: Georgia,* vol. 2 (Washington, DC: Government Printing Office, 1872), 1060.

29. *Testimony: Georgia,* vol. 2, 734.

30. *Testimony: Georgia,* vol. 2, 812–813.

31. *Testimony: Georgia,* vol. 2, 1096.

32. *Testimony: Alabama,* vol. 2 , 1186.

33. Parsons, *Ku-Klux,* 78–79.

34. Robert Muchembled, *A History of the Devil: From the Middle Ages to the Present,* trans. Jean Birrell (Cambridge: Polity Press, 2003).

35. *Testimony: Alabama,* vol. 1, 574.

36. *Testimony: Georgia,* vol. 2, 603.

37. Anita Stampler and Jill Condra, *Clothing Through American History: The Civil War Through the Gilded Age, 1861–1899* (Westport, CT: Greenwood Press, 2011).

38. *New York Times,* February 25, 1861, p. 1.

39. Ernest B. Furgurson, *Ashes of Glory: Richmond at War* (New York: Alfred A. Knopf, 1996), 325.

40. *Testimony Taken by the Joint Select Committee to Inquire into the Condition of Affairs in the Late Insurrectionary States: Mississippi,* vol. 2 (Washington, DC: Government Printing Office, 1872), 667.

41. *Testimony: Alabama,* vol. 2, 859, 863.

42. *Testimony: Mississippi,* vol. 2, 778–779.

43. *Testimony: Alabama,* vol. 1, 118–120.

44. Frances Osborn Robb, "'Two Men in Ku Klux Klan Disguises': A Photograph from Reconstruction Alabama," *Alabama Review* 70, no. 3 (July 2017): 239.

45. Matthew Harper, *The End of Days: African American Religion and Politics in the Age of Emancipation* (Chapel Hill: University of North Carolina Press, 2016), 51.

46. *Speech of Hon. James H. Harris on the Militia Bill* (From the *N.C. Standard*'s Phonographic Reports), HathiTrust. https://catalog.hathitrust.org/Record/012193087.

47. Thomas Nast, *The Democratic Hell-Broth, Harper's Weekly,* October 31, 1868, 704.

48. *Testimony: Georgia,* vol. 2, 682.

49. *Testimony: Alabama,* vol. 1 , 275.

50. *Testimony: Mississippi,* vol. 2, 696.

51. Alexander, *Reconstruction Violence.*

52. Thomas Nast, *Let Us Clasp Hands over the Bloody Chasm, Harper's Weekly,* September 11, 1872, 732.

53. Christopher Lyle McIlwain Sr., "United States District Judge Richard Busteed and the Alabama Klan Trials of 1872," *Alabama Review* 65, no. 4 (October 2012): 285–286.

54. James Melville Beard, *K.K.K. Sketches, Humorous and Didactic* (Philadelphia: Claxton, Remsen, and Haffelfinger, 1877), 154–155.

55. David W. Blight, *Race and Reunion: The Civil War in American Memory* (Cambridge, MA: Harvard University Press, 2001).

56. J. P. Dromgoole, *Yellow Fever: Heroes, Honors, and Horrors of 1878* (Louisville, KY: John P. Morton, 1879), 7.

57. Judge J. F. Simmons, *The Welded Link: And Other Poems* (Philadelphia: J. B. Lippincott, 1881), 19.

58. "A Negro," quoted in Bradley G. Bond, ed., *Mississippi: A Documentary History* (Jackson: University Press of Mississippi, 2003), 144.

59. Norvel Blair, *Book for the People! To Be Read by All Voters, Black and White, with Thrilling Events of the Life of Norvel Blair, of Grundy County, State of Illinois* (Joliet, IL: Joliet Daily Record Steam Print, 1880), 32.

60. Katherine Smedley, *Martha Schofield and the Re-education of the South, 1839–1916* (Lewiston/Queenston, NY: Edwin Mellen Press, 1987), 159.

61. Rev. Hollis Read, A.M., *The God of This World; The Footprints of Satan: Or, the Devil in History* (Toronto: Maclear and Company, 1875), 2.

62. Read, *The God of This World*, v–vi.

63. Read, *The God of This World*, 20.

64. Read, *The God of This World*, 106.

65. Read, *The God of This World*, 472–473.

Epilogue

1. Jefferson Davis, *The Rise and Fall of the Confederate Government*, vol. 1 (New York: D. Appleton, 1881), v.

2. Davis, *The Rise and Fall of the Confederate Government*, vol. 1, 398.

3. Jefferson Davis, *The Rise and Fall of the Confederate Government*, vol. 2 (New York: D. Appleton, 1881), 161–162.

4. Roy Morris Jr., *Ambrose Bierce: Alone in Bad Company* (New York: Oxford University Press, 1999).

5. Ambrose Bierce, *Tales of Soldiers and Civilians* (San Francisco: E. L. G. Steele, 1891), 21–40.

6. Bierce, *Tales of Soldiers and Civilians*, 41–54.

7. Ambrose Bierce, *The Devil's Dictionary* (New York: Albert and Charles Boni, 1925).

8. Carter Jackson, Texas Narratives, vol. 16, part 2, p. 180, in *Born in Slavery: Slave Narratives from the Federal Writers' Project, 1936–1938*, Library of Congress, http://memory.loc.gov/ammem/snhtml.

9. Delia Garlic, Alabama Narratives, vol. 1, pp. 129–131, in *Born in Slavery*.

10. Clifton H. Johnson, ed., *God Struck Me Dead: Voices of Ex-Slaves* (1969; reprint, Cleveland, OH: Pilgrim Press, 1993), 161.

11. Quoted in Lawrence W. Levine, *Black Culture and Black Consciousness: Afro-American Folk Thought from Slavery to Freedom* (New York: Oxford University Press, 1977), 34.

12. Quoted in Levine, *Black Culture and Black Consciousness*, 193.

13. Mary Armstrong, Texas Narratives, vol. 16, part 1, pp. 25–27, in *Born in Slavery*.

INDEX

160